the

BEETHOVEN
FACTOR

Other Books by Dr. Pearsall

the

BEETHOVEN FACTOR

the new positive psychology

of

hardiness, happiness, healing, and hope

Paul Pearsall, Ph.D.

HAMPTON ROADS
PUBLISHING COMPANY, INC.

Cover design by Tiffany McCord/Jane Hagaman
Cover dome: ©2000 Digital Vision/PictureQuest;
sheet music: ©1999 StockByte/PictureQuest

Hampton Roads Publishing Company, Inc.
1125 Stoney Ridge Road
Charlottesville, VA 22902

434-296-2772
fax: 434-296-5096
e-mail: hrpc@hrpub.com
www.hrpub.com

If you are unable to order this book from your local
bookseller, you may order directly from the publisher.
Call 1-800-766-8009, toll-free.

Library of Congress Cataloging-in-Publication Data

Pearsall, Paul.
  The Beethoven factor : the new positive psychology of hardiness, happiness,
healing, and hope / Paul Pearsall.
      p. cm.
Includes bibliographical references and index.
  ISBN 1-57174-397-9 (alk. paper)
  1. Resilience (Personality trait) 2. Self-actualization (Psychology)
  I. Title.
  BF698.35.R47P43 2003
  158.1--dc21

                                        2003010769

                    ISBN 1-57174-397-9

                  10 9 8 7 6 5 4 3 2 1

        Printed on acid-free paper in Canada

Dedication

With aloha for my wife Celest on our 39th wedding anniversary.

Mahalo for always keeping me hardy,

making me happy, helping me heal,

and never letting me lose hope.

Contents

Acknowledgments

When a new scientific movement begins, the tradition is to acknowledge the father or mother of the breakthrough. As the new positive psychology comes to life, it is impossible to credit one individual for its birth. Pioneers such as Eric Erikson, Abraham Maslow, Carl Rogers, George Valliant, Aaron Antonovsky, Mihaly Csikszentmihalyi, Suzanne Ouellette Kobasa, and many others were urging us for years to take a less pessimistic view of the human psyche. Among the more cynical philosophers, poets, and composers, there have always been those calling us to a more joyfully optimistic view of the human character.

Many psychologists feel that a 1999 meeting in Akumal, Mexico, signaled the emergence of the positive psychology described in this book. It was at this meeting that the former president of the American Psychological Association Martin E. P. Seligman gathered some of his colleagues for a discussion of the possibilities for a new positive psychology that might help us savor living rather than just survive in a stressful world.

At a summit held the next year at the Gallup Organization in Lincoln, Nebraska, he and Donald Clifton, Ed Diener, and Corey Keyes cochaired the first Summit of Positive Psychology. It was at this meeting that some of the key elements of what might constitute a positive psychology were mapped out.

As all of this was going on, dozens of creative researchers already were studying concepts such as resilience, benefit-finding, hardiness, trauma-induced growth, explanatory style, and the nature of human strengths and virtues. I present this new field to the lay public with an immense debt to all of these scientists for their creative brilliance and scientific courage.

This book was inspired not only by great thinkers but by my great family that saved my life and causes me to thrive. My wife, Celest, is one of the strongest and most positive persons I have ever known, and it was her support in the early 1970s that allowed me to challenge the established pathological "fix-it" model to establish one of the first positive psychology programs to be offered at a major hospital. My brilliant son Scott has been a model of hardiness by overcoming the ignorance and insensitivity he faced due to his cerebral palsy. My son Roger has shown resilient happiness through the stresses of his learning disabilities. My deceased father, Frank, taught me that healing was much more than fixing, and my mother, Carol, continues to lead a hopeful life even as she spends her days gasping for air with damaged lungs and a weakened heart. My Hawaiian *'Ohana Kuhai Hālau O Kawaikapuokalani Pā 'Ōlapa Kahiko* continues to teach me that, as Mark Twain pointed out, the ancients have stolen our best new ideas. All of these people are my coauthors.

This book has had to endure its own severe challenges. After the manuscript was completed and I was ready to spread the good news about a new positive psychology, totally unexpected and unprecedented obstacles to its publication almost killed it. My family would not let me give in, pointing out that I should heed my own words and seek benefits amid the trauma. That benefit was my discovery of Hampton Roads Publishing Company, Inc. Publisher Robert Friedman, my editor Richard Leviton, publicist Tiffany McCord, and the rest of the staff combined their considerable strengths and experience to make this book even stronger and get it to press in some very difficult times in the world. It is for all the people mentioned here that I hope this book will meet its goal of helping you experience growth through stress to savor a truly positive life.

The Beethoven Factor—A Prelude

"We do not think, we are barely conscious, until something goes wrong."

—C. S. Peirce

There stood Beethoven, gravely ill and totally deaf. Eyes closed, he kept conducting the orchestra even after they had ceased their performance and the audience had risen to its feet in thunderous applause. As a singer stepped from the choir to turn him around to see those whose shouts of "bravo" resonated throughout the concert hall, tears of elation filled his eyes. Perhaps the worst loss a composer could experience had been the catalyst for a remarkably adaptive creativity that allowed him to transcend his tortures to become immersed in the thrill of conducting the premiere of his Ninth Symphony, the "Ode to Joy." At that moment, and not only in spite of but because of his adversity, Beethoven had experienced the thrill of thriving through adversity.

- Are there lessons to be learned from how this man so crossed by fate could not only rise to the occasion of his suffering but become so elevated by it?

- Do we all have the Beethoven Factor within us as a remarkably powerful capacity to thrive in our daily life, and to live far above the languishing that too often characterizes the hurried, distracted trance of modern living?

- Is there comfort to be found in the examples of thrivers like Beethoven, whose crises taught them to lose themselves so completely in passionate appreciation for the present moment that they have no time to regret the past or fear the future?

- Can we transcend life's worst physical and emotional obstacles by realizing that our most magnificent human strengths are fired in the crucible of adversity?

- Can we go bravely through the indecencies of the human condition by realizing that a full life is less about a gifted life than about discovering the zest sparked by an effortful, challenging, and painfully frustrating engagement in the catastrophes of living?

- Can we adopt the enlightened optimism of thrivers through crisis who have realized that the key to feeling vibrantly alive requires embracing the necessity of the full sorrow, pain, and unavoidable losses of the darker side of life?

- Can we come to lead our daily lives, as described by psychologist William James, as "souls with a sky-blue tint," those who have grown through what he described as "the slaughterhouses of the human condition" to "passionately fling themselves on the goodness of life in spite of their hardships"?

- Can we learn perhaps the most valuable healing lessons of those who have thrived through adversity—the ability to regularly make the ordinary sacred?

- Even before we suffer terribly, can we live daily with the intensely authentic life appreciation of those whose pain awakened within them evolutionary thriving skills that rest unrecognized within each of us until something goes horribly wrong?

- Before it is too late, can we live as if we realize what thrivers know: that in the final analysis it will not be what we have done that matters most, but who we were with?

- Can we calm ourselves with the thriver's knowledge that strength is defined not only by perseverance and victory but also by knowing when to be an enlightened quitter who gives up, lets go, disengages, and moves on to different goals with new meanings for what constitutes a successful life?

- Has our fixation on recovery and the resilience of returning to where we were before our crisis blinded us to our "thriveability" and its states of flourishing and savoring our everyday living?

- Should our role models for success include those who have had the worst lives and not just the best, the thrivers through crisis who seem to have lost everything, yet end up with that which so many more fortunate persons seem unable to find?

- Unlike thrivers, are we living in a trance of distracted languishing through our lives, mistaking the absence of negative feelings for the presence of very positive ones and the reduction of stress for the joy of savoring?

- Is their new hope and inspiration to be found from crisis thrivers who live as William James suggested, "on the sunny side of their misery line," men, women, and children who have discovered the paradoxically instructive relationship between agony and ecstasy?

- In addition to PTSD (Post Traumatic Stress Disorder), is there also a PTTR or Post Traumatic Thriving Response due to SIG, Stress Induced Growth?

- Can we find comfort from the Beethoven Factor that promises us it will not be the absence of negative experiences that determines a richly experienced life, but how we transform ourselves through our worst times?

- Is there an entirely new science and more positive psychology that confirms the reality and power of the Beethoven Factor, goes beyond the dysfunction, denial, repair, and recovery approach of most self-help programs, and offers proof that there is a much richer, joyful, loving, gentle, and fulfilling way to live our lives?

The answer to all of the above questions is an unqualified yes, and the new science of positive psychology described in this book shows us how. Positive psychology took root at a small meeting of psychologists in Akumal, Mexico, in 1999. These scientists felt that, just as individuals can languish in their lives, so can an entire field of science such as psychology or psychiatry. Since its inception, psychology has been about remediation and repairing the worst conditions, and it has largely ignored what is strong, right, and wonderful about the human spirit. Even the few psychologists who did focus on such issues seldom had a scientific interest or took a research approach to learning about the light side of our humanness. As a result, when people wanted to reflect and learn about the good life and how to live it, they turned not to psychologists, but to philosophers, poets, and novelists.

The emerging field of positive psychology seeks to redress this imbalance; and what it is learning about our innate ability to thrive, flourish through, and savor living —in spite of and often because of our suffering—offers an entirely new view of who we are and how we can be.

The Eighth Deadly Sin

Psychology has aimed too low. It has generally accepted recovery as its goal while neglecting our immense innate capacity to thrive because we have suffered and to become better, stronger, and wiser than we were before we experienced catastrophe. Its attention to dysfunction, codependence, pathology, recovery, healing, and repair has made it possible to better treat broken-down people; but psychology has done very little to prevent people from breaking down in the first place, or to help us understand what it means to move up and be elevated. It has focused on the downward rather than upward psychological trajectory.

Research in the new science of positive psychology shows that, in spite of the hundreds of self-help books and self-improvement programs based on the old psychology of repair and recovery, more than 75 percent of us are "failing to flourish." Instead of living in flourishing's state of consistent positive feelings and joyful eagerness about our lives, work, relationships, and the world in general, it seems that most of us are languishing through our lives. Even if we are too busy to know it or too tired to care, we are in effect regularly committing the eighth deadly sin, called *acedia*.

Acedia was removed from the list of deadly sins in the sixth century by Pope Gregory the Great, but this sin of living with fatigued apathy, cynicism, ennui, and general spiritual weariness is still committed by millions every day. In fact, languishing now far exceeds depression as the number one emotional problem in the Western world. Unlike those whose life crisis led them to discover the capacity to thrive, flourish, and savor, three of four of us are missing out on the full gift of being alive. If are willing to learn from the thrivers, we don't have to wait to be shocked awake by a major life trauma.

Languishing is the opposite of thriving. It is a state in which an individual is emotionally and spiritually fatigued from trying to keep up with the accelerating hyperculture, and generally devoid of highly positive and optimistic feelings toward living. The steady hurrying hum of the electronic world, and the busy lives for which this dull drone has become the pulse, have hypnotized us into a state of spiritual stupor. We have failed to realize that we will never get there from "not here," but those who have thrived through trauma have awakened to learn to be very much here, and what "there" means.

Languishers committing the sin of acedia tend to live in a quiet and often unrecognized despair resting just beneath an ever thinning veneer of chronic, distracted, energy-draining business. Unless life deals them a dreadful blow, they seem unaware of the hollowness and emptiness of their spirit. Amid the tangible plenty reflected by a ballooning gross national product that measures everything except that which thrivers have learned makes life worthwhile, they fail to thrive.

The new field of positive psychology has discovered that those who have known the worst of life often learned how to find the best about living. Based on the experiences of these thrivers who have discovered their own Beethoven Factor, this book presents a template for thriving through what doubtless will be the increasingly stressful and painful times ahead. Unless we learn the lessons being discovered by the new positive psychology and the upward psychological trajectory it shows is within us, it is likely that we will continue to live on the carousel of dysfunction, denial, repair, and recovery. We will be resilient enough to live in a chronic state of serial recoveries from the crises that surely await us, but never quite wise or spiritually energized enough to know how to thrive because of them.

Thriving is defined as reconstructing life's meaning in response to life's most destructive occurrences. It is not only rising to the occasion but being raised by it. As one of the thrivers I interviewed put it, "Think of thriving as the five Cs. Think of it as the ability to transform a life Catastrophe into a Catalyst for a Creative Change of Consciousness. I only wish I hadn't waited until I almost lost my life to realize that I was not yet fully alive."

Thriving is experiencing a renewal of faith, energy, trust, hope, and connection just when doubt, cynicism, fear, fatigue, and alienation seem at their worst. It is not just bounding back, but up and beyond. It is the emergence of a new creative spirit through and because of the darkest times, a spirit that can guide us to the Beethoven Factor so we too can creatively conduct our daily life as an ode to joy.

Preface:
Awakening to a More Authentic Life

"All natural goods perish; riches take wings; fame is a breath; love is a cheat; youth and health and pleasures will vanish. Ultimately, the skull will grin at the banquet, but there are those who live habitually on the sunny side of their misery line."
—William James

The Path to Paradise

The path to paradise winds through hell. I've traveled that path, and I bring you seven pieces of very good news:

- The crises in your life are necessary, indispensable for a full and authentic life, and ultimately among the most significant and inspiring events in your life.

- Only those who have learned to thrive through crises, or learned from those who have, can fully understand what it means to flourish and deeply savor every moment of their lives.

- You have untapped innate evolutionary strengths, made not only to carry you through any trauma but also to help you become stronger and elevated by it.

- Because of your natural thriveability, there is nothing that can happen to you that has to prevent you from experiencing a deeply meaningful and profoundly more joyful life.

- You have a psychological immune system capable of dealing with the emotional stressors of your life, and it can become stronger each time you suffer through adversity.

- The worse your life seems, the more the possibility for discovering your innate ability to relish every precious moment of it.

- Feeling like quitting in the face of adversity can be a sign of strength through giving up impossible goals and seeking new purposes and meanings for what constitutes a truly authentic, full, and joyfully shared life.

Research in the new field of positive psychology shows the above statements to be true. It reveals that we were made not only to suffer but also to become much stronger because of our tribulations. The evidence is clear from this new and more optimistic view of our thriveability that life's worst misery can serve as a cosmic wakeup call to pay more attention to living's profound majesty. They are invitations to, in the words of positive psychology, stop languishing and start flourishing. They are opportunities to discover the ancient evolutionary thriving skills of our ancestors that made them the fittest survivors and allowed them to pass on to us the thriveability that lies waiting within our spirit.

If you're going through a miserable time in your life right now, take heart. Unless you choose to ignore your natural thriveability, you are more than up to the challenge. Fascinating new research has revealed that the times that try our souls are precisely the times that can awaken them. They are the opportunities when we can learn to—again using the words from positive psychology—"savor" our lives as never before by regularly basking and luxuriating in, marveling about, and giving sincere thanks for our moments here on planet paradise.

If things seem to be messed up in your life right now, take heart from the new positive psychology. Its research shows that you are probably on the verge of discovering that you were barely conscious all along and it is time to wake up. One of the thrivers I interviewed was a 14-year-old boy looking forward to a college scholarship in soccer. During his team physical examination, he was diagnosed with a tumor of the bone in his leg, and faced amputation. With the humor and upward psychological trajectory of most thrivers, he told me, "Yep, I'm really messed up. But nobody says they're messed down, do they? So, I guess I'm on my way up."

If life has handed you a dirty deal, it may also have handed you a new lease on life in the form of new goals, new meanings, and an authentic feeling of being alive that you have not yet experienced. You may be ready to learn that your regrets about your past and worries about your future have caused you to lose sight of the present where happiness grows. You may be ready to learn what the new positive psychology is discovering; we all have the capacity not only to survive and recover from terrible crises, but to thrive and flourish more than ever because—as Oliver Hardy was fond of saying when Stanley Laurel led him into yet another catastrophe—you may be on the verge of going through "another fine mess."

To Languish or to Flourish: That Is the Question

I've experienced firsthand the fact that no matter how unfairly cruel and hellish life seems to be, we have an inborn psychological immune system that allows us in some way and at some time to triumph over the terrible and make life at least as wonderful as it was miserable. Like an untested physical immune system, the psychological immune system can become weak and lazy when it is unchallenged for too long. Just as we do, it can begin to languish instead of flourish.

I've discovered that the lessons in thriving don't have to wait until we are forced to learn them the hard way. By learning from those who have already faced adversity and been transformed by it, we can learn to appreciate the moments of our lives, and learn the two most important lessons thrivers have to teach us. We can learn to savor life by making the ordinary sacred, and flourish through it by realizing that it is who we are with and not what we do that ultimately will matter most.

We're all suffering, but some of us may be too busy to know it. That's what languishers do. They are too much going places to truly "be" anywhere. Unless a major catastrophe slams them awake, they too often continue going through the motions without deep and joyful emotions. Even if languishers do eventually recognize the seriousness of their problems, they tend to settle for living in a state of recovery or return to the low-level normalcy of their prior life.

Until some major life crisis draws their attention to the magnificently chaotic nature of being alive and they elect to flourish through the rest of their lives, they become acclimated to what one of my patients described as "suffering in comfort." They slide back and forth between the states so well known by traditional psychology: dysfunction, denial, and recovery. They fail to experience the hardiness, thriving, flourishing, and savoring that positive psychology has recently discovered are our ordinary, natural gifts of a life of thriving.

Our modern lives are so hectic that we may not realize we are languishing. Unfortunately, more than 75 percent of us between the ages of 25 and 74 do not fit the criteria of positive psychology's "flourishing life," defined as a state in which the individual feels persistent positive emotions and experiences excellent physical, mental, and interpersonal relationship health.[1] Further, the *Journal of the American Medical Association* reports that more than 75 percent of Americans are now officially "diseased," according to current diagnostic criteria.[2] Positive psychology's interest is in the often forgotten flourishing 25 percent who seemed tuned in to their Beethoven Factor.

Traditional psychology and medicine have so compulsively concerned themselves with the search for our weaknesses and vulnerabilities that Dr. Clifton K. Meador of Vanderbilt University warns that sooner rather than later we will witness the extinction of the last well person.[3] How could such a smart and rich culture end up this way? The answer is that even with all we have accomplished, we too often languish rather than flourish, and recover or survive rather than savor and thrive.

Positive psychology is revealing that the answer to "there must be something more" is a clear and resounding "yes, there is." We can learn from those who have learned to thrive through their agony that we need not languish any longer. We don't have to mistake being busy for being truly alive, or fall into the stagnant reactive consciousness of weary indifference, pessimistic apathy, and cynical emptiness that comes with too much stuff and too little spirit and too much doing and too little being. We don't have to keep mindlessly and often wearily going through life automatically reacting to the stresses and strains of daily life while losing sight of what it means to lead an authentically rich and zestful life.

If you listen to their lessons, the thrivers you will be reading about can teach you what it takes in order to thrive in your own life and before you experience the impetus of the severe pain these thrivers have known. Before God sends you a hammer blow, their lessons can serve as the feather that draws your attention to what it means to thrive for the rest of your life.

We can learn the secrets of a thriving life from those who have already been to Hell and back. In their journey, we can find the way to paradise, even if that paradise may not be the one we thought we were pursuing. We can discover what helped these individuals, strengthened by their pain, to awaken to their ability to find a more meaningful, calmer, confident, happier, and loving life. We can learn the wisdom and caution behind Oscar Wilde's statement, "To live is the rarest thing in the world. Most people exist, that is all."

A Dickens of a Life

Through the many crises in my own life, I have become aware that the worst times can lead to the best of times. They can serve as spiritual alarms to awaken our ordinary magic to become stronger and more vibrantly alive. From the intensity of my own pain, from my interviews of and clinical work with others who have known great suffering in their lives, and recently through research from the newly emerging science called positive psychology, I have discovered the full magnificence of the gift of our ability to thrive.

Beyond blind optimism or trying to cling relentlessly to a forced positive attitude, I have come to understand that each of us has within us not only a physical immune system but also a powerful psychological immunity. This remarkable system is at the foundation of our innate thriving response, defined as total joyful immersion in the simplest aspects of our daily living. We can awaken to that inborn response, and those who have found it through their times of misery can help lead the way.

This natural thriveability is a kind of mental, emotional, and spiritual alchemy through which we are able to turn life's most bitter pills into an elixir that helps us not only overcome but transcend our agony. It allows us to come to see the world with a renewed confidence, enduring faith, and unrelenting joy that makes us feel almost invincible.

Like most people, I've led a "Dickens" of a life. When I read Charles Dickens's words, "It was the best of times. It was the worst of times," I often think that he was describing not only my life but all lives. Listed below are some of my own worst of times. They are some of the misery milestones along my path through Hell to paradise. Before you read about what I came to call my "thriving teaching trials," I suggest you take some time to reflect on the trials and tribulations in your own life and how necessary they may be to the fullness and richness of your life now. As upsetting as these events may have been, ask yourself if they were not in some ways essential in making your life more authentic, vibrant, meaningful, and joyful.

- My mother tells me that I barely survived my birth. I was taken from her for days, underwent several surgeries for damage to my head and body, and was very sick and frail through most of my preteen years. As I began to strengthen, it seemed that I so intensely treasured the opportunity to go to school, to play music, to read and write that my teachers thought of me as driven. My peers often saw me as "too intense," "strange," or a "misfit." Like most thrivers, it seems that because I had such a difficult time coming to life, I've learned to continue to try to keep becoming more alive—and this is the essence of thriving.

- I have known the unrelenting agony of my bones being eaten away by cancer and learned to treasure the painless moments I will never again take for granted. The ordinary aches and pains of daily living and symptoms of a cold or flu have become like familiar friends, whose annoying traits are outweighed by the value they add to our lives; reminders that my immune system continues to work its daily miracles that allow me to feel so totally alive.

- I have experienced the depth of depression when I saw my two impaired sons struggle against cruel discrimination. One has cerebral palsy, the other a severe learning disability. I saw the tears in their eyes when they endured the harsh reality of what they could never do and, more often, what an insensitive and intolerant world refused to allow them to do. From that sadness grew the proud joy of relishing the simple and ordinary childhood accomplishments too often taken for granted by parents of healthy children.

- I have known total blindness when both of my retinas became detached. When they were surgically reattached, I realized that I had been partially sighted all along, not because of any ocular problem but rather from lack of attention. For the first time, I began to see and cherish the most ordinary daily sights that had been right in front of me all along. Sunsets, traffic lights, gray days, and the faces of my loved ones seemed clearer and more vibrant than I had remembered before my sudden blindness. I wonder now how many others are blind but don't yet know it.

- I felt a helplessness, numbing emptiness, and sickening anger when two robbers almost killed my dad. He was carrying bags of food for our Christmas dinner to his car when he was shot. I went from despair to elation as I heard he would survive, and from that time forward never missed the chance to look deeply in his eyes, listen to his voice, watch as he walked, and take plenty of time to enjoy every moment I shared with him.

- A few years later, as I was comforting one of my own patients who had lost his father, my secretary called me to the phone. I heard the words that all of us dread the most. "I'm so sorry," said a nurse. "He's dead. Your dad had a massive heart attack and fell dead on the cafeteria floor here at work." From that sense of the sudden chilling finality grew my ability to embrace my dad's memory, my mother's life, my own life, and the life of all those I love with a depth and loving urgency that those who have not suffered such sudden close loss may not yet feel in their hearts. For me, every day without such a loss is a day I am allowed to keep making new memories and to celebrate the physical presence of my loved ones.

- I have known the heart-wrenching helplessness of trying to comfort my wife when she was told that her father had been found lying dead in a pool of blood from a burst aneurysm. Each time we have comforted one another, we have grown closer to share an almost overwhelming sense of the value of every living moment together. We have developed a kind of adaptive unity, what we've come to call our "couple's confidence" and our "creative couple coping." I have seen this same mutual thriving in many loving pairs who have learned to thrive together through the most severe and repeated adversity. My wife and I often wonder why so many couples fail to recognize the potential of a shared psychological immunity, treat their intimate relationships so casually, and sacrifice them so willingly.

- My wife and I struggled to understand my wife's mother after her stroke. She maintained her mental faculties, but felt agonizingly trapped in a body that would not allow her to speak. Until her death, she had tears in her eyes as she constantly struggled to be understood. I struggled in much the same way as I lay dying on a respirator, and we have never again taken for granted the gift of speech and the reassuring comfort of feeling heard and understood.

- My wife and I have known the emotional, mental, physical, and spiritual fatigue of being chronic caretakers. We have spent most of our lives fighting against the barriers of discrimination encountered by our sons and caring for my seriously ill mother, yet this lifelong giving seems to have awakened a deeper sense of connection between us and with all of our loved ones.

- I have known the profound sense of fear upon being told I would certainly die of cancer. I have known the terror of being told after my cancer went into remission that I would die anyway. They said I would die from suffocation caused by a deadly virus allowed to attack my lungs by my chemotherapy-and-radiation-weakened immune system. That fear of dying has led to my feeling of being more alive than I ever imagined possible, and I treasure every breath. Life seems so much more real now, and I think often of author James Fowler's words, "The more absolute death becomes, the more authentic life becomes." My confrontation with my own mortality resulted in my eagerness to write this book to get the attention of those unaware that they may not yet be leading a truly authentic life and may be squandering their chance to thrive.

- After nearly dying of cancer just at the time when I was experiencing publishing success, I had become too weak to write or promote my books. When I attempted to return to writing books, I was told by many publishers that my career was essentially over. One editor candidly told me that there was "a concern in New York that I would be a difficult author likely to die before I could finish and promote another book." I was also told that my story and the stories of the other thrivers you will read were "just too depressing and negative to sell." I finally abandoned my efforts to explain the nature of thriving and managed to publish *Making Miracles,* since reissued under the title *Miracle in Maui.* This book describes the details and science of my miracle survival from cancer, but it did not fully explore the issue of thriving. I finally found a publisher that understands what it means to thrive, and the book you are reading now is my attempt to share the wonderful news that thriving is an option for anyone who chooses it.

Remarkably Ordinary

As I write these words, I still feel the pain left from cancer's devastation of my body and the lingering sadness of these life challenges. But going through these experiences seemed to awaken my psychological immunity and my natural capacity to thrive through any trauma. They made me realize the wisdom of psychologist William James's observation that we need both the sunny and dark sides of life and a place for sorrow as well as celebration. They remind me that we need a place for radical pain to reawaken us to the grandeur of life's simple pleasures.

In my own life and work, I had discovered the value of what I called "SIG," or stress-induced growth. My suffering refreshed my memory about the importance of looking for inspiration from those who learned to thrive through crisis. As a clinical psychologist, I had designed and directed one of the first positive psychology programs. In 1973, my clinic was awarded the Rush Gold Medal from the International Psychiatric Association for achievements in preventive psychiatry. However, our program had more than a proactive "mental illness" approach.

Beginning in 1972 at Sinai Hospital of Detroit, what I named the Problems of Daily Living Clinic (PDLC) offered help based on the idea that mental health was much more than the absence of mental illness. The multidiscipline staff and I rejected the illness ideology emphasis on pathology and replaced its terms such as "patient" and "treatment" with words such as "client" and "program." Our goal was much more than the absence of sickness. We wanted to help launch people toward a life of what positive psychologists now call "flourishing."

Before its close in 1987, when I was diagnosed with cancer, we saw hundreds of people who learned to do very well in the context of risk. They came to savor their lives because of their struggle through adversity, not just overcoming it. The program emphasized what a person did, thought, and felt, not what a person "was" or "had." Our approach was based not on the sick and what made them that way, but on the savoring and how they did it. The people who came to us were often struggling, and our objective was to never leave them floundering in the relief from their pain. We wanted to help them move toward flourishing with the confidence in their character. We wanted them to see strength as not only perseverance and winning but also knowing when to gracefully give in, move on, and grow.

The PDLC was in place years before the 1999 gathering in Akumal, Mexico, where positive psychology formally took root. It was at that meeting, called by psychologists Martin Seligman and Mihaly Csikszentmihalyi, that the new field of positive psychology was born. These two men are positive psychology pioneers you will be reading about later, psychologists who joined with other like-minded scientists to propose a psychology based on helping persons move from languishing through hectically busy but empty lives to flourishing in more loving, joyful, and fulfilling lives.

When I completed my clinical psychology internship in 1968, I felt disenchanted with the predisposition toward pessimism about the human spirit. I had long felt uncomfortable with its diagnostic manual that had grown from 86 pages in 1952 to more than 800 in 1994. (I'm happy to report that the first *Handbook of Positive Psychology* published in 2002 is 829 pages in length.)[4] I felt that the pains and pleasures of living were located not inside individuals but primarily in the interactions between individuals and their world. Psychology seemed too "pathologized" for me, and my new clinic was my attempt to offer a more positive approach. My current suffering called my attention back to the immense strengths and virtues of the human spirit and to understanding not only what is weakest about us but also what is bravest. I became eager to write about the new positive psychology that was moving away from a preoccupation with repairing the worst things in life to building upon the best qualities of life—a new psychology of thriving.

Like the other thrivers you will be reading about, I know I am much more alive now and much more in love with life and with those who are in my life. I offer these examples of my own suffering not for sympathy or as evidence that I am in any way exceptional, more courageous, stronger, or naturally optimistic, or have had a tougher life than others, have a more positive attitude, or am wiser than anyone else. I offer them to encourage you with the news that, like the other thrivers you will read about, these dark times led me to discover the same thriving response that rests within your own consciousness. I offer them because I have learned that we are all capable of much more than resilience or a return to our pretrauma state. I have learned that settling for survival wastes valuable creative thriving energy.

I have learned that we are capable of coloring our souls not with bleak darkness of despair and hopelessness but with what William James called the "sky-blue tint" of those who transcend the "slaughter-houses and indecencies of the human condition" to "passionately fling themselves onto the goodness of life in spite of their hardships."[5]

The thriving response is as ordinary as it is powerful. It may be more easily recognizable by those of us whose attention has been demanded by what one of my patients called "the serial suffering of multiple miseries." But you don't need to wait for your turn at life's inevitable traumas to learn the flourishing of those who thrive. You can realize the power of your own psychological immunity and "thriveability" right now. You can decide to live every moment of your life in thriving mode and realize your own Beethoven Factor by taking a moment to experience some very simple but important thriving tasks.

- You can appreciate the simple fact that you can see these words (or feel or hear them if you are visually impaired) on this page and are able to think clearly about them, question them, and decide how you will interpret them.

- You can pause now, rest this book on your lap, take a deep breath, and relish your ability to breathe freely and on your own.

- You can place a phone call to a parent or grandparent, say "I love you," and try to store the sound of their voice forever in your heart.

- As if you may not be able to see again, you can look more lingeringly or caress more slowly the faces of your family.

- You can hug and hold your loved ones as if you may never again be able to feel their touch.

- You can smell the fresh air, see the bright colors, and listen to voices, music, and natural sounds as if you may never again be able to sense these simple delights.

By reflecting about these and other simple thriving tasks, you can begin to lead your life with less hurried disconnection, renewed vigor and zest, and enduring trust and optimism that there is nothing through the experience of which the human spirit can not only endure but thrive.

My many life challenges have taught me that we are made to not only endure the bad hands nature deals us. We are also made to be able to play our cards extremely well and more wisely and enjoy the game even when we don't win. I have learned that strength is not only "knowing when to hold them" but also "knowing when to fold them," give up, give in, and move on to other goals. In the final analysis, none of our strengths helps us avoid our final end. Ours is a doomed enterprise, but we can go about it like Tennyson's Ulysses, "always roaming with a hungry heart."

If you are willing to consider the findings from the new field of positive psychology and the research on our innate psychological immunity and ordinary but powerful human strengths, you will discover that it is not an exaggeration to say that our lives are well under way and we are very late recognizing that the journey has started. Whether there is such a thing as a near-death experience or an afterlife or not, a nearer-to-life experience and a before-death flourishing through the moments of life are matters of our own choosing.

Why Is There Suffering in the World?

"Why me? Why do I have to suffer so?" Like many thrivers, I asked this question over and over during my many tribulations. It is a version of the question that has persisted throughout history, "What is the purpose of suffering and evil in the world?" There are many ways to seek answers to this most difficult of questions, and each of us must find our own answer in our own way. This book provides an answer that other thrivers I interviewed and I have found. It is one that I hope will help you in your search for your own answer. It is derived from my own life trials, my work as a psychologist helping those who have suffered terribly, the dramatic stories of other thrivers you will be reading about, and the new research in optimum human functioning called positive psychology. For me, the answer is that life is made difficult so it can be made more authentic, real, and intensely meaningful. We suffer because we breathe, and asking why we must suffer is like asking why we must exhale. There is no life without it.

It seems that our lives may be torn apart so that we will learn not only how to weave them back together again but to cherish more every moment of our gift of life. As a Hawaiian elder told me, "God sometimes tears at the fabric of our life so that we will learn to be better weavers and to show us how to more deeply appreciate being given the chance to weave. We may not see the final pattern, but we are wise if we try to find new patterns and become more patient and creative weavers."

Going through the good and easy times of living can constitute periods of spiritual rest and renewal, but it can also result in a kind of spiritual languishing that is the exact opposite of the flourishing of the thriving response. It seems that the meanings of life are found not only within our blessings or during times of blissful meditation. They are found not only through perseverance and overcoming obstacles, but also through knowing when to give up, quit, and seek new and different goals and purposes in life. Thriving is not entirely or perhaps even mostly about victory. As you will read, it is also about allowing ourselves to be overcome, going with the flow, and accepting and learning from defeat and what follows from it. Giving up has a bad reputation in modern Western thought, but all of us quit sometimes and none of us will go through life without encountering numerous insoluble problems. The art of creative disengagement and seeking new goals and meanings is as much a part of thriving as persistent effort and a "never say die" attitude. Sometimes, thriving involves saying "die," welcoming death, and creatively thriving and even flourishing through its transitional processes.

Positive psychology has learned that thriving depends upon our vigorous struggles with the pain and challenges in our lives. At the good times, we are already experiencing joy. It is during the tough times that we are given the opportunity to learn as Beethoven did through his deafness. We can learn how to experience joy more deeply, meaningfully, regularly, and independently of life's lucky breaks, hard-earned rewards, and always temporary physical well-being. It is at the difficult times that we can come to appreciate what we could be grateful for almost all the time, an ordinary but enchanting joy in sharing with others the gift of being alive.

Toward a Positive Psychology

In the following pages, I will introduce you to the new science of positive psychology. After decades of a pathology-oriented psychology that primarily concerned itself with our darkest selfish motivations, corrupt unconscious processes, countless vulnerabilities, and attempts to repair and heal, a new positive psychology is emerging. It is interested in how innately strong, wonderfully adaptive, and basically very good we are. It is about more than finding and repairing what is wrong with us; it is also about identifying and nurturing what is good and great.

Instead of trying to identify and explain our weaknesses, positive psychology is dedicated to freeing us from the healing arts' psychoterrorism that constantly warns us of our corrupt unconscious, emotional and mental vulnerabilities, and ways of living on the edge of recovery. It is interested less in what threatens our lives than in what makes life worth living, less in our engrained weaknesses than our natural strengths. It focuses not on our frailties but on our natural human powers and virtues. It is concerned less with explaining why we get sick and more with why we stay well. In its most simple form, positive psychology aims to help us flourish rather than merely exist, and it finds its evidence not only in the lucky well but in those who have been to the dark side and found new light.

The primary characteristic of positive psychology is its emphasis on our generally upward psychological trajectory and our natural psychological immunity. It researches how we come to function so well instead of why we can seem so dysfunctional. It attempts to understand why so many people who should be feeling terrible manage to feel so wonderful, and how to enjoy life rather than avoid death.

To validate the findings from positive psychology about our natural talent to thrive, I will present the true stories of often horrible tragedies that led those who endured them to come up with the same explanation for why bad things happen to us as I did. By sharing their experiences, the thrivers you will read about have done some suffering for you. They have gone through versions of some of the same challenges you will face and come out thriving. Through their own words and in their own ways, they can teach you how their life crises led them to a more authentic life, a life you can lead now even before you face your own traumas. These superstars of thriving can help you point your own psychological trajectory upward by providing a pretested template for thriving.

Into a Deeper Universe

One of my test readers for this book is a cardiologist. His comments about my book suggested to me the concept of the increased authenticity that suffering can convey to our living. After completing his reading of an early draft of this book, he said:

At the beginning of your book, I almost didn't want to read it any further. It really was starting to make me uncomfortable with the problems in life I knew I was going to face sooner or later. I even felt sort of uncomfortable and a little guilty that I hadn't suffered as badly as your wife and you and the others you described have. But then I began to feel I had to keep reading for my sake and my family's sake. Somehow, it seemed that the quality of my life—no—our life, depended on it. Your story and the stories of those thrivers you wrote about who suffered so seemed in many ways to feel alive in the way I wished I usually did. They seemed to be immersed in their lives rather than just leading them. It was strange but in a very weird way, I sort of envied you and them for the kind of life suffering seemed to have opened up for you. I guess I related to that kind of life because of my experiences in the cardiac intensive care unit. Some of my patients who were confronting their own death seemed strangely more alive than those of us trying to keep them alife. Like the cases in your book, their lives had suddenly become so totally authentic. Your book made me decide that I had to make my life and our life more authentic now. I didn't want to wait for a disaster to teach me to thrive. I wanted a more authentic life before something major had to wake me up to it.

One of the first positive psychologists was William James. He wrote, "Those who survive great illness or great loss are twice born. They have drunk too deeply of the cup of bitterness ever to forget the taste, and their redemption is into a universe two stories deep."[6] I hope those of you who are suffering deeply now will find some solace, comfort, and confidence in the new psychology presented here and its promise of a unique form of invincibility. I hope those of you who have not yet sipped from the cup of life's bitterness will be able to learn from those who have and begin now to deepen your experience of living.

Comedian Art Linkletter is an example of a thriver. He has known tragedy in his life, but he still has managed to find his path to paradise on Earth. His words about his thriving summarize the orientation of positive psychology. When asked how he managed to thrive through so much adversity, he responded, "Things seem to turn out best for people who make the best of the way things turn out." Who are these people who are making the best of their lives? What is the nature of the ordinary magic that constitutes their capacity to thrive and helps them lead a life of meaning that is at least two stories deep? These are the questions with which the new positive psychology concerns itself.

Our worst life traumas may be cosmic alarms offered to awaken us to the full authenticity and challenging but wonderfully vibrant chaos of living, but we don't have to wait for these alarms in order to learn to thrive in our daily life. One of my patients was an opera singer and poet who developed cancer of the larynx. She was a thriver who flourished through her suffering. She said, "Tell your readers this for me. Tell them not to languish through their lives until something threatens their lives. Tell them to stop stressing and start savoring. Tell them not to wait until something makes them sob bitterly before they find the song in their soul and sing it. My only regret now is that it took my cancer taking my life before I recognized that I was taking and wasting my life every day. Cancer is faster and more painful, but it works the same way."

This now-wiser woman's words suggest that, by discovering our God-given talent for thriving, we will be able to avoid the sense of regret for a life not fully lived or not ever knowing we were never truly totally alive. They suggest the purpose of this book as expressed in the warning contained in Oliver Wendell Holmes's lament, "Alas for those who die never having sung and with all their music left in them."

Paul Pearsall, Ph. D.
Honolulu, December 2002

Introduction:
From Suffering to Savoring

"We believe that a psychology of positive human functioning will arise that achieves a scientific understanding and effective interventions to build thriving in individuals, families, and communities."
— *Martin E. P. Seligman and Mihaly Csikszentmihalyi*

A Psychology of Thriving

What if there was a group of people who had discovered the secret of how to live a joyous, deeply meaningful life no matter how much stress, and often because of the problems they had endured in their lives? What if this group had learned how to be invincible to the worst crises and had become stronger, more creative, and happier because of their suffering? What if these thriving souls had discovered the ancient secrets of hardiness, happiness, healing, and hope programmed within us as often neglected evolutionary gifts?

I've found that group. They are men, women, and children of all ages from around the world who have learned how to turn life's traumas into spiritual triumph, have shown the capacity to thrive in the way most of us long for, and now offer all of us secrets for savoring our lives in ways we may not even have imagined.

The hard-earned wisdom of this seemingly invincible group offers even those of us who have not yet suffered deeply a priceless gift. They offer us insight into our largely untapped abilities to rise to any occasion and show us how to lead a pleasant, good, meaningful, and full life no matter our circumstances. The lessons from these thrivers show that hard times can be the best of times to discover strengths we never knew we had, and to discover the guidelines for becoming stronger, happier, wiser, and more in love with life precisely because life itself often seems so unloving.

This hard-earned wisdom constructs a template for thriving in our own daily lives by suggesting trauma-tested guidelines for a much more authentic, full, and joyful life almost totally free of the nagging fears, daily anxiety and weariness, and omnipresent stressors of life's increasingly hectic pace. It offers a way to awaken from what seems to have become our trance of distractibility and daily fidgeting that too often leaves us feeling too busy to love and too tired to care.

The new positive psychology proposed by psychologists like Martin Seligman, Mihaly Csikszentmihalyi, Suzanne Ouellette Kobasa, Aaron Antonovsky, and the other scientists you will be reading about are not proposing a "happiology" or positive thinking warmed over. It is not a New Age philosophy that preaches always thinking good thoughts and loving our inner child. It is a rigorous scientific endeavor that looks at the importance and timing of constructive negative thinking and balances this with rational positive thinking. It conducts careful studies of those who have risen to and been raised up by the worst of occasions and found clues for how we can all come to savor life in the way they do. Its focus on our highest potential serves not as a replacement for but a major supplement to and counterbalance of traditional psychology's persistent focus on identifying and fixing our vulnerabilities.

Positive psychology is not concerned with popular psychology platitudes such as positive enhanced self-image or "high self-esteem" that have served as the basis for most education curricula and psychotherapy. In fact, its studies have shown that high self-esteem can be a severe obstacle to our ultimate well-being and happiness. Unconditionally loving themselves no matter and sometimes because of what they do, mass murderers, drunk drivers, racists, and school bullies all measure high on self-esteem.[1]

Positive psychology has learned that a negative self-image is as essential to health and well-being as a positive one, and that insulating ourselves or our children from critical "negative" thoughts and feelings of shame, guilt, self-recrimination, rational pessimism and depression, and deserved low self-regard only results in it being harder to feel authentically good about ourselves in the long run. It has learned that positive feelings and high self-esteem alienated from the exercise of true character and the real application of constructive strengths leads to life disappointment and even serious depression. It has discovered that if we don't deeply feel failure when it is fact, and fail to dislike ourselves when we do things that are not likeable, we can never feel authentic mastery when it is real.

In essence, positive psychology has learned that self-love should be conditional. What thrivers learn, and what positive psychology has shown really counts for a thriving life, is the development of earned self-regard based on identifying and applying our unique strengths to grow personally through our worst tribulations and overcome our worst fears.

The men and women of World War II are often referred to as the "greatest generation," but positive psychology has learned that they are made of the same stuff all of us are. They faced a time in history that evoked within them the same ancient evolutionary strengths that are within all of us. Whether other generations can be great requires clear recognition of the magnitude and threats of the real crises that confront us and then identifying and applying our innate thriveability to grow stronger and better through our pain.

Savoring Life

Positive psychology shows that we can feel invincible to the stressors and traumas of life and actually use these challenges as impetus for much more than a pleasant life of evanescent physical pleasures. It points the way to overcoming the most frequent modern emotional disorder—languishing, or "going through the motions" in life—and teaches us how to flourish by embracing the ordinary as sacred. It instructs us about the good life invigorated by a sense that we have faced our worst fears, discovered and acknowledged our most glaring weaknesses, realized our most powerfully adaptive strengths, and used the latter not only to carry on but to grow stronger and wiser than we ever imagined we were or could be.

One of the questions I asked clients coming to my Problems of Daily Living Clinic was, "Are you savoring your life?" The new field of positive psychology is essentially the study of going from languishing to flourishing and surviving to savoring. Positive psychologists Fred B. Bryant and Joseph Veroff at Loyola University pioneered the study of the "savoring" skill.[2] They have found that luxuriating, basking, relishing, marveling, and thanksgiving don't have to be things we do on vacation or on special occasions and holidays. Like other positive psychology researchers, they have found that these are ways we were made to live every day.

Positive psychology has discovered that it seems to be the particularly tough times in life that are the best suited for bringing out our "savorability." We seem to have the innate capacity to come through life's crises to lead a daily life in which we intentionally make ourselves much more regularly aware and appreciative of the joy of living.

The thrivers you will be reading about in this book managed to go from suffering to savoring. You can learn four components of savoring from them. They know the comfort of *basking* in earned praise, the loving feeling of *thanksgiving* to those who fill our lives with gratitude for their loving, the thrill of *marveling* in life's daily pleasures to such a level that we lose all sense of ourselves and time, and the comfort of *luxuriating* in the most simple sensual pleasures from which our attention seems so often distracted. The thrivers I studied were first and foremost recognizable by their ability to live their lives in accordance with these four components of savoring and to live them with an intensity that matched or exceeded the level of the suffering in their lives.

Joy from the Inside Out

Since its beginnings, psychology has assumed that happiness is essentially the result of good fortune or hard work. It attributed joyfulness to outside factors and essentially to the absence of sadness and stress. It has tried to understand well-being by studying those who aren't well. Its objective has been normalcy through the absence of pathology. But this book looks at the high-level well who have learned that happiness is much more than absence of sadness. It examines the experiences and lessons of those who have learned that what we accept as a normal life may be the major obstacle to a more authentically gratifying life.

In my studies of thrivers who learned to savor their lives, I have discovered that the suffering, depressed, and suicidal seek much more than recovery from their pain. When I saw them as my patients, I learned that they wanted much more than a return to normal. Like all of us, they wanted to feel much more than "okay again." They were in search of glee, not just the cessation of gloom. Like persons who had known a kind of spiritual starvation, they wanted to be able to not just taste life again but to savor it like never before. They wanted much more than to get rid of their symptoms—and this is the goal of positive psychology.

This fascinating new field has discovered that happiness is not just the absence of unhappiness or the presence of lucky circumstances. It reverses that assumption by saying that unhappiness is the absence of our natural state of happiness. It's sometimes called the psychology of optimum human functioning, and what it is learning about us offers confidence that we can deal with what worries us most, and it offers great comfort and hope regarding our capacity to thrive throughout our lives no matter what happens to us.

The new positive psychology begins with the assumptions that we are strong, adaptive, resilient beings capable of growing through any problem. It views our unconscious processes as being characterized by love and caring, not selfish greed. It sees our memories not as repressed nightmare-like imprints but as positive past associations to a generally loving and positive family life. It considers our capacity to adaptively and creatively construe our lives as capable of turning any challenge into an adventure in our continuing development.

Recovery or Discovery?

A trip to the positive psychologist's office begins not with the question, "What's wrong with you?" but, "What's right?" It's not concerned with what is or could go wrong with us. There are plenty of sources to frighten us about our dysfunctions, phobias, compulsions, codependence, suffering inner children, repressed memories of abuse, sexual problems, disorders and addictions, and human frailties and threats to our well-being. The assumption of pathogenic psychology seems to be that we are all either in denial of or recovery from some deficit in our lives, but positive psychology is interested less in how we can recover than in why so many of us seem to discover ways to flourish in our lives.

Positive psychology focuses on the unappreciated ordinary magic of our innate human strengths and virtues. It looks for the best within us and examines our capacity to thrive, defined in the research as our innate ability to flourish despite and because of our life circumstances.[3] Since the late 1980s, research in this growing field has been overshadowed by the negativism of the pathology orientation. Even so, positive psychology shows that, in spite of the stress and unavoidable transitional trauma that come with being alive, the majority of us still manage to maintain a general state of high adaptability and achieve increasingly joyful bliss.[4] But due to their training or perhaps a personal disposition that draws them to their field, many psychologists and other mental health professionals have failed to pay attention to all the good news that positive psychologists are offering.

Even most popular books that offer paths to happiness seem to assume that we must first overcome some basic flaw in our character or resist the gravity of our general pessimism and malaise in order to reverse our downward psychological trajectory. Positive psychology challenges the assumption that we are somehow flawed persons living in a world that is just too tough and cruel a place for a wise person to be persistently happy and positive. It asserts that our emotional trajectory is generally moving upward and that we can, if we choose, live in a highly adaptive state of discovery rather than chronic recovery.

Over the last hundred years that psychology and psychiatry have been healing disciplines, popular philosophies, cultural mythologies, and forms of secular religion, their pathogenic orientation has focused on risks more than resources. Philosopher Albert Camus captured that orientation when he said that the foremost question for philosophy is why we should not kill ourselves. Positive psychology suggests that this question can't be answered by curing depression, studying the chronically depressed, or accepting the idea that we are basically weak, dysfunctional beings prone to despair and in need of therapy. It suggests that we should remain alive because no matter how bad we feel, we have resources, strengths, and virtues that can help us learn from and through our sadness so we savor life again. Instead of studying the depressed, it focuses on the elated and tries to learn from those who have shown the capacity to flourish despite trauma in their lives.

Pre-Fall Psychology

One of my music teachers once told me that Mozart's music was so splendidly wonderful that it might have been written before the Fall. Nearly every ancient culture has a mythology of a primordial time when humanity lived a simple, joyful, and magical existence in attunement with Nature.[5] They teach that this Golden Age came to a sudden end—the Fall when our human consciousness somehow became separated from its divine source and the innate goodness and loving kindness that characterized it.

Psychology reflects the cultures from which it springs, so it has embraced the idea of our Fall. One of positive psychology's founders, Dr. Martin E. P. Seligman, refers to the view that happiness is somehow undeserved and inauthentic as the "rotten to the core" view of human nature.[6] Psychology has long assumed that something about us went wrong and that we have fallen and are constantly struggling to get up. It thinks that some innate weakness and evil narcissism still lurks just beneath the surface. It still embraces Sigmund Freud's ideas that we are governed by a selfish id barely controlled by a fragile ego. Without a shred of scientific evidence, it is convinced that whatever it was that caused the apple to get bitten is still there in the form of an archetypically damaged and weak character.

Even when one of us rises to the occasion to show apparent extreme altruism, pathogenic psychology distrusts what it sees. After Eleanor Roosevelt dedicated much of her life to helping people who were black, poor, or disabled, several pathopsychologists wrote that she was only compensating for her mother's narcissism and her father's alcoholism.[7] When we seem too happy for too long, pathopsychology assumes that we must be in some form of denial or regression to be cured only by facing the gloomy "realities" of life and failings of our own psyche.

Pathogenic psychology assumes the worst about us, seeing us as basically selfish beings driven by animistic impulses pulsating just beneath a thin veneer of social politeness. Without strong evidence, it begins with the assumption that negative emotions are automatic and natural, while positive emotions are short-lived rewards derived from hard work, good fortune, or stringent control of our dangerously negative unconscious.

In its eagerness to be of help to those with serious psychological problems, psychology and psychiatry have paid most of their attention to the diagnosis and treatment of pathology and the attempts to control the sinister undercurrents of our unconscious processes. These fields have made remarkable progress in establishing causes of emotional distress and in developing various therapeutic and pharmacological interventions that treat formerly untreatable mental illnesses. They have generally failed, however, to concern themselves with what constitutes and leads to high-level mental hardiness.

Positive psychology is applying the powerful scientific method used for so long by those in search of the abnormal to the study of the normal thriving people living their lives in relative happiness. The word "pathology" derives from the Latin, meaning "the study of the passions," and positive psychology sees growth in the suffering often thought of as associated with the word "passion." It is looking for our capacity for an ardent love of life that can come from enlightened suffering.

In its emphasis on our flaws and frailties, psychology seems to have lost its appreciation for the basic nature of the subjects of its study. It has failed to see their beautiful inner passion for a happy life, the ordinary magic that keeps them going on a generally upward psychological trajectory no matter what life events set them temporarily back.

Unlike astronomers who are awed by what they see, physicists glorying in the paradoxes of the quantum world and buzzing particles they can't see, or anthropologists marveling in the creativity and adaptability of ancient civilizations, psychologists and other health care professionals seemed to lose sight of their reverence for the thriving human spirit. The word "pathology" also refers to the study of the abnormal, so pathogenically oriented psychologists look for neuroses, complexes, and unrelenting sexual impulses held in check by repression. They overlook the normal everyday magic and remarkable adaptability of the human character.

Beware of Health Terrorism

Modern medicine has firmly embraced psychology's pathogenic view, or perhaps the reverse is true. Maybe psychology's attempt to emulate what it sees as the scientific respectability of medicine accounts for its pathopessimism. Whatever the reason, medicine and psychology study those who are ill; they see their vulnerabilities, and constantly warn us about our weaknesses. As I mentioned earlier, in 1999, the *Journal of the American Medical Association* reported that 75 percent of Americans are now officially "diseased," according to current medical diagnostic criteria.[8] From this point of view, we will soon see the extinction of the well-person species. Because of my research and clinical work in psychoneuroimmunology, I am often asked to speak to medical students. When I recently asked one of my students to define a "well" person, she answered, "Someone we have not yet thoroughly medically evaluated." Such is the dominance of the pathogenic model in medical training.

Modern medicine's pathogenic view results in a subtle but pervasive kind of health terrorism constantly warning us about the newest risk to our health.

Here are some examples of the current health terrorism based on the pathogenic point of view:

- Health terrorists warn women about the ever looming threat of breast cancer, but seldom remind them that 95 percent of them will die of causes other than breast cancer.

- Based on the ever present "nutrition pyramid" designed by attorneys working for former Senator George McGovern, we have been told for years to eat a low-fat, high-carbohydrate diet or die young. This is the exact opposite of what current research is now revealing about the danger of too much carbohydrate and the myth that eating fat makes us fat.

- While warning us to go on a low-fat diet, medical terrorism doesn't report that those of us who have a reasonably healthy weight and blood pressure would add only about 30 to 90 days to our lifespan by doing so.

- It warns us of the threat of high cholesterol, but seldom counterbalances this danger with the fact that we need cholesterol to stay healthy and to have a pleasing sex life.

- It nags us to be trim and have buns of steel, but it doesn't encourage us with the news that having a butt larger than our waist might be a sign of good health. (While a potbellied apple shape can be a danger sign, a pear shape isn't.)

- It tells us that chocolate is not good for us, but it doesn't report that some of the fat in chocolate (unfortunately for chocoholics, not the most abundant fat) actually lowers cholesterol levels or that chocolate contains a substance that helps fight tooth decay.

Health terrorism and its assumptions about our vulnerabilities have taken much of the fun out of life. It constantly warns us about our weak points and how those things we enjoy the most might kill us. The new positive psychology suggests that we are much stronger than we think and have been told, and it suggests that we don't have to lead our lives in the role of the worried well or health hostage.

Lessons from the Health Reprobates

With the exception of catastrophic trauma and immediate threats to our lives, much of what keeps us alive or kills us remains a medical mystery. People who by all medical predictions should die young often don't, and those who it seems should not too often do. The field of positive psychology suggests that the answer to this paradox may rest in part in learning less about why we get sick and die and more about why we don't become ill and why we thrive.

Here's a simple test you can try to see how needlessly pessimistic the pathogenic or "sickness vulnerability" view can be. Think of relatives who lived in reasonably good health into their 80s. Now answer this question about that person. Did they seem constantly worried about their diet or lack of aerobic exercise, vigilantly eat a high-fiber, low-fat diet, work out at the gym three times a week, and have regular physical exams and medical testing? For must of us, the answer to this question is no.

We all have relatives who violated almost every health warning and lived long and well. We also know of people who seemed to religiously try to follow every health warning and directive and yet died young. There is something more that causes us to be healthy, and that something more is the concern of positive psychology.

Health terrorists fail to look at "the other group" in their research. For example, researchers have shown that being overweight, not exercising, having high blood pressure, and smoking result in about a 30 percent chance that we will die prematurely. They fail to ask about the other group, the 70 percent who despite engaging in these unwise behaviors don't die prematurely. They show little interest in the 50 percent of those people with three or more of the major risk factors who will not die of a heart attack.[9] This pathogenic view causes us not to be able to see a healthy forest because we are too busy looking for diseased trees.

Of course, no one should ignore commonsense medical advice. Women should get mammograms, none of us should smoke, and we should move more, eat less, and get more sleep. We should stop doing the obviously stupid things that might kill us and start doing the clearly wiser things that enhance our chances to live longer and well. Nonetheless, there is something to be learned from the health reprobates who seem to be able to thrive despite their sometimes cavalier disregard of medicine's dictums. What lessons do they have to teach us about thriving? Positive psychology addresses this and many other questions, and attempts to reverse the prevalent reductionist and negative orientation of the health sciences by trying to learn from ordinary day-to-day thrivers.

Questioning Koch's Postulate

One of the fundamental precepts in modern medicine that underlies the pathogenic view is Koch's postulate. It derives from the work of nineteenth-century Nobel prize–winning German physician Robert Koch. He was one of the first researchers to identify a specific cause (the tubercle bacillus) for a specific illness (tuberculosis). Later, French scientist Louis Pasteur set forth his germ theory agreeing with Koch that a single outside agent causes disease.

Koch's pathogenic view was based on the germ theory idea that injecting a given bacteria or virus into a person causes the disease related to that outside agent. Avoid the cause and live, or kill the pathogen that has found its way inside us and cure the illness. The "injectee" seemed almost irrelevant, so the capacity to thrive despite attack was not considered. We became seen as ever vulnerable targets, not strong and resilient beings capable not only of surviving but of thriving through an outside attack.

The problem with Koch's hypothesis is that, with the exception of intravenous drug use or sudden and overwhelming infection, bacteria, viruses, and other outside agents usually have to deal with *us*. That is, they have to make it through our bodies' immune, neurohormone, and other defense systems. The same is true of psychotoxic agents such as outside sources of stress that have to deal with our strong psychological immune system, which you will read about later.

We are much stronger than Koch and Pasteur assumed. We have the capacity to thrive through attacks on our system. Outside agents may be necessary for us to become sick, but they are not sufficient. For example, the majority of those who test positive for the tubercle bacillus never develop tuberculosis. Most who are infected with the influenza viruses don't develop the flu.[10] Most of those who go through terrible psychological events don't develop serious mental illnesses or become dysfunctional. There is clearly something more involved here than one outside factor challenging a passive, reactive, vulnerable human system.

Louis Pasteur himself, the man who taught us how to keep the germs out of our milk through pasteurization, came to question his germ theory and the "outside cause on a vulnerable system" idea. On his deathbed, he is reported to have said, "The microbe is nothing, the soil is everything." He meant that the body's strengths and vulnerabilities are equipped to deal with the bacteria, viruses, and other invaders that challenge it. Whether or not he actually said these exact words, he did begin to question the exclusively pathogenic model of life and health; and positive psychology is asking these same questions. What about the nature of the "soil"? Is it stronger and more resilient than we have ever imagined? Positive psychology is studying our psychological terrain and discovering that the answer is yes.

A Little Negativity Goes a Long Way

As stated earlier, positive psychology does not suggest that we can or should always try to think positively. It shows that we need our negativity but must be alert not to let it dominate our thought processes or direct our lives. Some degree of our negativity may be a form of superstition based on the idea that we are somehow asking for trouble and daring the universe to trip us up when we start thinking too positively. It may also help us get through the stress and strain of daily living by keeping us on the lookout for the worst and causing us to be pleasantly surprised when something better happens. But a little negativity goes a long way.

Our negative thinking and feelings may often seem more immediate and pressing. They may have been designed that way in order to override our positive, easygoing emotions because when we need them, we usually need them in an unexpected emergency. Or, perhaps we have come to take our more subtle positive feelings and thoughts for granted because we have become used to them as a part of what makes life worth living day to day. In either case, positive psychology suggests that we look more carefully at our positive thinking that causes us to thrive. It suggests that, by doing so, we can learn how to rediscover the joy of living, loving, and working.

Warning! This Is Not a Self-Help Book

This is not a self-help or how-to-do-it book. I will offer tests and simple science experiments you might want to try to help you learn more about the thriving response, but all you really have to do is read and reflect. You may find that there will be something about the thrivers' stories that awakens your own psychological immunity, but there isn't a set of steps you have to take, assignments you will have to do, or a program you will have to start in order to realize your natural psychoimmunity. You will not have to keep a diary, write assignments for yourself, or set aside time every day to do something.

This is a book about growing through, not coping with, adversity. It's about learning lessons from the new research in positive psychology that teaches you how to thrive by gradually developing your own unique explanatory system, not by copying or trying to comply with someone else's.

This is not a book about the popular idea that "tough times never last but tough people do." With the exception of their decision to tap into their natural ability to construe events in such a way that their lives became enhanced through their pain, the thrivers I interviewed didn't seem to be naturally tougher than most of us. What strength they had derived from the very same natural thriving magic that is within each of us, the ability to decide to fully engage our problems, learn and grow from them, and become stronger because of them.

You will read about thriving superstars who honed their thriveability to a fine art, but they were only developing a talent we all have. Some thrivers did seem to have been born more easygoing, laid-back, ready to creatively figure their way through their problems, and naturally upbeat. But other thivers who were not so naturally thriving-talented still managed to thrive in their own way and time.

It is a mistake to see thriving as an extraordinary response. Many of the invincible people whose stories you will be reading sometimes whined, cursed, felt sorry for themselves, questioned God and their faith, blamed others, asked "why me?" and did all the things the self-help books often say we should not do when faced with a challenge. However, through it all they remained engaged with their problem, protected their core identity, and kept seeking and finding new adaptive meaning in life and about themselves. They were in a state of discovery, not recovery.

There are no quick fixes offered here. I will offer lessons from research in positive psychology and the stories of the thrivers that will show you ways you might tap into the power of your own psychological immune system, but thriving is more process than goal and more an evolving philosophy of life than a step by step program.

A Guide to Thriving

This book is divided into two sections. Part 1 describes the new field of positive psychology, the nature of thriving, and the ways in which your psychological immune system works to make thriving possible. It is the theoretical part of the book that presents the research and true stories that substantiate the existence of our inborn thriveability.

If you are currently in the midst of or anticipating a serious crisis or tragedy in your life, you may want to read part 2 first. It is offered in the form of a "thriver's guide" that presents life lessons learned by those who have already realized their thriver's invincibility and from the groundbreaking research of positive psychologists. After reading the Thriver's Manual, return to read part 1 so that you will be able to understand the theory and science behind the thriving response.

There are many "survival guides," but part 2 is a "thrival guide." It is designed to invite you to consider the four primary distinguishing characteristics of those who thrive through crisis—hardiness, happiness, healing, and hope. The book ends with an illustration from my study of thriving, the important influence of a thriver role model who influenced our lives and provided emotional momentum for an upward psychological trajectory.

Most thrivers report remembering one strong, nonparental adult who served as their thriving role model. While parents can of course also serve as thriving models, most of those who thrived said they had an additional person in their lives who showed them how to be invincible. One of my thriving models was my grandmother. The thrivers I interviewed often identified grandparents as thriving models, and my grandma was no exception.

To summarize and review the ideas about thriving, I end with a discussion of a special life lesson list given me by my grandmother Leita Schlieman when she was dying. She had suffered terribly in her life, yet was one of the strongest, happiest, and most invincible women I have ever known. She was far from perfect and had the same flaws we all do, but she seemed to thrive nonetheless. Whenever any of her family complained about the dirty deal reality was handing them, she would laugh and say, "Just remember, you don't have to face reality. You have to make reality deal with you."

Grandma and my aunts and uncles would often sit with us for hours listening to the radio. Much as we stare at the television screen now, we would all look at the small place where the station numbers on the dial glowed. It was an exercise in the kind of creative consciousness associated with the thriving response. As we looked at the dial, we could form our own images from the sound. One day when Beethoven's "Ode to Joy" came on the radio, Grandma said, "Listen carefully to that deaf man's music. Always remember, you are much stronger than anything that can happen to you, so you must never allow life to play you. No matter what happens, always be the composer of your own life's symphony."

I hope you will pause a moment before continuing your reading of this book to think about a thriving role model you may have had in your own life. I provide my grandmother's words at the end of this book as a way to rekindle memories of those who taught you how to thrive. I hope this book will cause you to recall and re-embrace the lessons of that special person who, like Beethoven, despite the trials and tribulations and all the frailties of being human, still managed to thrive.

PART I
Thriving through the Tough Times

"The mind is its own place,
and in itself can make a heaven of hell,
a hell of heaven."

—John Milton

1 A Life Fully Lived

"You gain strength, courage, and confidence by every experience in which you really stop to look fear in the face. You are able to say to yourself, 'I lived through this horror. I can take the next thing that comes along.'"

—Eleanor Roosevelt

Lessons from a Lucky Dog

When I was dying of cancer, I often read the classified ads. Reading about the ordinary, simple daily issues of life seemed to offer some comfort and hope that perhaps someday I would be free enough from my pain to become concerned about such often silly and mundane things. One ad caught my attention and caused me to reflect on the nature of positive psychology's thriving response, our innate ability to flourish through and often because of the trauma in our lives. It read, "Lost Dog. Blind in left eye, one ear, no tail, patches of hair missing. Recently hit by a car. Answers to the name Lucky."

I laughed to myself as I thought about the contradiction between the poor dog's name and his life experiences. As a reflected on his plight, I began to think there might be some wisdom to be gained from this simple ad. I thought about the strange paradox that this dog had gone through a series of terrible experiences yet was lucky enough to be loved and longed for by his owners. I wondered if he was aware on some level of the value of his living because he had endured so much. Did he know he was lucky just to be alive and to be missed? I wondered if he could know in some dog-consciousness way that he had been more fortunate than most dogs to have a family who helped him through so many problems. This dog had been through the mill but had apparently been ready and willing to get on with life. He was at the very least a survivor.

I kept the ad on my bed stand for weeks and I still have it. One day when my nurse was about to throw it away, I decided to call the number in the ad to see if the dog had ever been returned to its owners. I was reluctant to call for fear I would only upset the family if the dog had been lost for good, but I made the call anyway. A little girl's voice answered and I asked to speak to her mother or father. She said, "If you're someone else calling about Lucky, we already have him back. He's fine and playing with us."

The mother came to the phone and I explained who I was and from where I was calling. She expressed her concern for me and reassured me that Lucky was "a very lucky dog and is really thriving [her word!] on all the attention he's getting." She added, "You should know that his name before all of his problems was Ralph. We changed it when he kept coming through all his troubles and seemed happier than when he was just a Ralph."

I reflected for hours about what this woman said. I thought how in a strange way with which I was still mentally grappling, I too was lucky. I certainly didn't feel lucky to have cancer, but even at the worst of times I felt a delightfully baffling sense of being more authentically and intensely alive than when I was consumed in my busy career. I felt fortunate to feel an even deeper love for and from my wife and family, a love I wonder if enough of us fully realize until there is very little time left to savor it. I told myself then that I would be sure to tell this story in the book I hoped to write about the thriving response.

Six Reactions to Life's Challenges

To learn more about thriving, it is helpful to first understand its place in the cycle of our response to the challenges in our lives. Since the 1980s, psychology has been studying the stress, relaxation, survival, recovery, and more recently the resilience response. In the late 1990s, a sixth response was identified by positive psychology: our natural thriving response, defined as stress-induced growth.

Here are six human responses to the stress and strain of life:

• When we perceive a life event that goes beyond our presently conceived capacity to cope, our *stress response* kicks in. Unlike the following five responses, this one is automatic. Because our brain's primary mission is to keep us alive, it sends us into our primitive "fight-or-flight" mode without much mental input from us. All but our basic survival body systems shut down, and we enter a generally catabolic or "energy-burning" lifesaving mode.

- Several years ago, Dr. Herbert Benson of Harvard University described the opposite of the stress response, a natural human response he called the *relaxation response.*[1] When we intensely mentally focus, meditate, or pray, our metabolism slows down, our blood pressure drops, our heart rate lowers, and our brain calms down and enters a less aroused and agitated state.

- A third response to life's challenges is *survival.* When we are under severe stress and threat, mechanisms in our body and brain go into lifesaving action. The brain shuts down the body systems we don't immediately need and activates those systems we must have to stay alive and survive an immediate threat.

- A fourth response is *recovery.* During this response, the body's systems return to balance and the damage done by its prolonged warlike state begins to heal. If we are truly recovering, we may even experience the relaxation response.

- A fifth response*, resilience,* involves completed recovery and full return to a "pretrauma" state. The person is no worse off for the wear and tear and is able to function again in ways that may surprise those who have not experienced such trauma. Resilience is the body's and mind's capacity to bounce back completely and unharmed from the trauma they have endured. Our physiological immune system makes it possible for us to repair ourselves and return to our prestress level. Resilience is essentially getting back to our normal state and a level of functioning typical of most people who have not been under stress.

- A sixth response, and the focus of this book, is the *thriving response.* This response allows us to bounce back beyond normal and to function stronger and more joyfully than we did before our trauma. It occurs because we have a powerful psychological immune system that acts in much the same way as our physiological immune system. This system has its own set of rules and ways of dealing with the emotional "antigens" that can "infect" our consciousness.

Our sixth response is a "tend-befriend-comprehend" reaction to life's challenges that allows us to go beyond the stress, relaxation, survival, recovery, and resilience responses. It is much different from the more familiar "fight-or-flight" way of dealing with stress. You will learn later that one of the distinguishing features of thrivers is that they seldom either fight or take flight when a crisis strikes. Instead of fighting, they know when to quit and move on to other goals and interpretations of their situation and life in general. Instead of taking flight, they more fully engage in life. Rather than trying to escape, they reconstrue their situation and look for new ways and places in their lives to more fully engage. Rather than relaxing, they go into mental and emotional action and go toward or sometimes around instead of retreating from their challenges. They are heartened by their memories of their most loving and cherished connections even if their stressful situation distances them physically from them.

They become "consciousness creators" in the sense that they decide what will or will not be on their minds and do not reactively surrender their consciousness to the negative power of whatever is happening to them. Perhaps most important of all, they know how to be enlightened quitters who can withdraw from their struggle and select a new goal within a different life perspective.

Thrivers are characterized by their high mental alertness, emotional responsivity (not just "reactivity"), and their spiritual engagement through their quest for meaning in their crises. Once trouble happens, thrivers become more like students and philosophers than patients, victims, or warriors. They are made stronger by their adversity because they keep learning from it and are engaged with it long enough to thrive through it or seek new goals and objectives. Rather than just trying to get past or cope with the stressors in their lives, they look within their problems and themselves to create new ways of explaining and enjoying life.

Charles Carver, professor of psychology at the University of Miami, is a leading researcher studying our sixth or thriving response. He offers a technical definition for this response that distinguishes between resilience as essentially a process of recovery and thriving as a "better-off-afterward" style of dealing with severe stress. He defines someone who thrives as a "person who experiences the traumatic or stressful event and benefits or gains in some way from the experience and can apply that gain to new experiences, leading to more effective subsequent functioning."[2]

The key phrases in Carver's definition are "benefits," "gains," and "more effective subsequent functioning." Thriving is getting stronger because of our trials and tribulations. It's developing a new explanatory system, a new way of disputing our own pessimistic interpretation of what is happening to us that allows us to maintain an upward psychological trajectory. If another person unfairly accuses us of something, we gather information to dispute the challenge. Developing a new explanatory system is a creative form of personal disputation that allows us to come up with new ways of viewing our situation. As Carver points out, thrivers apply the gain they seemed to make through their strife to enhance their dealing with future experiences in their lives. Fortunately, we can learn to apply what these thrivers learned to our own lives without going through the pain they endured.

How Alive Are You?

Are you alive? If you answered, "Of course!" think again. Do you feel so vibrantly alive that you are regularly moved to tears of joy by the simple grandeur of ordinary things? Do you laugh to the point of tears several times a day? Do you smile contently with eyes in full squint and feel your heart warmed when you think of how loved you are and how others know you love them? Does it seem that you are so vibrantly full of life that you feel almost invincible? This is how thrivers feel.

You will be reading in the following chapters about a group I came to call "the invincibles." They were men, women, and children I met at my lectures around the world, patients who came to a clinic I founded in the Department of Psychiatry at Sinai Hospital of Detroit, and my fellow cancer patients I met while undergoing my bone marrow transplant for Stage IV lymphoma. All these people had done much more than survive or recover from almost unimaginable life traumas; they had managed to thrive because of them.

Many of the cancer patients who did not survive still seemed to thrive before they died. They became much stronger on all levels than they were before their adversity, and applied the emotional and mental gains they had made during the course of their cancer to the course of their dying. They often seemed much more fully alive than many of the distracted and hurried people who visited and cared for them. They knew when to fight and, perhaps more importantly, when to disengage and move on to other life meanings and goals. They radiated an invincibility that offered perhaps the greatest assurance and comfort any of us could hope for, the fact that we are capable not only of amazing resilience but also of thriving through our tribulations to give our living and even dying meaning and therefore more manageability.

You can learn the lessons from these thrivers and apply them right now to have a more authentic, vibrant daily life. You can learn to see, hear, feel, smell, and touch the world with the joyful intensity that thrivers do. You can relate to your loved ones with the urgent caring of a thriver even before you are faced with the possibility of not being about to hold and hug them again.

One of the thrivers I interviewed for this book was a 67-year-old grandmother. She had suffered a severe stroke that had left her speechless and able to walk only with the assistance of a cane in each hand, and even then only with great difficulty. Her story illustrates the thriving response.

While visiting her daughter, she had watched helplessly from the front porch as her four-year-old-granddaughter had darted into the street and was killed instantly by a speeding drunk driver. Unable to shout a warning, she had seen the inevitability of the tragedy but could do nothing about it. It took her what seemed like an eternity to join the others sobbing at the side of the fallen child. Unable to voice her horror and grief, she could only sob uncontrollably.

Even after such a dreadful experience, this grandmother seemed to have a zest for living that her family said was more than she had shown even before her stroke. She remained active in campaigns against drinking and driving, and volunteered at her church in the day-care center. After she had responded in a frail handwriting to all of my questions, she added a note. It said, "I hope you don't feel sorry for me. I am a very lucky mother and grandma. My memory and love for my granddaughter are so very strong. She is always in my heart, a heart I think is stronger now because it was so terribly broken."

Positive psychology suggests that even when we are not fully aware of it, our natural psychological immunity is trying to keep us on an upward psychological trajectory. The lessons from the thrivers teach us how to tune in to that inner positive momentum to enhance and even accelerate our generally positive life course. Fortunately, we don't have to go through a crisis to learn how to thrive through and because of one. We can study the reactions of those who have dealt with crises in their lives and start applying their wisdom and experiences to the daily minicrises and nagging aggravations that we too often allow to rob us of a fully authentic and joyful life. We can gain momentum for our upward psychological trajectory by learning what positive psychology has learned about thriving.

When crisis strikes, my interviews and research and the research of others indicate that we experience a crisis cycle (see figure 1).[3] This cycle incorporates the five human responses to stress listed above. One of these five phases in the crisis reaction cycle is the thriving response through which we can turn a crisis into a "consciousness catalyst" for a happier and more energized life.

The Kindling Reaction[4] (Worsening)

When crisis strikes, most of us tend to react by first adding our own emotional fuel to the fire of distress. Even though Benson's relaxation response is always an option when we're under pressure, most of us are too stressed by the pressures of the present moment to try it. Instead, we react like kindling wood being added to a fire. At least for a while, we think in ways that cause our prob-

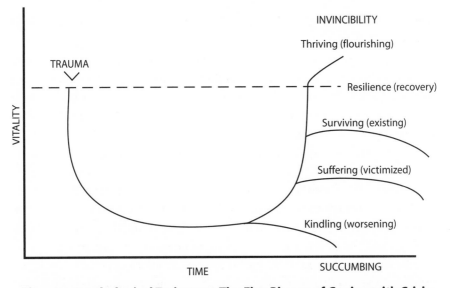

Figure 1. Psychological Trajectory: The Five Phases of Coping with Crisis
When trauma strikes, we respond with five crisis-coping styles. *Kindling* is over-reacting that worsens the problem and can result in ultimate succumbing to the adversity. *Suffering* results from feelings of persecution and being victimized that, if not corrected, can also eventually lead to succumbing. *Surviving* is return-ing to a subnormal level of daily existence in which we are "making it" but not growing in vitality. *Thriving* is finding new meaning in life, growing stronger physically, mentally, emotionally, and spiritually, and maintaining a generally upward psychological trajectory to increased psychoimmunity and invincibility. (From "Resilience and Thriving in Response to Challenge: An Opportunity for a Paradigm Shift in Women's Health" by V. E. O'Leary and J. R. Ickovicks, *Women's Health: Research on Gender, Behavior, and Policy,* I, p. 127. Copyright 1994 by Lawrence Erlbaum Associates. Adapted with permission.)

lems to heat up and become more intense. We become angry and even aggres-sive. We blame others or degrade ourselves and throw at least a mild mental tem-per tantrum. We become our own and our problems' worst enemy. Problems not only "happen to us" but we start happening to them through our overreactive catharsis, or what psychologists call "venting."[5]

Popular psychology teaches us that we will feel better if we "vent" or "get it all out" when we are frightened, upset, or angry, but research says differently. Just as junk food tastes good but is not good for us, venting makes us feel tem-porarily good. In the long run, however, it is terrible for our health. Catharsis is seductive because it gives us some quick, temporary relief from the tension we experience, but venting eventually takes a toll on our psyche, our body, and everyone around us.

The one thing we can be sure of when we let all our anger or negative feelings out is that we will become even angrier and end up making ourselves and others feel worse. Psychologist Diane Tice studied 400 men and women and the strategies they used to escape their foul moods.[6] She found that "venting" caused anger and other negative feelings to worsen and last longer.

We are not hydraulic steam machines that need to have our pressure released to prevent explosion. Thrivers learn this fact of life and tend to severely reduce their venting as their lives go on. Under pressure, the first thing they do is nothing. Instead, they reflect and try to construe their way through their challenges. In place of "letting it all out," they work on trying to figure things out. They don't curse the world; they try to discover new ways of construing it.

The act of construing is the process of mentally interpreting and framing life events in our own way. One of our most distinguishing and powerful human traits is our innate ability to interpret and assign meaning to what happens to us, to focus our attention where, when, as deeply as we decide, and to be the masters of the content of our consciousness.

Positive construing is the opposite of worrying. When we worry, we are most often in at least a mild version of our stress response. Psychologist Thomas Pruzinsky defines worry as "a state in which we dwell on something so much it causes to us become apprehensive. Worry is the thinking part of anxiety."[7] Thriving is the mental and emotional opposite of worrying because it involves construing a way out of and beyond a real and existing problem, not ruminating about what may be in store for us. Thriving is a way of thinking that reflects the statement by author James A. Garfield, "I have had many troubles in my life, but the worst of them never came."[8]

Author A. J. Cronin wrote, "Worry never robs tomorrow of its sorrow; it only saps today of its strength."[9] Worrying is one of the most mentally exhausting things we can do. It is like racing the engine of our car when it is in neutral gear. Thrivers seem to remain strong-willed and strong-minded because they seldom worry. If they do, it is in the form of presenting themselves with options and looking for strategies, not just making a mental list of potential disasters. They do not allow their mental energy to be drained away by ruminating about what might happen, and instead focus on construing ways to deal with what is happening. Author Arthur Somers Roche wrote, "Worry is a thin stream of fear trickling through the mind. If encouraged, it cuts a channel into which all other thoughts are drained."[10]

Research on the kindling response and its underlying worrying shows that they are functions of the lower emotional parts of our brain.[11] They are emotional and mental evolutionary leftovers that can help when they come in small doses that end with an adaptive strategy for dealing with a problem but not when they dominate our thinking. Our primitive forebears who worried the most tended to be more vigilant and more likely to survive, but our modern world has elevated worrying to an art form or kind of mental hobby. When we refer to "multi-tasking," worrying is usually one of the tasks that drives us to keep going for fear we might fail. We ruminate about "what if or what's next " so much that we miss out on "what's happening now" and the opportunity to enjoy, learn, and grow from it.

If they worry at all, thrivers do so quickly and efficiently. They pay attention to any negative thoughts and check them for hints as to what to avoid or do, but then they move quickly beyond them. One of the thrivers was a psychologist who had recently discovered the research data on thriving. She said, "I worry, but what worries me most is when I start worrying about worrying. I used to worry that I was worrying or even worry that I was not worrying enough. It sounds stupid and funny for a shrink to say that, doesn't it? Now I do what I call wiser worrying. I don't go round and round about a problem. For me, a worry is like a memory or reminder. I think about it and then try to figure out something to do about it. For me, a worry is an alarm to do something or figure something out. I think most worrying is being nervous about the future and frightened by the past, so I want to pay more attention to the now. Worrying really takes you out of the present, which is where you need to be if you're going to solve a problem. I think I've become a wiser worrier lately. I think and then try to come up with a new way of thinking."

One of the thrivers was one of my Hawaiian extended *'ohana* (family). She was 98 years old when she gave me a paper with the words "Why Worry?" she had written in Hawaiian calligraphy on the top. She had seen more tragedy and loss than most of us will experience if we had two lifetimes. She seemed to have every reason in the world to have become a chronic worrywart, but she clearly expressed in her words a thriver's orientation to worry.

Her note said, "About 40 percent of what we worry about will never happen. Another 30 percent concerns old decisions, which we cannot change. About 12 percent is related to criticisms of ourselves that are not fair and made by people who feel inferior to us. Another 10 percent of our worrying is related to our health, and worrying only makes us sick. About 8 percent of our worrying is worth the effort because it can help us find a starting point for doing something about whatever it is that is worrying us. If we resist wasting our time on the useless 92 percent of our worrying, we can get busy doing something about the 8 percent that needs our full attention."[12] Coincidentally, my interviews indicate that 8 percent seems to be a good estimate of the maximum amount of mental time thrivers spend on worrying.

Another destructive side effect of "kindling" or "losing it" is what getting stuck in this phase of crisis reaction does to those around us, the very ones we need to help us thrive. No matter how personally we feel the sting of adversity in our lives, crises happen to systems, not individuals. As hurt as we feel, we never hurt alone.

Although he didn't know it at the time, an example of the danger of venting for those around us was provided by one of my high school teachers. To make his point about how we can fall victim to elements such as the weather and the cycles of the moon, my high school biology teacher wrote the word *zeitgeber* (German for "time-grabber") on the chalkboard. It refers to a well-known biological fact that all living things become "entrained," or seem to fall into sync with the events around them. We feel sleepy at night because our time seems "grabbed" *(geber)* by the influence of nighttime *(zeit)*. When we engage in the kindling response, we become *zeitgebers*. Our emotional state becomes so intense that it grabs us and everyone around us, leading to feelings of guilt and helplessness.

When a trauma strikes, most of us are kindlers for a period of time. This is because of what psychologist and marital therapist John Gottman calls our "emotional flooding."[13] Seeing a problem that seems to exceed our adaptive skills can cause us to go into a "catabolic" or energy-burning state. In the period of one heartbeat, our heart rate quickly accelerates by as much as 30 beats a minute and stress hormones instantly begin to surge through our body. We flood our system with stress hormones, our judgment becomes clouded, and thriving becomes out of the question.

Two persons in a relationship who both tend to "flood" and therefore act as "cokindlers" often end up consuming their own relationship and not being able to thrive through their problems. Dr. Gottman reports that, based purely on the presence or absence of a flooder, he can predict with 94 percent accuracy which couples who come to his laboratory will have marriages that fail to thrive and will end in divorce.

Author Daniel Goleman describes the effect of flooding as being "emotionally hijacked," taken over by emotions of despair and anger and their accompanying stress hormones; something we all experience from time to time in our lives.[14] Unless we have become aware of our capacity to thrive, our threshold for suffering becomes lower and lower and we begin to waste essential life energy trying to put out the emotional fire we ourselves are fueling.

One of the invincible people I interviewed was a truck driver paralyzed in a rollover accident. He had experienced a heart attack and blacked out, and his truck tumbled down the expressway. He had been a powerful flooder most of his life, but eventually learned to calm down and thrive through his adversity. He said, "I learned that getting things off my chest meant I must have been putting a lot of weight there that was choking my heart to death. I could go off in an instant when someone got to me. Trust me, if you get away from what pisses you off for awhile, your PO quotient goes way down. My philosophy now is 'Don't suppress it, don't express it, just go someplace and sit down, shut up, forget it for a while.' Maybe then you can try to make some sense if it all."

The Suffering Reaction (Victimized)

If we realize that most of us kindle for a while when crisis strikes and that we can get past this stage by simply shutting up, stepping back, and taking the time to construe our way through our problems, we can begin to calm down and think more rationally. To reduce some of the negative physical side effects of our stress response, we might even be able to try the relaxation response.

Even though the so-called victim mentality has been criticized and can lead to extended suffering, it may also be a necessary phase in the crisis coping cycle and a way to relax a little before engaging our problem. When we move from the kindling to the victim stage, we become a little freer of the agitation of the catabolic stress hormones that rob us of our mental and emotional energy. For a period of time, we move from fighter to feeling victimized. We feel sorry for ourselves and may sulk and withdraw into self-pity. One of my fellow cancer patients pointed out the necessity of a little self-pity when she said, "Look, if I can't feel sorry for myself when I'm dying of cancer, can anyone tell me when I can? I think I'm entitled to feel like a victim at least for a little while. It gives me a break from being a warrior in the battle against my cancer."

Because thrivers' emotional momentum remains on an upward psychological trajectory, thrivers pass through the victim phase of the crisis cycle relatively quickly. For them, it is a brief pause allowing them time to clear their mind to get ready to work on construing their way through their difficulties. Like all of us, they feel like victims. But they eventually come to realize that the answer to the question "Why me?" is "Why not me?" or "It's just my turn." They begin to construe their situation in a more constructive light and move out of this suffering and self-pitying stage. If they don't, they end up dragging themselves and those who love them down with them.

Just as the stimulating agitation of ventilating or catharsis feels good for a while but is actually destructive, the social sympathy and seductive calming effect of feeling victimized can also feel soothingly good. Eventually, however, being a victim for too long damages our chances to thrive. Because we have stopped fighting and given in, we may temporarily stop the flooding and enter a more "anabolic" or energy-conserving state characterized by a slower and steadier heartbeat and more relaxing neurohormones. But we can become as addicted to this calmer, relaxed, and more passive state just as easily as we can to the stimulating catabolic state of kindling. My interviews indicate that some people in crisis begin to "yo-yo" between the kindling and victimizing reactions. Their bodies are eventually negatively affected by the strain of the constant ups and downs they are put through.

Because it is our biological nature, we are all entitled to kindle and be a victim for at least a little while, but being a helpless victim for too long eventually pushes away the very people we need to help us thrive. Just as kindling can spread to our social support system, clinging to victim status for too long can cause our family to feel responsible for our feelings, exhausted by our neediness, helpless to do much to change our feelings, and at least unconsciously angry and tired of living with a martyr and the burden of our passive submission and self-pity. More distant acquaintances can become even more distant when they begin to sense their own vulnerability to whatever problem we are experiencing. Health care workers don't want to feel like failures, and being a constant victim can remind them of how little they know or can do to help.

The wife of the paralyzed truck driver referred to his early adjustments to being unable to feel or move his legs. She said, "We all felt really sorry for him for a while, but we got sick and tired of what we called his pity parties. It seemed that his being a victim was becoming a way of controlling us or even blaming us. I didn't know what to do to help him and began to feel exhausted by him. I'm ashamed, but I got so I wanted to slap him out of it."

There is another caveat regarding chronic victimhood. Victims make terrible actors. If we feel in our heart and soul that we are truly victims, no amount of feigned courage or repeated "don't worry about me" statements will fool anybody who cares about and knows us. They can sense how we are feeling, and that is why sharing—not dumping—our true feelings and being aware of the feelings of our partners-in-thriving are crucial aspects of the thriving response. If we are aware of and try to get through the first two crisis reaction stages as quickly as possible, the result is the increasing social support and caring that comes from people who feel comfortable, competent, and safe enough to get close to us again.

Thrivers seem "systems sensitive." They understand that while they may be the current "primary target" getting the full brunt of a crisis, everyone around them is eventually influenced by and will have to deal with what has happened to them. They seem to sense that they themselves might become stressors for someone else.

Unless they acknowledge and move beyond it, people in the victim phase of the crisis cycle eventually begin to feel helpless to halt their emotional sinking. Their physiological immune system may parallel the surrendering status of their psychological immunity, thereby lowering both their emotional and physical stamina.

Describing his take on the crisis reaction stages, one of the invincibles said, "I think kindlers keep fueling the fire of stress, but by just sitting near the fire and allowing themselves to be burned by it, I think victims become fuel for the fire, too."

The Surviving Reaction (Existing)

After we have rebelled against and then felt victimized by a trauma in our lives, we can enter the phase of "making it." We begin to live in a weaker and more diminished version of ourselves that is never too far from returning to feeling victimized or kindling again. We feel "almost back" to where we were and manage to exist day to day. But even if we try to offer our bravest and most courageous front, those who know us best sense that we seem somehow less alive after than before our trauma.

Living as a survivor tends to result in a catabolic or "breaking down" process of the cells and tissues throughout the body. Unlike anabolic states such as thriving that build up the body, it is a process through which our energy resources can eventually be drained and depleted. Eventually it seems to feel that it takes "all we have" to keep ourselves above the victim phase. We tire easily, feel mentally and physically exhausted, and feel spiritually drained by trying to exist day to day. One survivor I interviewed was the widow of a rookie police officer killed on his first day on duty. She told me, "It takes all I can muster to just exist. I do it for the kids, but it's draining me. I get things done, but that's about it. There's not much energy in me to start the day, and by the end of it I have none at all. I'm a survivor, but I'm afraid most of me died with my husband."

Survivors are more easily accepted by society than kindlers and victims, but they can still make us somewhat uncomfortable. Because they have "found their place" and are not demanding too much with tantrums or angry outbursts or persistent neediness and self-pity, society welcomes and even praises survivors for their courage and endurance. However, eventually the mere presence of survivors of tragedy can remind us of the tragedy itself or tragedies that might befall us in our own lives. We withdraw, and the initial attention and accolades they received eventually diminishes.

The caveat at this stage is that just "making it through" and existing are ultimately never enough. They are a necessary transitional state either on the way back to the emotional worsening of kindling, the suffering of the victim role, or hopefully in the upward psychological trajectory toward resilience and eventually thriving.

One of the invincibles, a 42-year-old woman with multiple sclerosis, described the discomfort she experienced in being perceived as and feeling like a survivor. She said, "It was like everyone had you pegged. You weren't raising a stink about your condition and you weren't asking for their pity, so they could just smile and call me an 'MS survivor.' I was not going to let this damn disease leave me a survivor for the rest of my life. That's what you do on a desert island— you survive. Even if it kills me, I'm going to grow through this somehow. This thing might get me, but I won't give myself to it. It's going to have to come and get me, and I'm not going to make it easy for it. That's why I don't attend the MS survivors group. I'm thinking of starting the MS thrivers club."

The Resilience Reaction (Recovering)

Our natural resilience response helps us bounce back all the way to our pre-trauma state. We appear and feel none the worse for wear, and find the energy and reasons to return to our prior normal life. Because we seem to have "become totally ourselves again," people marvel at our resilience. They may not be aware of or understand what it takes to get to the full recovery phase of dealing with adversity, so highly resilient people can become "stress success symbols." This can result in a form of resilience envy or feelings of comparative stress-management inadequacy that in turn lead to emotional distancing between the resilient person and anyone who cannot relate to or trust in the miraculous power of resilience.

The crisis caveat at this phase is that highly resilient persons who truly recover do not receive much attention. Kindlers can mentally annoy us, victims can emotionally drain us, and survivors can serve as reminders of events we would prefer to forget. Resilient recoverers, however, tend to blend back into the everyday world so well that they are easily forgotten. Unless we hear their stories, the very nature of their resilience can result in a loss of some of their social support.

People in recovery will tell you that they often feel one crisis away from slipping back through existing to suffering and eventually kindling or worsening their situations. One resilient man who had battled alcoholism for 30 years said, "I'm in recovery. I'll always be in recovery. I know I can slip back in a New York minute, so I have to be on guard and never forget I am a recovering alcoholic. I sometimes feel as tipsy now as I felt when I drank. I feel I could fall back at the clink of a glass."

Popular psychology has created a worldwide recovery movement. It offers programs, descriptive terms and diagnoses, and has its own culture and explanatory system based on ideas of constant vulnerability, dysfunction, the danger of denial, and lost and found inner children. Our pathogenic medical establishment aims for survival and hopes for recovery. As reflected in the alcoholic man's statement, thriving is not often seen as an option when we surrender to a life of recovery.

In terms of the crisis reaction stages, each of us is free to choose our own disaster destiny. I do not want to seem an emotional elitist who thinks that only certain affective adjustments are the right ones. I am not implying that only those of us who have faced death can truly celebrate life, but I am suggesting that all of us can learn from the thrivers who have gone through terrible challenges. My interest in sharing the possibility of invincibility is not meant to imply that those who do not elect to live the highly energetic, constantly growing and dynamic, and totally absorbed life that comes with thriving are somehow unworthy failures who have not "seen the light." Perhaps our greatest human gift is that we are free to attend to our world in the way we choose.

For some, surviving or recovering may be more than enough. But for others, thriving offers a way to be and feel more authentically alive. After my cancer caused me to go through my own worsening, suffering, existing, and recovering, I highly recommend thriving.

The Thriving Reaction (Flourishing)

When we thrive because we have suffered, we not only bounce back, but up and beyond. In the words of positive psychologist Jonathan Haidt, thrivers are "emotionally elevated."[15] Elevation is characterized by warm, pleasant, tingling feelings in the chest, feeling the need to hold, hug, and help others, and feeling energized and optimistic about life in general. Along with words like savoring and flourishing, elevation has become part of the new positive psychology vocabulary.

As figure 1 indicates, we thrive when we surpass and transcend our prior level of functioning, regain and even accelerate our upward psychological trajectory, and seem to have mentally and emotionally benefited from our suffering. Because of our crisis, we seem to begin to flourish. Thrivers aren't masochists who seek or somehow endure pain better than others, but they do tend to be rational optimists who learn from it, know when to fight or flow with it, and when to give in and move on.

The rest of this book describes this sixth response, our natural thriveability as summed up here by one of the thrivers. "Bobbie" is a 47-year-old woman who suffers from lupus erythematosus, a chronic disease that causes inflammation of the body's connective tissues. Among other problems, it often results in being in constant pain and feeling tired, weak, and depressed. In spite of her disease, Bobbie is a community college professor, a mother, a wife, and daughter who also cares for her mother who is suffering from the severe stages of Alzheimer disease. Lupus can be a devastating condition, and its course and symptoms can be as varied and unpredictable as they are debilitating, yet she seemed more alive than many of the highly stressed young medical students to whom I asked her to speak.

I asked her to attend one of my grand round presentations about thriving, a lecture to the medical staff at Sinai Hospital of Detroit. When I finished discussing what I came to call the Beethoven Factor of elevation due to devastation, and my theory about thriving and the research findings from positive psychology that tend to support it, she offered her own definition of thriving.

Struggling to stand and short of breath, Bobbie said, "I know all you doctors care very much about us. You work hard to look for problems, to prevent our suffering, and to help us to survive and recover, but there is much more you are missing. We are all much stronger than you have been taught. We want to do more than get well. We want to get more well than we were before we got sick. We don't want to return to what we were. We want to go to new places in our lives because of what we went through. Otherwise, what was the point of it all?

"You are taught to fight against death, but you must also help us consider the thrill of living even when we are dying. You are taught that the patient should have a fighting spirit, and that sometimes helps, but you also teach us how to give up and move on and how to have a more open spirit. Look at me. Do you see only how I shake and appear so weak and frail? Is your diagnosis of my disease confirmed? Or, do you see my strengths?

"I know I am dying, but as I look around this room, I think I might be more alive than many of you. You all look so busy and so weary. No one asked me why I wanted to live. You all just assumed living is enough, but it isn't. You don't know about my mother I care for and who no longer knows me because of her senility. She is one of the reasons I want to live. She gives me purpose and the need to continue on. I know I am dying, but I am savoring the moments of my living in ways many of you young people may not yet understand. You may not even know that you may not yet be fully alive.

"I ask you to look more closely at those of us who are suffering and growing. Look not only at our disease but also for our strength and what you can learn from those of us who have chosen to thrive through our problems. I ask you to look beyond the face of my disease and into my mind and especially into my heart, because there is strength there you may be missing. Don't fear illness and death. Don't hate them, because they are natural and necessary. Try to learn from these things as I have. I know I am dying, but I am also more alive now than ever before. I hope you will join me."

As the nurses helped Bobbie struggle from the room, my students sat uncharacteristically silent. Several had tears in their eyes. Instead of the usual banter, theorizing, and showing off of knowledge of the disease process they had just observed, many of them seemed to be reflecting on their own lives. They had been taught the pathological repair model of medicine, not the thriving way to healing. In the context of their pressured, hurried, and problem-focused lives, they seemed to be wondering at least for this brief moment how someone so close to death could be so much nearer to life than they were. This is the wisdom of thriving, flourishing, and savoring that is the realm of the new positive psychology and the message of the following chapters.

2 Developing Your Talent for Thriving

"The hero is no braver than an ordinary man, but he is brave five minutes longer."
—Ralph Waldo Emerson

Gifted for Life

We all have a talent for thriving. I use the word "talent" because it captures the idea that thriving is a natural inclination or disposition based on our ancestors, who themselves rose to the occasion in their prehistoric struggle to survive. According to *Webster's Third New International Dictionary*, a talent is "a gift bestowed upon man,"[1] and the talent for thriving is perhaps our greatest gift. It is a gift we were given to help us become stronger when we are stressed and to be able to transcend the worst times in our lives to find a more meaningful and enjoyable life.

If we choose to develop this unique talent, it can provide the comfort and assurance that we are up to any challenge. By learning how to develop this most magnificent of all natural talents, we become able to grow through the hellish experiences that necessarily come with the privilege of living in a magnificently complex, randomly harsh, and mysteriously difficult world.

Resilience is defined in *Webster's Third New International Dictionary* as "an act of springing back, rebounding . . . the capacity of a strained body to recover."[2] This is primarily a physical definition, but it expresses the nature of psychological resilience. Thriving is possible because we are naturally resilient beings and, because we have such adaptive recovery powers, we have a place from which to become stronger than before we were psychologically strained. Resilience is our capacity for recovery to our prior state, but thriving is much more. It is our ancestral right to discover at the worst times in our lives a new and better way of understanding a deeper meaning of life. Thriving is defined in *Webster's* as "to achieve growth and prosper outstandingly, to flourish despite or because of circumstances or conditions." This is the same definition offered by positive psychologists studying our thriveability.

Most positive psychology researchers feel that the term "resilience" should be reserved exclusively to denote a return to a prior condition. Like psychologist Charles Carver, they feel that the word "thriving" should be used only to describe the "better-off-afterward" experience.[3] Thriving goes beyond rising to the occasion to being raised up by it. Positive psychologists see resilience as equivalent to recovery, so I use the word "thriving" to refer to our human capacity to do more than recover from a setback to a former state of relative well-being. I use it to describe our natural talent to move to a higher level, or super-resilience that allows us to feel more alive than before our trauma.

We experience the super-resilience of thriving when, in the aftermath of our crisis or because we have learned from those who thrived through their own adversity, we and everything and everyone around us seem infused with a fascinating, joyful new energy that makes us ask, "Why did it have to take this stress to make me realize how alive I could feel?"

Thriving's "better-off-afterward" reaction to trauma results in being able to answer "yes" to the "vitality signs" questions posed in chapter 1. It results from renewed attention to the simple pleasures of life so that we feel we are living more fully. It results from letting go of our anger at what seems an unfair world because we come to see how useless, destructive, distancing, and time-wasting our anger can be. It is loving and becoming more open to feeling loved because we have seen and felt what it might be like without that love. It results in paying renewed full and deep attention to what matters most because we now know and will forever remember what it might be like if those parts of our lives were gone forever. Because of our resilience and the thriving that builds upon it, we are allowed the remarkable opportunity to come back to new, more invigorated life when adversity begins to take the life out of us.

Stress-Induced Strength

We refer to many metals as being "highly resilient," but we would not describe a metal as "thriving." Some metals have sufficient elasticity to allow them to bend without breaking and then return to their original shape none the worse for wear. Human beings who are resilient can also "bounce back" to their original psychological and physical condition. Metals don't "thrive" by being made stronger because they have been severely stressed; but we can. When our "metal" is tested, some of us bounce back and others get much stronger. Psychological thrivers can become stronger because they have the capacity not only to endure spiritual, psychological, and physical stretching but to mentally engage with and grow emotionally and spiritually because of it. Resilience is recovering from stress, but thriving is discovering new energy because we have been stressed; and within this difference lies the deeper and more authentic life that comes to those who recognize and develop their talent for thriving.

Because they make for dramatic illustrations of my points about thriving, I will present several true stories of SIG—stress-induced growth. The persons who lived these stories are some of the superstars of thriving who serve as good models for a new positive psychology. They are like Olympians who hone their talent to the highest level; but even so, each of us possesses and can enhance our own unique talent to thrive. If we concern ourselves only with recovery and resilience, we miss out on the opportunity and the adventure of discovering the newer and more creatively adaptive meanings in life that ultimately make it more authentic.

The thriving superstars provide interesting examples for learning about the common everyday invincibility that rests within all of us. However, if we are to become thrivers, we must be inspired and encouraged but not awed by these stories. Thriving isn't finding "the answer" or accepting someone else's answers. It is a continuing process of searching for our own answers within our own value and belief system.

It is easy to identify people who are thriving. They seem somehow more vitally alive and to be embracing life more deeply and intensely than those who have not yet discovered their thriving talent. As the woman you will read about below pointed out, "I know someone who has learned to thrive when I see her. She will stand out as much more in love with life than the other people around her. You just get the sense that she is sort of invincible."

One such invincible spirit I interviewed had been the victim of a vicious home invasion. Two of her children were killed before her eyes and she was sexually assaulted, strangled, beaten, stabbed several times, and left for dead. She offered her own definition of thriving through crisis. She said, "Nothing makes you more alive than almost dying. Going through hell really helps you recognize that you should have appreciated the heaven on earth you already lived in. You never get over what we went through. In fact, you actually need to remember it because it is part of why you are able to thrive. It energizes you and makes you remember who you were and why you have to be strong. I think it makes you a little spiritually arrogant in a way. I guess that's because it makes you feel that if you handled what you did, you can handle almost anything."

Eleanor Roosevelt's words at the beginning of chapter 1, "I can take the next thing that comes along," express this invincible woman's feeling that came with her discovery of her capacity to thrive through tragedy.

Is Thriving Really Possible?

When I share the thriver's stories you will be reading, people often react with doubting amazement. I often hear the comment, "I don't believe it. I don't know how anybody could survive that, let alone thrive because of it. They're either a saint or living in a deep state of denial." Sometimes I am told that those who tell these stories are being disingenuous, melodramatic, or somehow acting or holding themselves up to be something they are really not. My experience is that those offering this skepticism have not yet had their turn at experiencing their own talent for thriving.

The thrivers I interviewed for this book did not consider themselves in any way extraordinary. In fact, it seemed that while so many others strive to stand out or to be seen as in some way extraordinary, thrivers value most their ability to be ordinary people extraordinarily enjoying an ordinary life. Perhaps because they have known such intense suffering, the opportunity to savor again the ordinary pleasures of living provides them the peace, joy, and comfort their crises reminded them they had been ignoring.

Thrivers do not see themselves as heroes, and are often reluctant to talk about their thriving, other than to say how wonderful life seems to them now. As you will read in chapter 5 in the example of Izzie, a man who survived and then managed to thrive because of the horror of a Nazi death camp, they are usually shy about sharing their stories and reject and even become impatient with and frightened by any attempt to distance them by elevation to a special status.

One of the objectives of their thriving through extraordinary adversity was to someday be able to again lead a normal and ordinary life, not the life of a hero. Because their suffering had made them feel so often terribly isolated until their resilience and thriving took over, it seemed that the one thing they feared most was to be seen as "outstanding" or "exceptional" people who were not seen as just like everyone else. They were often embarrassed by an awe they sensed from others and wished instead for a common daily life of simple pleasures.

The invincible people I spoke with told me their stories as interesting but not heroic biographies, and with the hope that those who have not yet known their level of suffering may glean some degree of comfort and optimism from their experience. Their message was similar to Emerson's in his quote at the beginning of this chapter, that any heroism was in their willingness and ability to remain mentally engaged with their adversity and maintain their sense of identity even when so many factors seem to be tearing it apart. Thrivers share their experiences not from the perspective of "Look what I did" but from the orientation of "Don't worry. Look at what you can do."

A New Vitality

You don't have to look to poets or philosophers to find a description of what it is like to thrive and become more fully and vitally alive every day. As I so often do, you can often find poetic and profound wisdom in the dictionary. *Webster's Third New International Dictionary* states that being alive is "a communication of a feeling of life, a blended verisimilitude of activity, verve, and interestingness . . . pulsating . . . stirring."[4]

One thriver offered a shorter definition. He was a young comedian diagnosed with cancer. I was speaking with him when a nurse entered his room to ask if she could take his pulse. With the humor that is so characteristics of thrivers, he joked, "No thanks. I need it." As the nurse placed her fingers on his wrist, he looked at me with tears in his eyes. He said, "You know. I've learned one thing in all this. Being fully alive is not just having a pulse. It's feeling like you are pulsating."

When pathogenically oriented doctors take your "vital signs," they are really only looking to see if you have any "danger signs." At best, they are looking for the resilience reaction, not the thriver's response. For example, cardiovascular stress testing is primarily a physical test that looks for signs of vulnerability, the ability of our heart to survive under stress, or an impaired recovery response. We are seldom asked about the real stress tests in our lives, the major losses and fears we have faced and how we managed to thrive because of them.

I suggest that we have set the bar for health far too low. We are capable of much more than freedom from illness, surviving sickness, or recovery from trauma. High-level wellness is much more than not feeling sick; it is feeling that we are savoring. We have an inborn psychoimmunity that provides us with the talent for such thriving. Here is brief checklist to see how well you have developed your talent for thriving.

- Do you feel more alive today than yesterday?
- Are you free from worry?
- Do people seem to be made happier by your presence?
- Are you laughing hard every day?
- Are you crying hard every day?
- Do you feel in love with life?
- Are you in love?
- Do you feel loved?
- Have you been made stronger by adversity?
- Do people turn to you for strength and comfort?
- Do you often feel overwhelmed by the grandeur and beauty of simple things?
- If you were to die today, would you feel you have fully lived?

The more items you checked from this list as true in your own life, the more likely it is that you are honing your talent for thriving. Even if you checked every item, life continually offers new ways to increase your savoring response. Don't wait for a life crisis to maximize your thriveability.

Multidimensional Thriving

In the language of positive psychology, thriving is a multidimensional systems event. As the above list suggests, it maximizes and extends the combined recovery power of the mind, body, spirit, and emotions, and involves loving connection with other people. On the simplest body level of human resilience, research in physical recovery shows that highly resilient people exhibit faster cardiovascular recovery from a highly agitated negative emotion or stressful event.[5]

My clinic staff and I conducted a simple experiment on the physical aspect of resilience and thriving. Several groups of our patients were asked to wear a small blood pressure monitor on one finger and a pulse meter on another. The results of the measurements taken by these instruments were then recorded on a small printer while they sat waiting for the blood test required of all of our patients. A look at the records of these patients revealed that no matter how much or how little stress was reflected in blood pressure and pulse rate prior to the stress of a blood test, some patients were more physiologically resilient and recovered much quicker than others. In fact, even after finally being poked by the needle, many returned to lower pulse and blood pressures than their usual daily average numbers.

When I interviewed each patient, something interesting emerged. Those who were the quickest to recover and even physically thrive, as shown in improvement in cardiovascular function after their stress, were also those who had gone through prior intense emotional crises, had been resilient, and eventually thrived. Those who were slower in the cardiovascular recovery were those patients who had come to our clinic for psychiatric problems not related to a specific serious life crisis.

Even though this "simple science" study does not meet the criterion of a random, controlled, double-blind study, it does give some indication of how the body recovers and shows its physical resilience. It indicates that experiencing your resilience may actually help strengthen it, and you will read in the following pages that this is also true regarding your mental thriving and the psychological immune system that makes thriving possible. Being stretched to your mental or emotional limits can result in decreasing your emotional recovery period and increasing your emotional resiliency response, and it can set you up for a try at thriving.

Scaring the Health Out of Us

One reason we seem to have so many kindlers, sufferers, survivors, and recoverers is the pathogenic orientation of modern society. A fearful, negativistic, pessimistic view of the human condition has worked its way into the fabric of our modern collective consciousness. Political scientist Aaron Wildavsky wrote, "How extraordinary! The richest, longest-lived, best-protected, most resourceful civilization, with the highest degree of insight into its own technology, is on its way to becoming the most frightened."[6] By learning about our natural resilience and the miracle of thriving, we can free ourselves from being held hostage by this subtle but pervasive psychological health terrorism.

The pessimism of the sickness model of life permeates our media. Morning papers or television news shows announce the looming of the next thing that threatens our survival. Except for the occasional "human interest story" reporting some survivor's extraordinary courage, most of what we hear and see reminds us not of how thriving, talented, and robust we are, but how vulnerable. We often seem to be a crowd of people in recovery, running in fear of the next source of dysfunction. The assumption seems to be that we are barely strong enough to withstand the challenges of a world we ourselves created; a species smart enough to create such a complex and stressful world should also have the capacity to deal with it.

Here is another simple science study you can do to test the validity of my assertion of the dominance of the pathogenic, pessimistic view of our human capacity. The next time you are in a bookstore, go to the self-help or medical books section. You won't have much trouble finding them, because they are usually quite large. You will often find the worried well there searching through the shelves for the latest best-seller offering guidance and comfort for whatever ails them. Read the titles of the books and ask yourself this question, "What human vulnerability is this book supposed to help?"

Even though you will read many upbeat titles, you will probably notice that most of the books are based in some way on an assumed human weakness or lurking threat to our vulnerability. Diet books are a good example. They offer weight loss programs and various ways to trim our body, and the assumption is that we are too fat, are shaped wrongly, have no self-discipline, or are in a constant battle of the binge or the bulge.

Izzie, the death camp survivor, said of these books, "I think a waist is a terrible thing to mind. I almost starved to death when I was in that Nazi prison. I don't worry anymore about controlling my appetite or my weight. When I step on the scale and numbers roll up, I feel relieved. It's like I'm becoming more and more alive. My body was healthy enough to survive the garbage we ate there, so I'm not that worried about dieting now. I'd sooner go to the cookbook section and find a book on tasty fattening food for the joyfully obese."

Persons looking for the secret of a transcendent and thriving life often turn to New Age thinking and contemporary psychology self-help books to find the meaning and purpose they seek. Because of psychology's and medicine's obsession with pathology, readers seldom find there the scientifically based paths to a thriving life now being offered by the field of positive psychology. As a result, these pilgrims in search of purpose are either left disappointed or led down numerous dead-end paths or find themselves fidgeting and searching for yet another psychological guru.

For every 100 journal articles on sadness, psychology offers one article on happiness.[7] As a result, even the most well-intended self-help expert has been left with little to draw upon in the way of carefully researched paths to a joyful life. Look carefully at these books, and you will note that many of them are based on correcting assumed weaknesses rather than on discovering and building upon what positive psychology now knows are our documented strengths.

Self-help books about sex offer seductive strategies for awakening an unresponsive partner or his or her body parts. Relationship books assume that we have to sort through hoards of losers and use special romantic maneuverings to find and seduce the one right partner for us. The genders are seen as coming from different planets, men are assumed to be after one thing and women something completely different, and avoiding or repairing relationship failure is presented much more often than books about thriving twosomes living and growing in long-lasting, loving, healthy relationships. Long-lasting marriages are applauded as romantic artifacts, while failed relationships and divorce are considered the norm.

Intense psychotherapy with gut-wrenching scenes of despair and emotional confessions can be seen on television talk shows, and the resident expert often assures the suffering that "life is difficult and full of strife" and that they had better "get real." Never mind that the research shows that constructive self-delusion is helpful and necessary and the key characteristic of depressed people is that they have gotten too real, aren't good at embracing "false hope," and are unable to creatively and unrealistically construe their life situation when they have to. It surprises me that so many of the most popular "positive thinking" gurus seem to know so little about the research from the field of positive psychology.

The pathogenic, negativistic view of the world has led to a society of the worried well doing all they can to survive for as long as they can. As you will read later, getting "real" can be the reason there is so much suffering, and may explain why so many thrivers relish their intentionally framed illusions.

The pathogenic orientation is often subtle, so you will have to do your self-help book experiment carefully. Authors, publishers, and editors know that most readers do not want to hear negatives because they already have plenty of them in their own minds. But beneath the self-help hype and optimism usually lurks the dire assumption that something or someone is broken or breaking down and needs immediate fixing or remediation. The series of books for "dummies" and the dysfunctional living in recovery are further testament to the dominance of the negative view of who and how we are.

One of my patients ridiculed my simple science bookstore study suggestion. He said, "Of course the books are problem focused. Nobody's going to write a book and then put on the cover the title 'You're Invincible, So What Are You Doing in the Self-Help Section?' or 'Don't Worry About It. Go Home and Enjoy Life,' or 'This Is a Self-Help Book, So Go Help Yourself,' or 'You're Much Stronger Than You Think, So Ask Yourself How to Do It, Not Me,' or 'To Hell with Recovery. That's Not Living,' or 'You're At Least As Smart As Me, So Think for Yourself.'" I answered, "I wish I could use a version of some of those titles. They reflect the point I want to make." There is much more right with the world than wrong, and we are much stronger than we are being told, think, or may have even imagined.

A Dynamic Explanatory Style

Illusion is coming back into style. Until positive psychology recently took root and the nature of human resilience began to be understood, the gold standard of psychiatry was the ability to face reality and avoid illusion. "Normal" thinking was defined as realistic and totally accurate in its perception of one's vulnerabilities, the world's threats, and the future's dangers. The ability to face the facts of life was seen as the ultimate criterion for being sane, and the more realistic people were, the more mentally healthy they were assumed to be. Research in the new field of positive psychology, however, shows that developing an explanatory style that seems to others to be an overly optimistic mental assessment of what we can accomplish, an exaggerated perception of our control of our own destiny, and most all what appears to be blatantly unrealistic optimism even to the point of self-delusion can be a part of the creative consciousness that allows for flourishing through life's challenges.[8]

We have an inborn talent for thinking from a thriving perspective, but our pathogenic assumption about lives and our ability to deal with them diminishes our capacity for thriving through crisis. We all have the capacity not only to be emotionally invincible but to become emotionally stronger and stronger under more and more pressure. If we are willing to fool ourselves and know we are doing it and do it just enough to allow ourselves a wider range of explanatory styles and new ways to find meaning in what happens to us, we can thrive through almost anything.

According to pioneer in positive psychology Martin Seligman, "Explanatory style is a theory about your past, your future, and your place in the world."[9] Thriving people decide that their lives are ultimately the result of the personal theory they construct about it and not the exclusive result of the external world. As one of the invincibles put it, "The talent to thrive is the ability to happen to the world instead of allowing it to always happen to you."

Thrivers are the architects of their own consciousness. They fashion their explanatory style and refuse to surrender it when problems strike. They become their own meaning-makers, mental illusionists who take whatever happens to them and transform it to find challenge where others see only disaster. Most of all, they reject the helpless victim orientation that has become so accepted in the pathogenic view.

Four Dirty Words

Positive psychologist William Banks refers to our neglect of our talent to thrive as "the new obscenity."[10] He wrote that the oft-repeated or at least implied phrase, "I can't help myself," reflects a surrender of the very quality that separates us from animals—our resilience response and our capacity to thrive through adversity.

The research in positive psychology shows clearly that we do not have to be victims or settle for mere recovery. We can thrive because, unlike other animals, we are not just reactors. We can use the skills that the positive psychologists are discovering constitute the super-resilience of the thriving response. We can construe, frame, make meaning, mentally accommodate, and determine the content of our consciousness.

The miracle of thriving is that we were made to be agents with free will. To offer up the "I couldn't help it" excuse squanders one of our most powerful human abilities, our capacity to deal constructively and effectively with almost any challenge by assigning our own meaning to it and using our innate emotional, physical, mental, and spiritual skills to develop that meaning.

Half-Empty or Half-Full?

Do you see the glass as half-empty or half-full? It's a well-known and overused question, but I suggest it is still a way of discerning the nature of our explanatory style and the trajectory of our emotional and mental life. It reflects the way we assign meaning to our lives, and ultimately whether we will be a sufferer, survivor, recoverer, or thriver.

Here is another one of my simple science experiments. It was designed to look at whether we have an optimistic or pessimistic explanatory style. The next time you have a drink from a full glass of soda or some other fluid, drink only half of it. Before you take your next drink, stop and seriously ask yourself, "Do I in fact see this glass as half-full or half-empty?" If you are drinking with someone who knows you well, ask that person how he or she thinks you see the glass. How you honestly answer the question says a lot about the meaning you are now assigning to your life and your thriving potential at this time in your life.

I asked most of the thrivers I interviewed for this book to take the "half glass" test with me. Those who had gone through a major life crisis and resiliently bounced back to thrive said they considered the glass half-full. More important, they seemed to answer the question with sincerity and conviction. All but one of my informal control group of nine medical students who said they had not yet experienced any serious difficulties in their young lives considered the glass half-empty.

The one student who said she saw it as half-full was a 42-year-old woman whose husband had died of a heart attack, and years later, her thriving had led her back to school to become a doctor. While the other students laughed in derisive disbelief, she firmly and insistently stated she saw the glass as half-full. The other eight younger students joked about the test. They said they knew the right answer was "half-full," but when I challenged them to answer reflectively and honestly, they looked at their glasses a little longer, thought awhile, and said the glass did in fact appear to be half-empty.

Again, my glass study is not acceptable as good scientific research. My medical students are certainly not a randomly selected control group to compare with my thriving patients. Except perhaps for the older student, they are pessimists in training and firmly immersed in modern medicine's pathology emphasis. Health to them is the absence of sickness, and illness happens when our health runs out. They are being taught to look for what's wrong and what's missing, so they don't make a fair comparison to thrivers through crisis who have learned to look at life more optimistically.

Don't Die Until You've Lived

During my internship in clinical psychology, a typically pathogenically oriented physician was taking four of my fellow graduate students and me on rounds to visit dying patients on the oncology unit. I did not know then that decades later I would be a patient dying on that same unit. He had just finished lecturing to us about the stages of dying, and gathered us together before rounding to say in a somber voice, "Remember one thing when you look into the faces of these dying patients. From the moment you are born, you begin to die. We all are dying, and the patients you will see are just being very obvious about it." As my fellow students nodded in agreement, I felt uncomfortable. I had been raised to believe the exact opposite.

My family lived as if birth was only the beginning of a process of spiritual development that transcended the physical limits of physical aging. I would learn later when I almost died of cancer that my family was right. From the moment you are born, you are offered the opportunity to thrive through life and give it meaning that transcends physical death. Even as I suffered the terrible pain and fear of cancer, I felt that I was born to live and thrive through all that life offers, no matter how stressful. I learned that learning to thrive allows us to be free of our fear of death because we give our lives a meaning that transcends physical endings.

You will read in the following chapters about my own thriver's story and the stories of other thrivers who know that the doctor was wrong. You will learn not about coping with the stages of dying, bereavement, grief, or loss, but about the stages of thriving through these processes. You will learn what thrivers know, that from the moment we are born, we can begin to thrive.

Avoiding PIDS—Psychological Immune Deficiency Syndrome

Resilience and thriving require knowledge about our psychological immune system. As you will read in chapter 7, much as we have a remarkable physical immune system, we have an emotional immune system always working for us. It provides the energy of our thriving talent. Like our physical immune system, unless we act or think in ways that interfere with it, it usually does its job quietly, automatically, and reliably. Our physical immune system is maintained primarily by our behaviors such as diet and exercise, but even it is influenced strongly by the meaning we give to events in our lives.

Our psychoimmunity is primarily nurtured by the meaning we assign to our lives, and when we take a pessimistic, pathological, half-empty, survivalist view of where we fit into the scheme of things, we can experience PIDS, psychological immune deficiency syndrome. We weaken our emotional immunity when our explanatory style results in messages about our lack of faith in our ability to deal with adversity. In a sense, our negativity discourages and talks our immune system out of working as hard as it can for us. As a result, we end up interfering with our natural resilience response and allowing ourselves to be battered about helplessly by the slightest emotional antigen. Thriving becomes out of the question, and we become only sufferers, survivors, or recoverers.

Freedom from Brain Abuse

Imagine for a moment that you actually "are" your own body. Imagine that you are receiving the messages coming from your brain every moment of every day. How would you feel working under the command of a brain that sees the world and thinks the way it does? Would you feel stressed, frightened, bothered, and constantly under the pressure of staying alive? Or, would you feel calm, content, and gently, optimistically, and joyfully going about the business of dealing with any stress of daily living? Would you feel encouraged and comforted by your brain, or harassed or even abused by its mortality phobia? Would you feel invincible and ready for anything, or vulnerable and defensive for the next threat?

With every thought you have, you are sending what physician Bernie Siegel calls "live messages" to your entire body.[11] The chaos and randomness of the universe provides most of the colors of your life, but it is you who ultimately, consciously paint the picture and mentally "frame" whatever happens to you. Your meaning-making, your "explanatory style," is the coordinator of your psychological immune system. How you "frame" or construe what happens to you determines most of the emotional, physical, and spiritual impact of any life event. Your internal dialogue about life and its challenges determines whether you are a survivor, in recovery, or thriving.

Thriving Tendencies

You will read in chapter 4 that there are people who seem to have an inborn tendency to thrive. Their upbeat, outgoing, and uninhibited temperament causes them to respond with a generally optimistic explanatory style. The good news, however, is that our temperament does not have to be our destiny. We can learn about our own thriving response from more naturally thriving persons and get some new ideas about improving our own thriveability.

While there are those who have a tendency toward thriving, all of us have a tendency to get stuck in the way we see the negative things that happen to us. It seems that our general explanatory style regarding the good things that happen to us keeps changing throughout our lives, but that our view of negative events tends to remain essentially the same.[12] Thriving ultimately depends on a very flexible explanatory style, so being stuck in one style when it comes to life's challenges inhibits our psychological immunity.

One of the thrivers commented on the challenge of explaining the good and bad things that happen to us. She said, "Anybody can explain why good things happen to them. What is difficult is explaining why the bad things happen to us and why good things seem to be happening to bad people." Because a highly flexible explanatory style is a keystone of the thriving response, we must resist our tendency to cling to the ways we frame the negative events in our lives.

Combing through the teenage diaries of people now in their 70s, researchers found that explanatory style for good events was highly dynamic.[13] Good events were interpreted at one time as "just good luck" or "sheer fate" and at another time as due to some special skill of the diary's writer. Explanatory styles of bad events remained unchanged, with diary writers who seemed to be perpetual pessimists staying that way. Thriving requires a more adaptable construing of the negative events in our lives. As one of my interviewees said, "Anybody can explain why great things happen to them. It takes real creativity to find meaning when things go sour."

Obstacles to Thriving

It is becoming increasingly difficult to thrive in a world that seems to be constantly scaring us to death. Most of what we enjoy has some danger associated with it, but we seem surrounded by killjoys and pleasure police who are intent on spoiling our fun.[14] Almost every day, someone spoils our fun by pointing out how vulnerable we are to clogged arteries, the nagging of repressed negative memories, and an array of dangers waiting to take advantage of our human frailties. Psychology tells us that our families are dysfunctional, we are in either denial or recovery, and that we are natural-born victims; but there is a new psychology emerging, one that helps free us from being hostage to the sickness or prevention model of living.

This book is intended to offer an escape route from the current health terrorism. It presents the evidence that we are much stronger than we are being told and than we ever may have imagined. Not only does our physiological immune system offer us immense resistance and resilience, but also our psychological immune system provides us with the ability to thrive in the face of the threats to our lives. Loss of a loved one, life-threatening illness, financial disaster, or the many impacts of the various forms and sources of terrorism around the world may seem to be challenges we can only hope to survive, but in fact they and other life challenges are the necessary catalysts for learning to thrive through life.

Instead of looking at the sick to learn how to stay well, positive psychology looks at the well for lessons about how to stay mentally in charge of the quality of our life experiences. The fact that we are made to actually thrive through our worst times cannot be understood by learning from those who have studied the origins and cures of pathology. It is learned and applied in our lives by looking to the often forgotten happy well, not the worried sick or the experiences of the prematurely dead.

The Forgotten Fit

Because of our modern focus on sickness, dysfunction, and pathology, recovery often becomes the most we can hope for. When researchers say things such as "86 percent of those who ate meat several times a week were shown to develop some extent of arterial blockage" or "73 percent of children from broken homes have trouble in school," they forget to tell us about the other percent, the thrivers who become stronger because they encounter physical and mental health threats.

Dire warnings worry us, but they don't seem to do much to significantly change our behavior. Despite warnings of the danger of eating meat, most of us still eat it, but we do so with a "glutton guilt" that interferes with our enjoyment of a juicy steak and makes us feel as if we are hopeless health reprobates slowly but surely killing ourselves. Most of us know our parents were far from perfect, but until the recent emphasis on dysfunctional families and scarred inner children, we thought we had become stronger because of our upbringing and all its flaws.

Professional pessimists are pathogenically oriented killjoys. They are constantly looking for trouble, and in doing so have until now ignored the forgotten percent of regular meat eaters who never develop heart disease and the thousands of children from terrible homes who have become successful at work, great parents, and happier in their own marriages than their parents seemed in theirs.[15] Researchers tend to forget the thrivers, but the lessons from this group of forgotten fit are at least as important as the ones from the sick, suffering, or recovering.

Where are the forgotten thrivers? They are not usually found in hospitals, therapist's offices, motivational seminars, or attending weekend self-actualization retreats. They are silent flourishers going about their lives with joy and resiliency.

Most of the books dealing with the issue of well-being are based one way or another on studies of the unhappy, disturbed, suffering, or sick. Some books focus on survival and recovery and the occasional extraordinary survivor, but there is much we can learn from the ordinary invincibles. They are not just a lucky few statistical outriders whom we can only envy. Their way of seeing the world can teach us much about how our psychological immune system can help us thrive.

Positive psychology tries to learn about the heart by asking those who ignore many of the heart-smart warnings yet do not develop heart disease. They want to know more about the children from the most dysfunctional families who seem mentally and emotionally healthier than those who came from more advantaged backgrounds. The challenge for positive psychology, however, is that these thrivers are too busy enjoying life to be coming to clinics and laboratories, so if we want to learn from them, we have to look for them.

They are much too involved in enjoying life to come to us to talk at length about how to live.

Thrivers are more likely to be found lying on the couch eating potato chips than panting on a treadmill at the health club. They are more likely to be sitting quietly on their porch watching the day go by than attending a seminar on personal power. You may find a few of them running in marathons, but more of them are likely to be walking joyfully at the end of the race or sitting on the curb with their families watching in amusement as gaunt-looking runners pant past in their knee braces. You are more likely to meet one of them while strolling along a garden path than in the aisles of a health food store. I met some myself while standing in line at an ice cream parlor. They are not worriers, so don't expect them to be up-to-date on the latest reason they should not be eating ice cream.

The following chapters describe not only the emerging field of positive psychology but also the completely different worldview that an optimum-oriented rather than deficit-focused psychology embraces. Looking for what has made life so wonderful for those for whom it had seemed so terrible is much different than looking for life lessons from those who have succumbed to the stressors about which we are constantly warned.

The Salutogenic Approach

The opposite of the pathogenic, or "problem-focused, negativistic, sickness-oriented," view of the human experience is what pioneer positive psychologist Aaron Antonovsky calls the "salutogenic orientation." Psychology's current "pathogenic" orientation is preoccupied with finding our weaknesses and vulnerabilities and then trying to fix them. Antonovsky coined the word "salutogenic" to refer to a point of view that looks for our strengths and focuses on maximizing them. It is concerned with identifying and building upon our best qualities rather than finding and repairing what is wrong with us. It is an approach that "salutes" life instead of pathologizing it. Rather than looking for symptoms of sickness such as depression about the past, languishing in the present, and pessimism about the future, Antonovsky's salutogenic approach emphasizes the source of satisfactions with our past, flourishing in our present, and hope, optimism, and faith in our future. It leads to an entirely different perspective on our day-to-day life that is free of fear for its length or liabilities. It results in an explanatory style that begins, maintains, and ends with the firm control of one's own skill at meaning-making.

Later in the book, you will read more about my clinic that offered brief psychological immune systems boosts to those who had already shown resilience. This clinic was based on enhancing explanatory styles and identifying mental, emotional, and spiritual resources, and promoting thriveability, not treating or preventing illness. The clinic staff had a slogan that said, "There are a lot of things that can screw you up, but you have the thriveability to construe them up."

Letting It Happen

A unique thing about thriving is that it seems the less you strive, the more you thrive. The meaning of the word "striving" is to fight, struggle, and compete against. In a culture that emphasizes the value of beating the odds, being a fighter, and struggling to get a piece of the pie, we often lose sight of how to enjoy the pie. Thrivers stand out as calm, content, and connected persons who are not trying hard to win or overcome anything or anyone. Because thriving is a natural, built-in response related to our psychological immune system, it works best when we are reflective and contemplative enough to create an explanatory style that allows it to happen rather than trying to do or strive or will something to happen.

Researchers in biofeedback have discovered that trying to "will" a change in blood pressure, a slower heartbeat, or more relaxed muscles does not effectively lead to those effects. We cannot will our physical immune system to be stronger, but we can think and find meaning in ways that allow it to do its natural work on our behalf. The same is true for our psychological immune system. If we apply some of the general rules of imagination and assigning meaning characteristic of the invincibles who have shown their high degree of thriveability, our emotional immune system will do its thing on our behalf.

Researchers have learned that when biofeedback works, it does so when the person feels that they "just let" relaxation happen to them rather than trying to "make" it happen.[16] In the positive or salutogenic view of life, we can be naturally relaxed, balanced, well beings who don't have to "try" to be that way. We only have to let ourselves "be" that way and stop getting in the way of our psychological immune system by striving to overcome adversity or be all we can be.

When you read about invincible people who seem to be the Michael Jordans of psychological immunity, remember that all of us have a powerful emotional immunity that can kick in when we need it. All of the thrivers I interviewed said that their experience of invincibility was subtle and seemed to happen over time. One of them said, "It's like you get in the zone. You don't actually try to get there, but it's kind of magical. It just kind of happens."

Thriving does not require performing the correct visual imagery or writing or saying a list of positive self-affirmations. Learning how to thrive through crisis is not a matter of competing against the odds or ourselves. It is a matter of remaining mentally, emotionally, and spiritually engaged in adversity long enough to allow the innate and naturally resilient psychoimmunity to work its magic for us. It is learning to find meaning in the face of senseless cruelty, to see when we are blind in ways the sighted have not imagined, feeling more intensely when we are numbed by disease or emotional trauma, and as Beethoven did, hearing again when something has rendered us deaf to the wonders around us.

Psychology has learned a lot about what can make our moments miserable. If we put our mind to it and suspend our denial for a while, most of us can list several things or events that we think threaten our well-being and can make us miserable. If we run out of things to worry about that might hurt us or shorten our lives, we only have to consult the evening news or newspapers to find some more. We have a pretty good idea what might kill or emotionally scar us, but we seem to know much less about the natural resilience of those who have been exposed to these threats and have themselves gone through what we fear the most to not only survive but also flourish. Until the new field of positive psychology, we paid much less attention to how so many people manage to make the moments of their lives grand even when they seem so grueling and who know how to accommodate to find a better mental match with their world.

Positive psychology is asking thriving questions. It asks: Who are the thrivers? Who are the sedentary carnivores that never develop heart disease or, if they do, find new meaning and joy in life because of it? Who are the children who come from the most dysfunctional and deprived families to become strong, happy, successful, loving people and parents?

Who are the parents with impaired children who seem to take more joy in parenting than those who were blessed with children without noticeable impairments?

Who are the men and women who have been assaulted, tortured, imprisoned, or exposed to the worst that humans can do to one another, and who end up being more content, calm, forgiving, loving, and joyfully connected than those who never know such horror? How do they do it? What can we learn from them so we can all do it? What is their secret of successful thriving through crises?

These are salutogenic questions, and the answers lie in our natural psychological immunity and the talent it gives us for thriving.

Doing Well without Trying Hard

In a modern world focused more on doing than on being, on living long at the sacrifice of life's simple pleasures, on coping more than celebrating, on living in recovery instead of celebration, on living in what often seems to be a perpetual state of victimhood to some real or perceived assault, and reliant on various self-help, how-to-do-it approaches for solving our problems, it may be difficult to understand and accept this book's premise that just knowing about thriving and how it works will allow your psychological immunity to strengthen and your thriving talent to be enhanced.

I offer the evidence for natural human thriving so that you may incorporate it into your own consciousness and therefore give consciousness support and a mental boost to your psychological immunity. If you will reflect on the evidence of our invincibility presented in these pages and incorporate the four components of thriving described in the Thriver's Manual presented in part 2, your own thriving can be awakened and be ready to go to work for you simply because you have literally changed your mind. The next time crisis strikes, you will have begun to think differently.

Just like your physical immune system, you don't have to keep telling your psychological immune system how to do its job. It "does its thing" naturally if you let it by thinking in ways that strengthen it and don't interfere with it by trying to present a good image or pretend to be strong. You don't have to fake it; you're much stronger than you think. By changing how you think about adversity and how to deal with it, you can learn to think even more strongly.

Much as a vaccination ultimately boosts your physical immune system, I hope the research and stories about psychological immunity will challenge you just enough to activate your own psychoimmunity and make you more immune to your next crisis. Once the brain that is so consumed with survival or recovery is "re-minded" of its capacity to thrive, it will become ready to realize its innate thriving talent and help activate our psychological immune system and make it ready to grow through all future challenges to our emotional immunity.

3 An Ode to Thriving

"Oh, if I were rid of this affliction, I could embrace the world."

—*Ludwig von Beethoven*[1]

How a Deaf Man Learned to Listen

At age 31, Beethoven had become suicidal. He lived in poverty, was losing his hearing, and wallowed in the depths of withdrawn despair and hopelessness. Twenty-three years later, utterly deaf, no longer suicidal, and, instead, energetically creative, he immortalized Schiller's life-affirming "Ode to Joy" in the lyrical chords of his Ninth Symphony. His transposing of Schiller's inspiring words, "Be embraced all ye millions with a kiss for all the world," reflected his remarkable ability to triumph over the tragedy of his hearing loss. He had triumphed over his tragedy to be able to construe the world in ways that can forever help all of us feel the joy he experienced by hearing his miraculous music.

Beethoven can be seen as one of the superstars of thriving. Like many of the other thrivers you are reading about, he did not suddenly transform himself from someone living in helpless despair to a person living in constant joy and elation. Like all ordinary thrivers, he continued to suffer through many terrible times and remained prone to dark moods through most of his life. In an 1801 letter to his friend Karl Ameda, he wrote, "[Y]our Beethoven is having a miserable life, at odds with nature and its Creator, abusing the latter for leaving his creatures vulnerable to the slightest accident. . . . My greatest faculty, my hearing, is greatly deteriorated."[2]

For years, Beethoven heard mostly humming and buzzing until, for the last and very productive years of his life, he became totally deaf. Through it all, however, his ability to creatively construe his situation allowed him to develop an increasingly more encompassing and adaptive explanatory style. As my grandmother told me, his way of creatively composing his life to be reflected in his majestic musical compositions can inspire all of us to discover our own thriveability.

In another letter Beethoven wrote to a friend five months after the letter to Ameda, he said, "You must think of me as being as happy as it is possible to be on this earth—not unhappy. No! I cannot endure it. I will seize Fate by the throat. It will not wholly conquer me. Oh, how beautiful it is to live—and live a thousand times over!"[3] His words capture the essence of how a deaf man learned to listen by continuing to lead a life as magnificently enriched as it was difficult.

Beethoven's ability to thrive though adversity rendered him invincible in the sense I have been using that word. Nothing, not even complete loss of his hearing and failing health, could stop him from leading an increasingly authentic and creative life. Even as he faced his death, his music and even his written words reflected his invincible spirit.

In 1802, his doctor had sent him to Heilgenstadt, a quiet rural village outside Vienna. There Beethoven reawakened his love of nature and composed many joyful, optimistic works, including his well-known, exuberant Symphony no. 2. He also wrote his last will and testament and instructed that it not be opened until after his death. This "Heilgenstadt Testament" is an ode to thriving and contains messages similar to those shared by the thrivers described in this book. On October 6, 1802, Beethoven wrote, "With joy I hasten to meet death. Despite my hard fate . . . I shall wish that it had come later; but I am content, for he shall free me of constant suffering. Come then, Death, and I shall face thee with courage."[4]

I use the phrase "the Beethoven Factor" to represent the nature of the thriving response because his life illustrates an often troubled but still creative consciousness characteristic of all the thrivers I interviewed. With their own unique thriveability, they all show the capacity to transpose potential disaster into unique odes to joy.

A Thriving Life

I refer to thriving as the "Beethoven Factor" not only because of the gifted composer's magnificent victory over adversity but because his invincibility also reflects the life-span view of thriving. When I speak of thriving as rising to the occasion, life itself is the occasion to which I refer.

Beethoven himself was far from being an enlightened guru, and though he thrived through his problems, he remained an ordinary man with ordinary vulnerabilities and liabilities. He never summoned the courage to tell others of his deafness, writing in one of his letters that he was "unable to say to people, 'Speak louder, shout, for I am deaf.'" He often tried to deny his problem and deluded himself by visits to all sorts of charlatans and quacks who claimed they could cure his deafness. As ineffective as these visits were, they also may have offered Beethoven brief spurts of hope and even moments of healthy self-delusion that bought him time to keep composing and offered at least a momentary placebo boost of creative energy that gave him some relief from his sense of hopelessness. They might have bought him time to think and frame his problem more adaptively and creatively.

Beethoven's deafness was a uniquely harsh kind for a musician and composer. It distorted subtle sound, turned low tones into an unintelligible hum, and made crescendos seem like an intolerable din. Nonetheless, he continued to create some of the world's most magnificent music. The more I read about Beethoven's thriving, the more I understand why my grandmother told me to listen carefully to the deaf man's music so I could learn ways to compose my own life.

As you have read, quantum leaps of thriving sometimes happen. However, most thrivers rarely recognize their invincibility in a short period of magnificent epiphany. Like Beethoven, they have periods of dismal lows and unrealistic highs. Through it all, thrivers maintain the key characteristic of thriving, their persistent upward psychological trajectory. They retain their creative consciousness and remain engaged with their crises to eventually make something constructive from them. Without losing their core identity, they keep searching for new and more adaptive expressions of it. It is within their struggle, not in their ultimate victory, that their thriving is experienced.

The Thriver's Psychoimmunity

My interviews with thrivers support what positive psychology has discovered about thrivers like Beethoven. They tend to have very strong psychological immune systems. Even at the worst of times, they seem aware on some level of the rules by which it functions.

The "Let It Go" Rule: Thrivers seem to know or have learned to let their emotions flow naturally rather than cling to them. They know that it's not being afraid, depressed, or anxious that destroys their lives; it's allowing oneself to get stuck in these emotional states. Beethoven's statement that he would not

"endure" his pain but that he would not allow it to " wholly conquer" and dominate his life reflects his unconscious awareness of this rule.

The "Have Faith, Calm Down, and Don't Despair" Rule: Thrivers have faith
that no feeling will last forever and that there is always an equally strong opposing
emotion for every emotion we experience. Like most thrivers, Beethoven seemed
to adopt an increasingly more inclusive and adaptive view of what constituted happiness. Even as he struggled with his loss of what for him was his most important
sense, he still wrote that he was "as happy as it is possible to be on this earth."

The "Suffer Wisely and Cheer Up" Rule: Thrivers sense that suffering is
essential for a truly authentic life. They seem to know that even when things
seem at their worst, they are much stronger than they think and will be stronger
on some level because of their pain. Beethoven's statement, "I can defy this fate
even though there will be times when I shall be the unhappiest of God's creatures," exemplifies his grasp of how the innate psychoimmunity operates and
that he seemed to understand the dynamic nature of emotions.

The next time you hear music composed by Beethoven, I suggest you do
what my grandmother recommended and listen to how it reflects the ebb and
flow of his emotions and his evolving joyful view of life and nature. Listen for how
the changes in volume and complex intonations and movements seem to be an
ode to thriving, a reflection of his lifelong effort to become creative through his
suffering. Listen for how music created by a deaf man might help you strengthen
your own psychoimmunity.

Four Psychological Immunity Reactions

Our psychological immune system is not separate from our physiological
immune system. They work together as one protective and life-enhancing unit.
They operate as a complex interactive loop between the brain, body, and mind.
Here are four of the ways in which our psychological immune systems works in
parallel function with our physiological immunity to allow us to experience the
Beethoven Factor.

Psychological Immunization: By going through several life traumas, a person
can become to some extent emotionally less sensitive to further trauma. As
Beethoven did, people who have gone through terrible stress can develop a psychological immune system characterized by a much less intense reaction to future
stressors than people who have not been "inoculated" against emotional "antigens."

Resilience researcher Charles Carver refers to this adversity-induced psychoimmunity as equivalent to a dose of chickenpox.[5] Because we have experienced

and then dealt with an adversity once, we can acquire a more practiced psychological immune system and at least partial emotional immunity to similar stressors in the future.

Beethoven went through several psychological traumas and various manifestations of his hearing loss. He repeatedly encountered the stress of dealing with various phases of going deaf and trying to disguise his diminishing hearing. What many saw as his natural reserve or creative preoccupation and absent-mindedness were often ways he kept trying to deal with the trauma that had struck him at his prime. He wrote, "How can I, a musician, say to people 'I am deaf!'" Because of his constant struggle of trying to deal with his problem, his psychoimmunity seemed to become stronger.

Beethoven never became totally immune to his life's crises. But like most thrivers I interviewed, he did seem to gradually become a little more immunized against those outside antigens that were invading his emotional system. As when we can develop mild flu symptoms when we are vaccinated against the flu virus, he still suffered, but perhaps not always quite as deeply.

Psychoimmunological Rapid Rebound: When we encounter severe trauma and manage to thrive by making our own meaning out of what happened to us, not only are we immunized against the next adversity, we also become better able to recover more quickly from it.

One of the thrivers I interviewed was a 26-year old television comedy writer who had experienced four nearly fatal heart attacks in less than two years. When I discussed the concepts of thriving and invincibility with him, he said, "Well, I know I'll never be invincible to heart disease. My great-grandfather, grandfather, and dad all died of heart attacks. But, when you've literally picked yourself up off the floor as many times as I have, you become a pretty good picker-upper yourself. I think you come back a little quicker each time."

Beethoven also had a history of being emotionally knocked down hard and often. He was often offered false hope to cure his deafness by those he would later call "cheaters and quacks." It seems he became a little more adept each time at picking himself up and returning to his creative work, despite what must have been repeated heartbreaking disappointment.

Psychoimmunological Hardiness: The third psychoimmune response relates to rising to an even higher level of psychoimmunity following an adverse event. Carver writes, "People who come to appreciate fulfilling aspects of life on a continuing basis after a personal trauma are also functioning at a higher level than they previously did. In this model, something about the experience of the adversity and its aftermath has taken the person to a higher plane of functioning."[6]

This is a description of thriveability, a stronger-than-ever psychoimmunity, and the upward psychological trajectory it makes possible.

In the aftermath of becoming totally deaf, Beethoven faced other crises in his life and work. He questioned his faith and the meaning of his life, writing that he increasingly felt "at odds with nature and its Creator" and "abused by the latter" for making him suffer so. From these depths of doubt and despair, Beethoven rose to even higher levels of thriving. After totally losing his hearing, he expressed himself with the enhanced emotional strength of those who have had their psychoimmunity boosted by severe hardship. His words stating that he was "as happy as it is possible to be on this earth" reflect that strength.

Lowered Expectations: Perhaps one of the most surprising findings from my interviews of thrivers was not that they seemed to develop stronger psychological immune systems that reacted less intensely to stress over time, that they recovered faster after a crisis, or that they somehow became even more psycho-immune and stronger due to their suffering. It was that part of their creative construing was their development of lowered expectations of both themselves and of life.

I had thought that thriving and a feeling of invincibility would be accompanied by raised expectations, and that was certainly often the case. However, most thrivers' psychological trajectory wavered, often dipping up and down even as its overall course was upward. They not only could find more to enjoy about life, but also adjusted their expectations downward when necessary to allow them to be much happier with much less. They lowered the threshold for being thrilled and forgave themselves for their shortcomings and the world for its random harshness. As one thriver joked, "It's a lot easier to feel great when you don't go around expecting life to be fantastic. The old joke is pretty true. Keep your expectations low and you won't be disappointed. Semi-great is good enough for me now."

Thrivers like Beethoven seemed to find strength to carry on and to refine their explanatory system by not only expecting more of themselves and the world but also learning to ask and expect a little less. They weren't always steadfastly committed to their goals or unrelenting optimists. They seemed to fine-tune their lives and become as realistic as they were optimistic.

No one knows if Beethoven would have written even more beautifully inspiring music had he not lost his hearing. We will never know what he could have done without the challenge of his deafness. But we do know that the eternal musical gifts he gave us seem to reflect a resilient spirit and creative joy that serve as examples for thriving.

Perhaps Beethoven was able to share his gifts not only because of a renewed commitment to the highest possible creativity but also because he was able to adjust and even lower his expectations of himself. Perhaps what we see as majestic works were, for Beethoven, compromises matched to his adjusted expectations, accommodations that were a part of his thriving.

Creative Accommodation

Developmental psychologist Jean Piaget referred to the process of making adaptive changes in our thinking to deal with life events as "accommodation."[7] Accommodation not only takes the form of mental upshifting and increased expectations, it can also involve mental downshifting when necessary to a less demanding view of the world and ourselves. It incorporates external circumstances and makes changes in our consciousness not only to fit them in but also to modify and strengthen the adaptability of our thinking.

Although we live in a modern world that encourages ever higher expectations, thrivers have a highly flexible accommodative style. Their explanatory systems allow them to not only increase but also sometimes significantly lower their expectations. Creativity and high-level adaptability can come from this kind of downshifting of goals just as it does from rededicated upshifting.[8]

In a culture that keeps encouraging us to get more, do more, and say yes, thrivers seem be able to "have less, do less, and say no" when their thriving depends upon it. One thriver I interviewed was a 16-year-old boy whose football coaches felt was destined to be a star. The night before he was to sign his letter accepting a full football scholarship to a Big Ten school, he was paralyzed for life by a drunk driver. He told me, "All the other guys in rehab are talking about their commitment to walking again. Not me. I'm learning how to accept the fact that I won't and figuring out ways I can have a great or maybe even a better life because I'm in a chair." It seemed clear that this courageous young man had lowered his aspirations but realistically raised his inspiration.

Thrivers are able to make a better fit between the random chaos of living and how they think about life and its meaning. They find meaning in life that makes it more enjoyable because their threshold for enjoyment can be lowered when need be and raised when possible.

Beyond Pollyanna

Thrivers are not Pollyannas. They are not blindly optimistic and are far from showing the often irritating feigned cheerfulness that can result from trying to comply with popular psychology's version of positive thinking. Their invincibility derives not just from their discovery of what they are able to do about their problems, but also from their acceptance of what they may never be able to do.

Any joy that thrivers gain through their suffering derives not from newfound super-strength, but from establishing a better and more comfortable mental match between the possible and impossible. One of the thrivers I interviewed paraphrased a well-known positive thinking phrase, "The possible we do immediately. The impossible takes a little longer."

After failing for years to regain her ability to walk after being struck by a car, this thriver said, "We have to learn what's possible, but impossible we have to learn to ignore. Like the other patients, I tried to be Ms. Positive Thinking at first. People sort of expect you to put on your game face and tell them that you will walk again, but I knew I wouldn't. People with my kind of injury just don't. I didn't want to waste my life like all the heroes around me by going after an impossible goal. I wanted to live my life now, not be on a mission that I knew would not succeed no matter how many people applauded me. I wanted to get back a normal life by figuring out as quickly as possible what was and was not possible for me in my case. As soon as I finally figured out what was going to be possible and how much I was willing to give to get to that point, I started to deal with my crisis in my own way."

We do not thrive because we finally accomplish the impossible or overcome tremendous obstacles. We thrive because we mentally remain engaged with our problem long enough to find meaning that helps us accommodate to whatever happens to us. We do not make miracles just by rising to new heights. We live a wonderful life by searching for the miraculous in whatever life has made for us. The young woman in the wheelchair said, "I hate it, but the whole thing about not feeling anything below my chest is sort of really a kind of ugly mystery to me. Somehow, I've got to figure out how I'm going to fit this into my life and not let it run my life."

A Consciousness Catalyst

For thrivers, traumas in their lives seem to provide a mentally motivating mismatch between their currently operative life theory and life's reality. This causes what psychologist Jean Piaget called "disequilibration," or a dissonance between what our life theory predicts should happen and what actually does. For thrivers, this dissonance is a consciousness catalyst that causes them to rethink their current theories and beliefs about the world and their place in it. The conscious acts of creation that constitute thriving require an accommodating mind, one that is constantly changing and made wiser by the events that challenge it.

Thrivers seem to know when their current explanatory style is too limited to handle their current crisis. They adjust it to create a consciousness of lowered expectations if they must and higher hopes when they realistically can. As illustrated by the following report from one of the thrivers I interviewed, a consciousness of adjustable levels of expectations can be one of the most important parts of thriving. I spoke with her in the crisis clinic at Sinai Hospital of Detroit a few hours after her own adult daughter had been badly beaten by her new husband on their wedding night. She had brought her daughter to the clinic because she herself had gone there in the past for help after her own experience with domestic violence and abuse.

"I learned my lessons about some men a long time ago," she said, crying. "In a way, one of the best things that ever happened to me was my ex-husband hitting me. He did it only once, but that was enough. It adjusted my view of what real love is and what it can never be. I tried to tell my daughter that. I told her she was being way too unrealistic about this guy and about what she thought love is. She was love-blind, but I saw it coming because I was looking for it. He was a hothead from the start and she knew it, but she clung to her romantic notion that she could change him when they got married. I was sexually abused by my father when I was young, and it taught me that there is a big difference between lust, love, romance, and real caring. She went for this hunk of a guy because she has the fantasy of the perfect man. I can tell you from experience that there is no such thing.

"You have to have more realistic expectations. You have to realize that the essence of love is really accepting imperfections. Unless you're perfect, and most of us aren't, you don't deserve someone who's perfect. You have to get real or you just set yourself up one disappointment after another. You have to try to find a pretty good match for you, but you won't ever find the perfect one."

When I conducted a follow-up interview with this woman, she reported that she is "reasonably happily married," and added, "and that's more than enough for me." I do not know what happened to her daughter, but I hope some of the mother's thriver's accommodating wisdom rubbed off on her.

Don't expect a personality transplant due to your thriving. If you are a generally joyful, happy person, you'll be much the same way no matter what crisis you face. If you're a perpetual grump and general annoyance to those you live with, you will probably still be that way after your thrive through your problems. The Beethoven Factor does not refer to a total personal makeover, only to the capacity to think things over and come out stronger and more adaptable from the process.

It Just Takes Time

Your physical immune system helps your body restore health, but it is your psychological immune system that helps you restore meaning, and it is a sense of meaning that we need most in order to thrive. We survive when sickness turns to health, but we thrive when suffering leads to meaning. By its very nature, new and creative meaning cannot come fast. With rare exceptions, it is less inspiration than prolonged contemplation. You have read that thriving is most accurately understood as a lifelong process, a kind of constantly changing style of life management. It's becoming an increasingly more creative storyteller, the story of your life.

In my interviews of older thrivers, one of their favorite sayings was, "It just takes time." They often bemoaned what they called "the impatience of people today" and "the modern world being in such a hurry." They were eager to share their experience that their own thriving always worked for them in the long run because they were able to "just wait a while." One veteran of World War II told me, "I think I'm just beginning to figure out how I feel about what happened to me in the war. I've been working on it for decades now, and I think I'm finally finding some meaning and closure. The process has been going on since I came home from the war. Something about the September 11 terrorist attacks seemed to help me find meaning in what we all went through back there on the beach at Normandy. It rekindled something in me that I remember feeling back then that kept me going. I guess it just takes time, but you have to be thinking and thinking during that time. If you're patient, you feel a little better because you know you are still working on it and it is not over for you. You don't want to be a survivor all your life.

"When they say I'm a World War II survivor, I feel like telling them that most of us have become much more than that by now. I think that's what might be causing the problem for the Vietnam vets. I think they are trying to figure it all out too fast. It will come to them. They have to stick with it even if it is a painfully long process. They can't expect so much of themselves so soon."

Keep Your Eyes on the Dash

I recently attended a funeral for Clay's mother. Clay is one of my closest Hawaiian friends. Like so many Hawaiians, he has managed to thrive through many trials and tribulations imposed on the Hawaiian culture by Western interference.

With hula, song, and humor, as well as tears, the funeral was a celebration of her life, and it seemed that those in attendance were actually learning to thrive with the grieving family through their experience of the passing of Clay's mother.

Each eulogy at the funeral seemed an example of thriving in progress. Each son, daughter, and grandchild shared their memories as they struggled to put the loss in the context of their own life and find some meaning in this old woman's death for their own living. As I listened, I looked down at the funeral announcement. Under the picture of Clay's mother were the numbers 1918–2001. A minister was speaking about a poem he had read about "the dash" and attending to the quality of our years between our birth and death. His words helped all of us find meaning in my friend's loss. I thought that "the dash" could be seen as a symbol expressing the place where thriving happens.

As I looked at the dash between the years under Clay's mother's picture, I thought about the ups and downs of this Hawaiian mother's life as they were told one by one by her loving family. I thought how, despite so many problems and years of painful cancer, this woman had managed to thrive. I thought how her life taught all who were there that thriving is ultimately found in the meaning we assign to the dash and the time it takes to thrive it seems to represent.

A Lesson from China

To summarize the elements of the lifelong thriving orientation of the Beethoven Factor and the points about thriving made in this chapter, I offer the wisdom of another thriving superstar. He was born in and spent most of his life in China. He had lived most of his life in poverty and oppression. He had been imprisoned in China for his democratic views and protest in Tiananmen Square. He had witnessed most of his friends being massacred or disappearing forever. He had somehow managed to talk his way out of prison and come to America to learn English in weeks, earn two academic degrees within a few short years, and become a highly successful businessman.

He had come to me for help in dealing with the loss of his wife to breast cancer and, within days of that loss, his own diagnosis of cancer. Reading his application for treatment, I expected to see someone who looked and acted as if he had been through the psychological mill, but he appeared upbeat, jovial, and energetic. Even when he cried, he still conveyed a strength of spirit that caused wonder and awe in the medical staff.

One night after a particularly difficult and painful chemotherapy treatment, I sat with him in his hospital room. I often did that with our dying patients, and it is from them that I learned so many profound lessons about the Beethoven Factor, the human capacity to find some level of cosmic joy amid all of our local pain. It was with these patients that I witnessed the power of our psychological immune system in action, even when the physiological immune system was under siege. It was among the dying that I met some of the most fully alive people in the world.

The Chinese man had tubes in his arms and his hair was gone. I held a plastic bowl near his mouth as he repeatedly gagged and vomited. Even in this awkward situation, he said in his typical joking style, "I'm sorry to put you through this with me, but I know you've been through this yourself. As you can know, what doesn't kill you . . . only hurts like hell." He spoke of his love for his wife and how he felt she was with him now more than ever and that she was somehow looking after him. He said his pain seemed to bring him closer to her because he was feeling what she must have felt with her cancer.

In his weakened voice, he said, "You know, the Chinese character for crisis is made up of a combination of the one for danger and the one for opportunity (see figure 2). I am in more danger now, but like all the other dangerous times, it seems to be yet another opportunity in my life. My wife's death stretched my spirit, but it did not tear it. It made me stronger to face this cancer. My own cancer has brought my wife closer to my soul. I might be with her in not too long, or again maybe she will have to wait a little longer. Who knows? I'm not getting rid of the false hope my doctors say I have, because for me hope is hope. You don't have to worry about facing reality, because sooner or later it will find you. But you can make a little of your own reality. I feel weak but in a way I know this is what life is supposed to be for my wife and me. You called it the Beethoven Factor in your lecture, and now I know why. He composed such beauty from the troubles in his life."

Figure 2

The Chinese characters representing crisis, danger, and opportunity are related. The left character *(Wei-ji)* represents crisis as containing danger. The middle character *(Wei-xian)* represents the danger that lurks in crisis. The right character *(Ji-yu)* represents opportunity. It contains the symbol for crisis *(ji)*. Together these symbols illustrate the ancient Chinese understanding of the relationship between crisis, danger, and opportunity that constitutes the nature of the thriving response. (Thank you to Mr. Hendri Widadi for drawing and teaching me about the meaning of these characters.)

After another bout of very severe nausea and pain, he took a deep breath and continued. "Don't think I'm not scared to death. I hate this cancer, I've cried until I have no more tears, and I'm embarrassed to tell you that I have sworn in Chinese at the doctors and nurses. I do not consider myself a fighter and I'm often more than ready to give up, but I'm still here so I guess I'm not supposed to go yet. I'm spending my time writing long letters to my wife, and she answers them at night in my dreams. I think I hear her sometimes, maybe as Beethoven heard. I don't think I could have listened this way without facing what I'm facing now."

A nurse came to inject more toxic chemicals into the man's intravenous line, and it seemed to sting him terribly. As he winced in pain, I tried to comfort him by pointing out that at least he was in one of the best hospitals in the world. He answered, "I think when you are sick you should not ask what is the best hospital for your treatment. I think you should ask instead if it looks and feels like the kind of place where you could die in peace. I think you should ask if it feels like a place of love and caring that is not afraid of death and can help you learn how to do it. If it is such a place, it is probably a very good healing place."

My patient showed all the characteristics of a thriver you have read about. His hardiness in the face of terrible pain, his humor in confronting the seemingly unending series of crises in his life, his patient hope despite his physicians' time-based insistence that he must "face reality," and his ability to construe or imagine ways of looking at his situation were always present when we met. And by the way, not only his healing but also his cure was complete. He recovered from his cancer, something one of his doctors called "unreal."

When I met him again after another one of my lectures, he told me, "My cure was not as big a deal as people make of it, but my healing was truly remarkable for me. It was such a difficult opportunity, and it is still going on. See, I have your list of the six rules of the psychological immune system to help me. I like to read them as I listen to your favorite composer, Beethoven." He showed me his laminated card with the six phrases written in Chinese. On the top were the Chinese characters for crisis, danger, and opportunity in figure 2. He said each of them first in Chinese and then in English. He smiled as he read, "Let go, have faith, calm down, don't despair, suffer wisely, cheer up."

This Chinese thriver continues as of this writing to be one of the most successful financial advisors in New York and often acts as an intermediary for American businesses trying to get a start in China. When I interviewed him again for this book, he said he would send me a quote someday that he felt summarized how he views and he hopes others will view the Beethoven Factor. By a coincidence of a magnitude that only a thriver will accept as true, it arrived as I was completing my writing of this chapter. It was a statement by Anwar Sadat that said, "He who cannot change the very fabric of his thought will never be able to change reality."

Like Beethoven, thrivers know how to weave and keep reweaving the fabric of their lives even when forces keep tearing at it. By constantly re-creating their own consciousness, they are able to do what Beethoven did. They remain the creative composers of their own consciousness.

4 Finding Meaning in Misery

"The lowest ebb is the turn of the tide."

—*Henry Wadsworth Longfellow*

The Man with the Blue Tattoo

I could see the faded blue numbers that had been burned into his wrist by a Nazi guard at the concentration camp. Everyone called him Izzie, and his modest, quiet nature and wry wit endeared him to all of us at the clinic. He was 86 years old, but had the handshake of an athlete, a devilish sparkle in his eye, and a healthy glow that made him appear half his age. Izzie had seen both parents and his sister dragged away in the middle of the night; he had been forced to watch his sister be raped, and he ran away with his eyes closed and his fingers in his ears as the Nazi soldiers shot and killed his family. He had been tortured, starved to the point of skin and bone, and had slept for more than a year in human waste with the unrelenting agonized cries of his fellow prisoners ringing in his ears.

By all medical standards, the physical stress of his ordeal should have killed him. By all psychiatric predictions, he should have been driven out of his mind from living minute to minute not knowing when the number on his wrist would come up and he would be killed.

Despite these appalling experiences, the man who went through them was in outstanding physical health, laughed often and heartily, and seemed more vibrantly alive and fully engaged in the joy of living than many who had never known such suffering. The way he seemed to relish every moment of his life made those who knew him reflect on why they themselves often lacked his profound appreciation of life's simple pleasures.

Izzie was a frequent visitor to my outpatient preventive psychiatric clinic at Sinai Hospital in Detroit called the Problems of Daily Living Clinic. I designed that clinic in the early 1970s as a place where ordinary "nonpatients" could come for help with transitional life crises before they developed into more serious psychiatric disorders. Izzie often came to talk with us about various hassles and stresses. It soon became apparent that we were learning and being helped by him much more than we were assisting him. He was never charged for his visits, and early on became our teacher rather than our patient.

Izzie had heard me speak at his temple. Originally he had come for help with dealing with his wife's pressure on him to stop operating his shoe and watch repair shop and just, as he put it, "Sit home and drive my wife Greta nuts." After his physical exam, required of all of our new patients, I told him how heroic he had been to survive the unimaginable horror of the death camp. He immediately and with atypical impatience firmly corrected me. Because all of our clinic counseling sessions were tape-recorded, I am able to reflect back often on his exact words as an essay on thriving.

"No, son," he said with tears welling up in his eyes. "I am not a hero. I am not special. What I treasure most is the opportunity to be a man again like all other men and not an animal in a cage waiting for slaughter. I did only what anyone could do. I was an ordinary man forced into extraordinary circumstances, and when that happens, there is something in your spirit that you can draw upon to help you. There were hundreds in the camp with me who showed their strength not by defying death but by learning how to welcome it and embrace their lives before they died.

"I ask, dear man, that you not confuse defying death as heroic or courageous. Doing so gives much too much undeserved power to the evil that imprisoned us. It was ordinary men, women, and children who proved they were invincible no matter what was done to them. Life is not only survival. Living long is mostly a matter of good luck, but living with meaning requires work. You must keep looking for meaning in life's misery, because if you don't, misery becomes senseless. If you can't find at least some meaning in your misery, then it is just plain misery."

Beyond Survival

I was mesmerized and inspired by Izzie's words. Everything he said confirmed all that I had learned then and have learned about thriving as I've continued to study it. His statement that what he called senseless misery leads only to suffering with no purpose, no end, and no way to keep growing and developing seemed to capture the central premise of thriving. It described the adaptive and creative framing and construing of events that turns tragedy into triumph and ordinary daily living into a wonderful life.

Izzie's expression of his desire to live and be seen as an ordinary man was echoed by many of the other thrivers I interviewed. It was the same message Olympian Matt Biondi had written about in his foreword to my book *Toxic Success*. When he experienced the positive yet still stressful winning of a series of gold medals, he wrote that despite his extraordinary success and admiration as an Olympic hero, his success only served to make him long to not be seen as a hero. He wrote that he "felt the need to be allowed to be vulnerable again and to become more a part of a full life again . . . to share in all the wonderfully ordinary chaos of life."[1] For Matt, success was a form of life crisis through which he learned to thrive and try to rediscover the more authentic life of an ordinary contented man.

Izzie's description of the strength and positive qualities of the human spirit also highlights the focus of the new field of positive psychology and the amazing life-affirming capacities it is discovering within each of us. His description of the possibility of becoming more alive even when death seems imminent struck a very personal chord in me later when I experienced that same sense of new meaning when I faced my own death from cancer. I learned firsthand what Izzie said about surviving, that it is often a matter of good fortune or strong genes, but thriving is much more. It is a matter of choosing a new way to embrace life beyond staying alive and to keep searching for meaning in our misery. I would feel the ordinary magic of human invincibility and my own capacity to extract new meaning from the worst mess I had ever been in, and Izzie's life and message would become further inspiration for the writing of this book.

In the late 1980s, I had lived for months with bald, pale, skinny children trying to play like any other children. Dragging all sorts of tubes and bags hanging from the intravenous stand they called their Christmas tree, they chased, laughed, and punched gleefully away at the controls of their video games. I saw one very sick child laughing and screaming in victory, telling anyone who would listen that she was seeing the space ships she was destroying as cancer cells and then "blasting them one by one into oblivion." I sat with old people doing their best to knit or play checkers as their hands trembled from the weakness of their cancer and its treatment. I joked with teenagers with multicolored wigs over their bald heads moving rhythmically through the corridors to music playing in their earphones, just as any healthy teenager would. I saw people of all ages so often talking about the sacredness of life that so many of their visitors seemed too busy to see. I saw them facing the possibility of their deaths not only with fear but with curiosity and developing wisdom and insight into their lives.

For so many of us, our cancer seemed to have made us cease any effort to be extraordinary and begin to relish the ordinary magic of the simple pleasures of everyday living. When I learned how to look, I could see meaning sprouting everywhere from the misery of cancer, and Izzie's words about thriving came to me again.

It took me more than ten years after healing from cancer to learn enough about thriving to be comfortable writing a book about it. It took me that long to collect the stories of thriving you are reading in this book. It also took me that long to comb the psychological literature of the new science of positive psychology, the field that deals with the ordinary invincibility of the human spirit rather than its vulnerability, flaws, and frailties.

The Father of Positive Psychology

I had been developing my ideas about the trauma-induced thriving I called the Beethoven Factor since before I designed and opened my clinic at Sinai Hospital. I had always felt uncomfortable with the gloomy pathogenic orientation of my clinical training, and often found myself in debates with my instructors about the true nature of the human spirit. I had seen plenty of examples of resilience and thriving in persons whom the clinical model I was being taught predicted should be candidates for therapy or even medication. I had seen my grandparents go through severe setbacks in their lives to be the happiest and calmest people I have ever seen. I had watched as my parents struggled through borderline poverty to make a joyful life for my brother and me.

It has always seemed to me that psychology was beginning with the wrong premise. I remembered my grandmother's encouragement that if we remain the composers of our own consciousness and do not surrender it to external circumstances, all of us are much stronger than we think we are. While the psychology I was being taught seemed to suspect and distrust our unconscious processes, I had been taught that we were the masters of our own mind. The psychology I was being taught was assuming sickness and vulnerability first and then trying to bring about health, but I sensed that we were all basically strong and healthy. I felt that the challenge in offering help to persons in distress was to help them realize, awaken to, and maximize their natural thriveability.

Like many of my fellow students during my undergraduate years, I had read all I could about Buddhism. When I learned that the name Buddha means the "Awakened One," I wondered what it was he had awakened to. I read about Buddha's Four Noble Truths and thought how encouraging they were regarding the natural resilience of the human spirit. As I look back on Buddha's truths now, they seem in many ways to be precursors for the new positive psychology. Buddha could be considered the father of this evolving new science. I paraphrase these four truths here in terms of what they meant to me as premises for a psychology of optimum human functioning.

- *Buddha's First Noble Truth is that everyone suffers.* Sometime in our lives, we all go through mental, physical, emotional, or spiritual pain. I thought that, if suffering has persisted through human evolution, it must be less an enemy than a necessary evolutionary process with some ultimately adaptive purpose.

- *Buddha's Second Noble Truth is that we create much of our own suffering.* In various ways, we all contribute to our own suffering by spending time and energy regretting our plight or wishing things had turned out differently. I thought that to regret what the First Truth says is inevitable, natural, and necessary might distract us from our capacity to find meaning and personal growth through our plight. I wondered if our focus on surviving might not prevent us from responding to trauma's challenge to help us thrive.

- *Buddha's Third Noble Truth is that we have a choice not to contribute to our suffering.* I thought this meant that our ultimate human gift is our ability to choose how we will perceive whatever happens to us. Positive psychologist Mihaly Csikszentmihalyi wrote, "The control of consciousness determines the quality of life."[2] Buddha's Third Truth and now the science of positive psychology show that experiences only ever really happen to us if we decide to allow them into our consciousness. What we do with them there is a matter of choice.

- *Buddha's Fourth Noble Truth is that there are ways we can go about changing how we think, perceive, and feel.* I thought this meant that one of our greatest gifts is that we can alter our own consciousness and frame the events in our lives in ways that help us thrive. I wondered if we aren't given our trials to allow us to learn how to triumph over them and to discover a more meaningful and joyful life in the process.

As positive psychology's research emerges, it does not seem overreaching to suggest that Buddha might be considered the father of the psychology of optimum human functioning. At the very least, his teachings provide a perspective for understanding what positive psychology is learning about our natural strengths. It seems that Buddha's truths are reflected in the wisdom of Mahatma Gandhi's teaching that the only devils in the world are those running around in our own hearts. He warned that it is within us that life's battles are ultimately fought and won.

Thriving Times

As I reflected about Buddha's First Noble Truth that everyone suffers, I came up with a "trying times" test. I wrote it when I was a senior at the University of Michigan, and later used it with our patients at the clinic to help them understand how Buddha's First Truth might help them put their suffering in a constructive perspective. I present my 40-year-tested Thriving Times Test here so you can see that you don't have to go through the experiences of the thriving superstars to have the opportunity at the stress-induced growth in your own life. I suggest that all of us necessarily go through various manifestations and levels of all twelve of these thriving times.

There are many "stress inventories" that list the major stressful times in our lives. One of the classic stressful life events tests is the Holmes-Rahe Social Readjustment Rating, which presents a long list of stressors such as the death of spouse, moving to a new home, losing a job, getting a new job, having a child, divorce, and so on. I wanted to use a list that was more general in nature and focused on our consciousness rather than our circumstances. I tried to arrange the items in a general life developmental task order that reflects the transitional times in our lives that can provide catalysts for a developing consciousness.

Thriving Times Test

Answer yes or no to the following questions.

1. ___ *Do you feel confidently independent?* We must grow through and overcome our fear and insecurity of being on our own in the world.

2. ___ Do *you feel comfortably interdependent?* We also must grow through our fear of being dependent in the world. Do you feel worthy of being loved in the way you need and want to be loved? We must learn to move from the

dependent love of our childhood to the mature interdependent love of adulthood.

3. ___ *Have you gone through a failed close interpersonal intimate relationship?* In some way at some time, we must learn how to turn a broken heart into a more loving, forgiving, and strong heart.

4. ___ *Have you had to deal with a major life disappointment?* We must learn that a full life is as much about growing through disappointment as it is experiencing delight.

5. ___ *Have you gone through serious concerns about your financial situation?* We need to find a level of calm contentment and resolve the conflict between the stress of our increasing wants and comfort of met needs.

6. ___ *Have you found fulfilling, energizing work?* Across the life cycle, all of us must eventually find meaningful, appreciated, rewarding work.

7. ___ *Have you known and overcome terrible fear?* In our own way, all of us are afraid. We must learn that what frightens can also come to embolden us and teach us where and to whom we must look to find our sense of safety and security.

8. ___ *Have you gone through very serious illness and severe emotional and/or physical pain?* We all eventually experience mental, physical, emotional, or spiritual illness and pain. We must learn through these times that curing or fixing is not always possible but that healing or becoming whole again is.

9. ___ *Have you formed a spiritual or religious belief system that helps you explain evil and cruelty in the world?* We all need to be able to mentally comprehend, emotionally manage, and find spiritual meaning in the often cruel chaos of the world.

10. ___ *Have you known and become stronger because of a deep personal loss?* We all become bereaved, know grief, and must learn to turn those feelings into new ways to value life and celebrate loving memories.

11. ___ *Have you felt total and complete vulnerability and helplessness?* We must learn how to find meaning when everything can seem so meaningless.

12. ___ *Have you faced and become comfortable with your own mortality?* None of us is truly free to live until we are able to find meaning in the inevitability of our own deaths.

Each of the above twelve consciousness catalysts represents an opportunity for thriving, the nature of a passage in life through which we will grow, remain static, or regress. Perhaps because of the severity and scope of their life trauma, the thriving superstars were able to answer "yes" to all twelve items. You may want to look at your "yes" answers and reflect on what lessons about thriving you may have learned. You also might want to look at your "no" answers, for these are challenges to thriving you are yet to experience.

Many of the thriving examples presented in this book may seem extreme. They include trying to thrive because of life-threatening cancer, paraplegia, violent crime, the death of a child, and the torture of a concentration camp. They are acute crises, but you can learn about your own thriveability from those who experienced them. Hopefully, most of us will experience much less drastic forms of trauma in our lives, but we will nonetheless have to deal with the same general issues identified in the items on the above list. I hope as you read about the more drastic examples of stress-induced growth, you will reflect on the general thriving themes listed above as they are contained in these challenges.

Hearing the Deaf Man's Symphony

I often listened to classical music when I was dying of cancer. Beethoven's Ninth Symphony was one of my favorites and often the favorite of other cancer patients. In my lectures about the Beethoven Factor of thriving to groups around the world, I sometimes play his music to illustrate his ability to hear more than he had ever heard before because of the trauma of his deafness. I speak of his creative thriving despite what could have been a devastating setback that ended his ability to compose forever. During my chemotherapy, I often listened to his Ninth Symphony to place me in a more creative frame of mind more conducive to finding meaning amid the madness of my cancer. It seemed to help keep the cancer from metastasizing to consciousness by overwhelming healthy and hopeful thoughts that would help me dispute cancer's assertion that it had become my life. One of my fellow patients diagnosed with a brain tumor also tried my Beethoven Factor music. She said, "It's horrible enough that the cancer's in my brain. When I listen to Beethoven's music, it helps keep it out of my consciousness."

Izzie had commented on one of my lectures during a visit to our clinic. "You see, you knew what I have been saying all along. You spoke to us of what you called the Beethoven Factor. You see, Beethoven ultimately did not survive. None of us do. But the meaning he managed to find through his misery helps us hear what he heard, the joy of living. Survival is always temporary, but the results of Beethoven's growing through his problem are within the notes of his music, and they are forever. Beethoven could not escape the physical prison of his deafness, but he was able to go far beyond its limitations. He managed to escape the prison of his deafness by finding new meaning in his life that freed his spirit, allowed him his own way to listen, and still helps those who will listen to his music find their own meanings in their life."

I thought Izzie was finished speaking and prepared to turn off the tape recorder, but he grabbed my hand and held it firmly. He had been smiling up to this point, but his face now appeared solemn, and I could see his eyes moisten with tears. He said, "I have something that might help you think more about your theories about thriving. The SS officers sometimes made prisoners who were musicians play Beethoven and other classical music for them. I remember thinking how ironic that was. The officers probably heard only notes and not the true meaning of Beethoven's music, or perhaps it was their only source of joy in their impoverished lives. Whether they knew it or not, I think they were more imprisoned than we were. They were held captive by the anger and evil of someone else's thinking. Their minds were not their own. We could sometimes faintly hear the music, but I think they were deaf to it." Izzie stopped talking, released my hand, and stood up. He walked to the window and finished talking while looking out at the autumn sunset.

"I remember the prisoner we all called 'the teacher,'" he said so quietly that I had to move the microphone closer to him. "Her name was Mosha, and most of us in the camp knew her. The men and women were always separated, but I saw her sometimes. Her face was scarred from beatings and her face was skeleton-thin and pale with deeply sunken eyes that had darkness all around them, but you could see that she had been a real beauty. Because she had not been cooperative and refused to play for them, they had placed both of her hands on a large rock and made a game of taking turns breaking each of her fingers one at a time with their rifle butts. After her torture that day, the women say she seemed more at peace than ever that night. She became weaker and weaker, and one morning we found her dead.

"Mosha had been a piano teacher before they took her as she was playing and teaching one of her students. They shot her student but kept Mosha alive to play for them, but no matter how they beat her, she refused. You could say she should have just played for them so she could survive, but her music was a sacred gift she would never give them. It was more important to her than surviving. Whenever Beethoven was being played for the SS officers, the women said that Mosha would always say in her teacher voice, 'Shush! Be quiet now and listen to the deaf man's symphony. If you listen as he did, you will hear the way to freedom.'

"Many times Mosha would shut her eyes so she could listen more intently, and tears would still squeeze out and roll down her face. She would not stop to wipe her tears and kept moving her hands and swaying her head back and forth as if she was conducting a large orchestra. She would say the same words about Beethoven that many of her friends in the camp came to know by heart. 'If you will listen to Beethoven, you will hear the way to freedom.' She spoke of Beethoven as if she had come to know him personally.

"Most times, we could barely hear the music coming from the officers' quarters and usually we could not hear it at all, only drunken laughter, but Mosha always said she could hear it. The weaker she became, the more she said she could hear it. She became more and more withdrawn and began to hallucinate. She would ask the women around her to listen for music that only she could hear, and they said she almost made them hear it too. They said she was losing her mind, but I think in a way she was finding it.

"One of the prisoners was a psychiatrist, and he said he thought she was decompensating and entering what he called a dissociated schizoid state, but she was still our teacher. On the night she died, they said no one but the teacher could hear the music, but Mosha said it seemed to be getting louder and louder. As she lay in her bed, she had closed her eyes and conducted the deaf man's symphony for one last time. She had come to the camp a teacher, but escaped it as a maestro."

Izzie stood silently by the window for several minutes as we both cried. He turned around and said, "You can turn off the tape now. I talk too much. I do think though, Doctor, that this may be what you mean by the Beethoven Factor."

Coming Out of Our Trance

If we are to discover our natural "thriveability" without the catalyst of the extraordinary distress endured by the invincible people described above, we have to first become aware that we are not thriving. We have to become alert to the near trance-like survivor style of thinking into which so many of us seem to have fallen. We have to be less consumed with trying to live a long life and more contemplative about how to discover an increasingly meaningful one.

Perhaps the dominance of the pathogenic model in our culture is perpetuated by our tacit acceptance that survival is enough. It may be that, because we are so constantly nagged about how vulnerable we are and about the many threats to our survival, we have lost confidence in the resilience, creativity, and adaptive power of our consciousness. I offer this book about thriving with the hope that most of us will not require the catalyst of a major life catastrophe in order to find that confidence again.

Every moment of our lives, we are in the process of creating the content of our consciousness, a process that positive psychologists call "meaning reconstruction."[3] Even as you read these words, you are deciding which of the messages you are receiving you will allow to become a part of your consciousness. Being aware that we are the creators of our consciousness is essential to awakening in time to thrive through our living.

The Joy of Fixation and Regression

Research in positive psychology now shows that the linear, step-by-step approach to life is a reflection of choice, not an automatic way of thinking. Even though I tried to arrange the items on my "trying times" list in a general life sequence, many readers may have noticed that they experienced these transitional developmental times in a different order or even passed back and forth through the list items at various times in their lives.

Two popular pathogenic words are "fixation" and "regression." Negativistic psychology assumes that life is characterized by a one-way series of development stages. Anyone who stops or goes backwards on this assumed set of stages is seen as at least temporarily emotionally disturbed or, more recently, "dysfunctional." While there are those with serious mental disorders who completely lose touch with reality or try to escape it through debilitating childish delusion, most of us are capable of a willful consciousness time travel. We can elect to dance back and forth along the memories and anticipations of our paths of life. Thriving requires intentionally and consciously staying awhile, joyfully lingering at, or revisiting and perhaps painfully learning from a given psychological time in our lives. In the creation of our consciousness, we need not be pushed or pulled along a preestablished course.

Those who thrive through their crises are able to make their own sense of what happens, put it in a creative context that fits their value and spiritual system, and then devise a management scheme that gives them hope. They may psychologically progress, fixate, or regress for a while, but the key is that they remain in charge of their own "meaning construction."

Shakespeare said that we are all acting out our own dramas on the stage of life. Survivors tend to be like actors taking direction, but thrivers assume direction of their own life dramas even when the scripts contain tragedies. Thriving is defined as *construing stressful events in our lives in ways that lead to new, higher levels of hardiness, happiness, healing, and hope.* To thrive or not to thrive is one of the most important choices we will make in our lives. Whether we lead or feel led by our lives is ultimately up to us.

Beyond Recovery

The human capacity to thrive through crisis has been described in literature and philosophical inquiry for centuries.[4] Ernest Hemingway's idea that "we become stronger at the broken places" has long been a theme in plays, poetry, and philosophy. Modern medicine and psychology, however, have often ignored thriving and limited their healing horizons to reducing suffering, promoting survival, and believing that all if not most of us lead lives of chronic recovery.

Author Wendy Kaminer wrote, "The religiosity of the recovery movement is evident in its rhetorical appeals to a higher power and in the evangelical fervor of its disciples."[5] Those who do not acknowledge they are in some sort of recovery are often accused of being in denial or even heretical, but this idea of the persistent need for recovery begins with the assumption that all or at least most of us are dysfunctional. Positive psychology assumes the exact opposite by viewing us as essentially functional beings capable of much more than a life damned to eternal recovery.

From the perspective of positive psychology's research, recovery is only a good beginning. We are capable of much more than freedom from pathology, just "getting back to normal," or living on the edge of regression to dysfunction. As Izzie told me, "When you write your book about thriving, you should tell your readers that thriving is really nothing new. People have been doing it since they learned how to think differently about hunting after they were chased back to their caves by a saber-toothed tiger. They probably sat down, caught their breath, and tried to think about the meaning of what just happened to them so they could hunt differently next time."

The Danger of Biting Bullets

The work of the positive psychologists is contributing to a slow but sure paradigm shift toward learning about health from the healthy rather than the sick. Science changes its mind very slowly, and the best the healing arts have had to offer to date has essentially been the "bounce back" survivor or resilience orientation and sometimes the heroic exception to the survival and recovery rule. The possibility of thriving still stretches the imagination of many scientists, but not that of those who have felt its power or seen it in a loved one.

The "pathogenic-survivor-recovery" orientation not only largely ignores the thriving response, it also contains some dangers and causes us to miss out on some of thriving's practical benefits. Glorifying the "bullet biters" who manage to survive against all odds can invite what psychologists Karen W. Saakvitne, Howard Tennen, and Glenn Affleck have described as "an implicit moral judgment on pain and bias toward sublimation and stoicism."[6]

If we assume pain is an enemy with no purpose other than to ruin our lives and that it must be erased as quickly as possible, we may interfere with the transformative role pain can play in our lives. If our healing heroes and heroines are only those who seem to be stoic individuals who have proven that they can "take it" and come "bouncing back," we fail to understand its sometimes "bouncing back and forth" nature.

Even worse, we can devalue and even berate the experience of those who show their own unique ways of thriving that do not comply with our bullet-biter's point of view. We might even unintentionally end up "blaming the victim" of trauma for not being mentally, emotionally, spiritually, or even physically strong enough to "take it."[7]

Psychologists Saakvitne, Tennen, and Affleck, wrote, "Our culture fosters denial of the long-term impact of trauma by urging victims to 'get over it and get on with it,' and by idealizing those who 'bit the bullet,' and thus does not recognize complex posttraumatic adaptations [i.e., thriving]."[8] My interviews indicate that the process of thriving is much more than being tough-minded and ruggedly defiant. In fact, most of the thrivers I've interviewed have not been "bullet biters" who have "gotten over" their trauma to live in an ever vigilant state of recovery. Instead, they seemed to have accommodated or taken their traumas in, processed them, and made them a part of a new, more vigorous, and adaptive consciousness. They are living in a state of discovery rather than recovery.

Thriving as Sound Economics

There is also a practical side to the issue of thriving, and practical usually means economics. If we fail to learn about the wonderfully complex nature of thriving, our society in general may miss out on what could be one of its most significant social and financial benefits. Because the skill of thriving and making something very good out of something very bad seems to be such a noble thing, it may seem crass to focus on its practical and financial benefits, but they are significant and important to the eventual thriving of our society.[9]

If medicine, psychiatry, and psychology limit themselves to seeking only to produce a group of survivors or recoverers, they fail to acknowledge and deal with the more subtle but important pragmatic side of thriving. Because they not only recover but also become stronger and more adaptive, patients may become less likely to be patients soon again in the future. By focusing on helping those who are dealing with adversity to not only rebound from but also exceed their pretrauma level of functioning, we help create a hardier population that puts less financial pressure on an already burdened health care system.

Because they become generally stronger after their illness or trauma, thrivers may also be less likely to relapse. If the goals of medicine and psychotherapy go beyond curing and recovery to learn more about stress-induced growth, clinics' waiting lists might shorten and waiting rooms could become less crowded.

If we can learn to apply the emerging lessons from positive psychology and the wisdom offered by those who have thrived, we might be able to help others enhance their own innate talent for thriving. If we focus on thriving, we can develop a new form of preventive medicine perhaps better called "enhancement medicine." Instead of "recovery rooms," we might have "thriving rooms" where patients go to be helped to find meaning in their misery. A society of thrivers would not only be a very joyful and creative place in which to live; it would also be much less expensive.

Don't Forget the Co-Thrivers

When I interviewed the family members of thrivers, they had their stories of their own thriving. Because they were not prisoners in horrible situations, personally going though the torture of a horrible event, or facing their own deaths, their stories may not sound as powerful or dramatic as the thrivers with whom they lived and loved. They were, however, thriving in unique ways. Their trauma was what was happening to someone they loved, and they were engaged in trying to find meaning not only in the suffering of their loved one but in the possibility of the loss of that person.

Aunty Betty Jenkins is one of my Hawaiian 'ohana (family.) As I was writing this chapter, her husband, Jack, underwent open-heart surgery. When I called Aunty to see how Jack was doing, she shared her struggle to find meaning in their adversity. Through her tears, Aunty described how she was thriving through her suffering.

She said, "It seemed so quiet at home and so lonely lying there in that bed without him beside me. I felt afraid and wondered what life would mean if I would lose him. I thought of how important he has always been to me. Of course, I always knew that, but somehow this brought it all more to my heart. All the little hassles and problems of life now seemed so stupid and unworthy of a moment's distraction from our loving. I always knew what Jack meant to me and what my family's support meant to me, but this has all made that meaning even deeper and broader. It has changed everything and deepened my love. I'm not going to take a single moment with him for granted again."

Behind every good thriver is another good thriver. In fact, these co-thrivers aren't behind, but consciously with, their thrivers. They may be doing their thriving in the shadow of someone going through a more obvious major catastrophe, but they are no less exercising their thriving talent. They are becoming a vital part of a thriving system.

Aunty Betty and her husband, Jack, wrote the foreword for my book titled *Partners in Pleasure*. The book describes the Hawaiian concept of *lōkahi*, meaning harmonious and enduring loving unity. It described the Hawaiian legend of the *naupaka*, a hardy plant that blooms with a half flower blossom. Legend has it that two Hawaiian lovers were separated and banished to live apart forever, the man in the mountains and the maiden at the sea. Upon hearing of their terrible fate, the maiden took a full *naupaka* flower from her hair. She tore it in half and placed one half behind her ear and the other half behind her lover's ear. Now, the *naupaka*'s flower blossoms only in one of its halves on the plants in the mountains and the other half on the plants that grow at the sea. This is representative of the timeless and enduring unity of love, the kind experienced by many co-thrivers.

I hope the many first-person reports about thriving offered in this book will in no way diminish the crucial role that co-thrivers play in how we find meaning in our misery. Izzie's wife, Greta, was a co-thriver. She always came with him to our clinic. She was quieter and much more shy than Izzie, and they often bantered playfully back and forth and argued about silly things such as the time left on a parking meter or if the TV weatherperson had said it was going to rain. She called him "old man" and he referred to her as "old woman." She told me, "I hope you're not going to put everything this old fool tells you in your book. People say he is so smart, but they do not live with this old fool. He is lucky to find his socks." Izzie laughed and said, "This old woman is the bane of my existence. If I didn't love her so much, I'd leave her tonight."

Izzie's and Greta's constant chiding of one another was evidence not of conflict but of deep trust and unconditional love. It was based on a mutual understanding, trust, and communication system born of going through terrible tragedies together. Izzie joked "Now, if you want to talk about just surviving, talk to my wife. She has her hands full just trying to survive living with me. I don't think even Beethoven himself could thrive through that. This poor woman suffers in such great silence." Saying this, they would both laugh, hug, and then kiss each other.

I learned years later that Greta had also been briefly detained in a death camp and that her entire family was killed in the Holocaust. When I asked her about her experiences, she said, "If I'm going in your book, you should tell them that a lot of thriving is done very quietly and privately. Many of us cannot or perhaps do not want to tell others about it. We all don't have the big mouth of this crazy old man."

My interviews with the spouses and family members of cancer patients revealed the same "silent suffering" of thriving Greta describes. I dedicate this book to the co-thrivers, such as my wife, Celest, who know suffering, thriving, and invincibility in ways that even those who are dying and enduring other hardships may never fully know. It may be that there is no greater pain to try to learn to thrive through than the unrelenting pain of someone we love.

A deeper meaning that often comes from thriving through crisis is a profound awareness that perhaps our greatest fear is to feel alone and unloved in the world. Thrivers know that the ones who love us and go so willingly with us in our search for the meaning of our misery help us conquer that fear. Even if these co-thrivers exist now only in our memory, they are in our consciousness waiting to serve as our guides. They are waiting like my grandma to help us thrive through our pain.

When I was trying to thrive through my dying, my wife, Celest, and my family kept me from feeling alone and unloved. Late one night when I was dying and gasping for air as my lungs began to fail, I could feel my wife's heart beating as she held my hand. It seemed to be a kind of music that calmed and comforted me like no medication could. Even at the time of such misery, I came to understand the meaning of Henry Ward Beecher's words, "Of all the music that reached farthest into heaven, it is the beating of a loving heart."

5 A Course in Thriveology

Are You Having Piloerections?

How many times a day do you have an emotional reaction that causes you to get goose bumps? If you answered several times, you're probably thriving. Goose bumps are what doctors call a piloerection, the involuntary erection or bristling of the hairs on your body. Hawaiians call this chicken skin. Every one of the thrivers I interviewed said that they often had goose bumps in response to the ordinary grandeur of daily life.

Piloerection happens when our arousing (sympathetic) nervous system is activated by our intense emotional response to a life event. It can occur when we feel chilled, feverish, frightened, or sexually aroused, but it is also a sign that we feel deeply moved by what we are experiencing. When our emotional reaction causes neurohormones to surge through our body, they cause our pilomotor nerve to stimulate our pilomotor muscles (pilomotion), resulting in the sensation that our skin is "crawling" and that our hair is "standing on end."

Because thrivers are so fully and deeply engaged in living, their threshold for goose bumps is significantly lower than for those who have not yet developed their thriving talent. For someone who is thriving, a simple sad story, a song on the car radio, or just the recollection of a very important moment easily elicits a piloerection. Such ordinary events also elicit the feelings of warmth and tingling in the chest associated with the elevation response discovered by positive psychologists. The hormones cause the vessels to dilate, and the heart becomes more open and warm.

Once they learned about the physiology of their chronic goose bump reactions and why they had them much more frequently after they thrived through their life traumas, my patients often joked about having piloerections. One man said, "I guess I was a little emotionally impotent before I got hit by that car and almost killed. Now I don't need any Viagra to have lots of piloerections."

Serious Symptoms of Good Signs?

By its very nature, thriving is a contradiction. It is about becoming stronger and being devastated at the same time and about rejoicing and suffering simultaneously. For example, if we see someone who seems in extreme pain, angry, and withdrawn, we might assume that person is not yet thriving, but we could be very wrong. As you read in the example of Mosha, she managed to thrive even at the times of her most severe pain.

One of my patients was an emotionally disturbed young woman. Like Mosha, she had several symptoms of what psychologists call "dissociation." She would periodically withdraw into herself, emotionally and mentally, sitting quietly and looking out to nowhere. She was extremely guarded in social situations, was easily frightened, had many phobias, and refused to date without several other people present to make her feel safe. According to her family, she seemed to often live in her own fantasy world. She held a job, was financially independent, but sat alone most of the time when she was not working. Based solely on appearance, she would not seem to be thriving, but that assumption would be very wrong. Thriving takes place in our consciousness and may not always show its process physically.

By looking only for some external tangible result of thriving, we can fail to learn about its full process and individual history. Because the result may not live up to our expectations of what a thriver should look like, we can fail to understand the unique thriving process that particular person may be employing. The woman above had suffered more than 15 years of almost nightly sexual abuse as a child. She had been beaten severely by her father, then a stepfather, and finally two uncles who had moved into the house. All of this took place with the approval and encouragement of her mother, and the story made national news when the guilty parties were arrested.

Our clinic staff tried to interview as many people as we could who had influenced the lives of our patients, and one of my associates interviewed our patient's former high school counselor. She told us that she had recently met her by chance at a local shopping mall and was "amazed at how she talked so thoughtfully and joyfully about her life now. She didn't look any different, but she seemed to be so much more calm and content than I ever could imagine anyone being after all she went through."

If we make the mistake of thinking that those who have symptoms of mental or physical illness are not thriving, we fail to fully grasp the full nature, range, and complexity of thriving. If we assume that pathology or severity of trauma excludes any possibility of thriving, we fail to understand the full potential of a creative consciousness totally engaged in construing a happier and more meaningful life.

Fifteen Thriving Dialectics

Dialectics refers to trying to reconcile seemingly contradictory positions to arrive at a truth. To fully understand thriving, we have to be willing to incorporate and include all of its many paradoxes and apparent contradictions into our concept of stress-induced growth. Based on the research in positive psychology and my interviews of thrivers, here are fifteen findings regarding the intricacies of thriving.

- *Thriving and the appearance of suffering are not mutually exclusive.* Someone who looks and appears to be feeling miserable can still be firmly and deeply absorbed in the process of thriving.

- *"Insensitive" people might still be thriving.* People who seem emotionally numb and even narcissistic can still be developing their thriveability. Someone who seems to have shut out the outside world can be doing some very important thriving work inside their own skin.

- *Thriving and denial are not mutually exclusive.* You can be in a state of deep denial and still be thriving. People who seem to be denying or avoiding their problems can be buying themselves some thinking time to work on their explanatory systems.

- *Thrivers aren't always likeable people.* Their intensified enjoyment of life and eagerness to grasp and embrace every moment of living can be off-putting to those living a more hurried and distracted life. Because they have learned how wonderfully miraculous life can be, they can come across as salespersons urgently trying to sell others on the idea of leading a more authentic, meaningful, and joyful life.

- *Thrivers aren't always energetically outgoing.* Quiet, withdrawn, pensive people can also be thriving. People who seem reticent about sharing their feelings and appear down and out may be in fact be on their way emotionally and mentally up. They might be in a profoundly important reflective phase of their thriving and consciously consumed in their efforts to develop and enhance their explanatory style.

- *Thriving almost always takes a long time.* While it can rarely happen suddenly and without any apparent explanation, thriving is usually a lifelong process. It's a process constantly in flux with many emotional hills and valleys along its generally upward psychological trajectory.

- *Sometimes thriving happens fast.* People who seem to be "doing too well much too fast" may indeed have managed to do just that. While thriving usually involves protracted self-reflection, abrupt, surprising, quantum leaps in thriving can happen and are not necessarily what psychologists diagnose as dissociation or delusional denial.

- *Thrivers can get very down on their way up.* On their upward psychological trajectory, thrivers can get very down for a while. Persons who seem to be depressed or are "kindling," thereby making their problems worse, may be in a temporary "down phase" essential to eventually moving more "up." Contrary to pathogenic psychology's view that depression is bad, it is a necessary and natural part of living. It is a time we all need for turning inward, reflecting, and trying to construe our lives in new and more adaptive ways. Like all of our emotions, it becomes debilitating only when it becomes permanent.

- *Dying doesn't prevent thriving.* Death ends life, but dying is a crucial transitional time in our living. One of my fellow cancer patients said, "I used to think so many things were so terribly important. Now that I'm doing it, I think that dying is probably the most important thing we do in our lives. I really can't think of a more important time to learn to thrive."

    People you may think are facing a thrive-resistant crisis may be thriving at the highest level. On my walks through the cancer unit on which I spent many months of my own life as a patient, I saw terrible sickness, pain, and dying everywhere. However, I also saw dramatic and moving examples of thriving. A curriculum in thrivology should require courses in thanatology, the study of death and dying. It should require a residency on cancer units and at hospices where so much thriving is always going on. If we elect to make it so, facing the end of our lives can be one of the most important mental, emotional, and spiritual catalysts for thriving in our lives.

- *Thriving does not require staying in control.* People who seem helpless, lost, disoriented, confused, and unsure of where to turn or what to do next can also be in the midst of thriving. They may be in an important "searching" phase in developing their explanatory style and trying out various ways of managing their lives. They may be testing to see when a different kind of control might work or whether the ultimate act of control is deciding not to struggle to stay in control and gracefully go with the flow.

- *Despairing and thriving can go together.* Feelings of deep despair can lead to thriving and may even be necessary for it. People who seem to have hit rock bottom and lost all hope and zest for living can be preparing to head emotionally upward in a different mental direction motivated by the new meanings and purpose discovered through the depths of their despair.

- *Thrivers can have low self-esteem.* Positive psychologists are learning that our self-esteem is nowhere as fragile and easily damaged as we have been told by pathogenic, negative psychology. Most of us have a mature inner adult, not a fragile inner child.

- *Thriving can involve shame and guilt.* Having a guilty conscience does not necessarily prevent thriving, and may often be essential for it. People who are feeling conscience pangs and shame as they look with anxious concern and deep regret at something they did in the past can be collecting data for a new explanatory system. They may need this "good guilt" and appropriate shame as emotional, spiritual, or mental energy for a new moral direction in life.[1]

- *The entirety of thriving is difficult to see.* One person's way of thriving through adversity may not reflect the true and full thriving resource available within the system in which that person lives every day. As down as that person may seem, there may be an experienced thriver at home helping them begin to learn how to thrive.

• *Thrivers can seem pretty weird.* They don't always have a good grasp on reality. Because thrivers have learned the art of enlightened denial, they can seem to be what one thriver's spouse described as "a little daffy and out there." They know that depression is due less to the inability to face reality than to not knowing when it is healthy to try to creatively and constructively escape from it.

Beware of Gurus

Putting this list in the form of a description of someone who might be thriving results in a surprising image. Thrivers might be persons who appear sickly or robust, angry or compliant, short-tempered or forgiving. They might seem to be suffering deeply, guilt-ridden and helpless, but also might seem almost giddy and totally in control of their lives. Sometimes a thriver might be someone who went through Hell on Earth and automatically, suddenly, unexpectedly, and for no apparent reason, became much stronger because of his or her predicament. Other times, a thriver might be someone who seems to have been gifted, lucky, and worry-free who suddenly and automatically "saw the light" and began thriving.

To see thrivers as guru-like, and thriving itself as limited to only supermen and superwomen who are always highly positive, even-tempered, highly energetic, and deeply interested in psychological concepts, is again to oversimplify the thriving response. As you have read, the last thing most thrivers want is to be seen as extraordinary or guru-like. Like Izzie, they don't want to stand out. They want to know the joy of peaceful blending in. Like the moody Beethoven, they aren't consistently peaceful philosophers with a perpetually positive attitude. Their distinguishing characteristic is not their extraordinary nature but their ability to tap into the same ordinary thriveability that rests within all of us.

One of my fellow cancer patients, Max, was one of the most grumpy, surly, cantankerous people I had ever met. He bragged that he was an "ornery, tough, obnoxious guy from the Bronx." He came into the hospital that way, generally made everyone's life miserable while he was there, and left in a huff when his cancer went into full remission. He had gone through horrendous pain and contracted several life-threatening hospital-induced infections during his stay. On the day he left, he said, "This hospital kills more people than cancer. It's like New York. If you can make it there, you can make it anywhere. I'm out of this hellhole."

Max seemed to "try on" several thriving styles while he was hospitalized. He would yell one day, close his door and sulk the next, and sometimes try to leave without medical clearance with the nurses dashing after him. I never heard him laugh or saw him smile, and was sure that he was the poster child for failure to thrive. On the day he was discharged and after hearing the wonderful news of his cancer's remission, he came to my room.

I was very sick that day and could barely lift my head. I had been one of the few people who had dared go near him, and we had spoken a few times late at night. He had told me how little he thought of my profession as a psychologist and of doctors in general. He said he thought all psychologists were crazy and that doctors were all "in it for the money." He came to my bed, and I thought for a moment he was going to insult me one more time before he left. Instead, he leaned over and gave me a gentle hug. "I really had these fools going, didn't I?" he asked. "It was my hobby to annoy them and my way of getting through this cancer crap." He had tears in his eyes, and said, "If you tell anyone I hugged you, I'll come back here and turn off your oxygen." He smiled, winked, shook my hand, and left.

A nurse came to my room, perhaps to see if I needed assistance after what she feared was another angry outburst from their problem patient. "I'm happy for him," she said, "but he's as much of a pain in the ass now as he was before he got the great news. He hasn't changed a bit. He just walked by our nurses' station with a big smile on his face and flipped us off."

From the perspective of the variations on the thriving theme I am describing here, I disagree. In his way and in his time, that first small demonstration of caring and vulnerability marked immense growth for Max through his crisis. He seemed to be in the midst of beginning to thrive.

So What in the Heck Is Thriving, Anyway?

After one of my lectures to a medical meeting about the complexities and apparent contradictions of the thriving response, a young medical student said, "So what in the heck is it, anyway?" The shortest, most inclusive definition of thriving that I've been able to come up is that *thriving is stress induced growth (SIG)*.

The emphasis in this five-word definition is on the word "growth," but that growth may be a form of mental, emotional, or spiritual becoming that we have not typically associated with words like "resilience" and "thriving." We all grow at our own pace, in our own way, and from different starting points. Thriving is moving mentally and emotionally up in our own unique way and at our own pace from wherever we may have been when we first encountered our thriving turning point. Perhaps most of all, it is the recognition that we have been languishing instead of flourishing.

I told the medical student that the only way I've discovered to determine if someone is thriving is to ask. That may seem a greatly oversimplified approach, but I've found that asking the question "Are you thriving?" usually elicits an interesting response. When I asked an extremely busy and pressured successful woman if she was thriving, she quickly joked, "Well, I'm able to sit up and take nourishment, if that's what you mean." I waited a moment and she added, "Wow, come to think of it, that is about what I'm doing. I guess right now the answer is no, I'm not thriving. That's why I'm working so hard now, so I can answer yes to that question later. But I guess I'll have to think about this, if I ever have the time."

To learn about thriving, you have to listen and really hear the person's answer when you ask if they are. If you tune in to not only what a person says but also how, and if you listen carefully for their general explanatory style and current philosophy of life, you will usually be able to recognize a thriver. If it seems to you that they are generally on an upward psychological trajectory and fully mentally engaged and attentive to life and why and how they are leading it, they may be thriving despite their current mood. Most importantly, if it seems to you that they are savoring their lives by engaging in regular basking, thanksgiving, marveling, and luxuriating, you will know they are experienced thrivers.

Do We Really Love a Challenge?

Thriving happens when we face a challenge, and a challenge always involves a significant change. We often say we love a challenge, but in reality we seem to dislike and often try to avoid the real changes in our lives that are the essential prerequisites for thriving. In his typical jokester style, Izzie said, "Change is inevitable, except from a vending machine." Another characteristic of thrivers is that they not only expect change, they come to seek and thrive because of it.

I define a life trauma as any event that significantly challenges our current explanatory system. It is anything that demands our attention, stops us in our tracks, turns us around, and causes us to rethink our lives or look for new meaning in it because of what has happened to us. A life change or trauma, then, is anything that impacts and changes the direction of our lives. Positive or negative, it is any challenge to our expectations and current explanatory systems.

Instead of trying to survive or cope with change, thrivers come to relish it. For them, change is something to be accommodated, digested, and processed, not something through which they try to quickly pass. The very definition of life is its dynamic state, and as Izzie pointed out, "Change is what life is for. Without it, you are dead even if you are still breathing."

Change is often painful because it demands that we give up the security of the familiar and comfortable. Change creates the disequilibrium that thrivers turn into catalysts for changes in their consciousness. It is the necessary challenge to their explanatory style that makes it keep growing and becoming more adaptive.

You may have noticed that it is usually just when things finally seem stable and going just the way you planned and predicted that something happens to mess things up again. The statement, "We make our plans and God laughs," reflects the inevitable chaotic nature of life for which our capacity to thrive was created.

Posttraumatic Thriving

One of my patient's traumatic experiences provides another example of the mysteries of thriving. Her experience came just when her life seemed to be finally going the way she had always planned. If there is a law of thriving, it is that a major warning sign of a big change coming in our lives is our feeling that everything is finally going exactly as we planned it.

Sharon showed remarkable thriving after a gang rape that left her near death. In fact, her thriving was so sudden and strong that her doctors were convinced that she was in deep denial or repression and suffering from a long list of other psychiatric problems due to her refusal to face the reality and pathogenic magnitude of her crisis. As one of them said, "She just is not facing the reality and seriousness of what happened to her. She will only get sicker if she keeps thinking this way. She can't survive this by how she's trying to deal with what happened." This doctor was more right than she probably knew, for Sharon would never be content being a survivor.

Sharon was a police officer and single mother. She was born in London and had been a police office there before coming to the United States. She changed her life completely to marry the American who brought her to the States. She had just stabilized her life after a bitter divorce from the man for whom she had given up so much, and had gotten her financial affairs in order. She had played fullback on one of the four football teams in a local women's league that had received national media attention. The rapists had held her captive for nearly two days and repeatedly sexually assaulted and beaten her. Only months after her horror, she had returned to a local community college to begin work on a degree. Even on the morning after the assault, she had spoken with a toughness and humor that made her doctors and nurses uncomfortable and eventually led to their diagnosis that she was in "posttraumatic shock."

Because she had been my patient a few years before, when she had asked for help during her divorce, I was called to "evaluate" and help "prescribe treatment for her." The referring doctor who called me said, "This lady is pretending to do well far too soon. She's trying to be macho about the whole thing, but I told her that this is not one of her football games. This is a real-life tragedy and she has to see it that way before she can survive and recover. If she doesn't face up to reality and bite the bullet soon, she's going to become a very, very sick lady."

When I entered the room, I was alarmed to see how badly beaten she was. Her eyes were almost swollen shut and deep purple bruises extended over half her face. Her jaw was misaligned, so her speech was muffled. She mumbled through her bandages, "Oh shit, now they've called the shrink. I think these wimps are too weak to deal with me and handle how I'm handling this, Doc. You've got to tell them that I'm not nuts, or at least not more nuts than you know I always am. I knew they'd call a shrink because they can't deal with how I'm dealing with this my way and how fast I'm getting over and beyond this. They keep saying, 'This is going to take a long time to get over,' but it hasn't. Damn it, I am over it. It's still there, but I really do feel that I'm on top of it. Get it? I'm over it because I got on top of it?"

She laughed and then stopped as she winced in pain. The nurse changing one of Sharon's bandages shook her head in disbelief at hearing humor at this terrible time. She gave me the "didn't we tell you she was sick?" look and left the room.

I sat next to the patient's bed and held her hand. "It just happened suddenly, Doc," she said, much more seriously now. "I can't explain it. They sent in some rape counselor who started telling me how I would or should feel and the stages I would have to go through to recover. 'Give it time, you've got to give it time,' she kept saying, but it didn't take me any time at all. She told me that I would survive this, and I told her that was not nearly enough for me. I told her I wanted more than to just survive and that I actually felt stronger than I did before, and then I threw her ass out."

I could see that for this time in this crisis and in her own unique way, this woman was thriving. I wrote on her medical chart, "Diagnosis: Thriving in process. Prescription: Do not disturb," and leaned over to gently hug her goodbye. She put both of her very muscular arms around me and began to sob. "It's my body that was raped, damn it," she said, "And I'll be goddamned if anyone is going to stop me from dealing with it in my way and in my time, not theirs. I got over it suddenly, and I can't explain that to them. I put up a mental wall so the rape wouldn't take over my brain. If I have to keep getting over it, I will. For now, this works for me and I don't need anyone to mess with how I'm handling this."

I sat back down and we talked quietly together about "her way" and not "their way" of thriving. As she dried her eyes, she said, "I should have known it. I finally had my life together. And you know what, I had just had the shopping day of a life-time. It is what every woman longs for. I had four heavy bags with not one full-price item in any of them. I had to put the bags down to open the car door, and that's when they grabbed me—and on the day after Thanksgiving, of all days. For the first time in my life, I had all my Christmas shopping done more than a month early. I should have seen it coming, because every time you think you're in charge of your life, life knocks you on your ass and beats the hell out of you. Hell, I'm a cop with a black belt, and the bastards still got me. Someday, some way, and no matter what that rape counselor said about letting it go, I know I'm going to get them. And even if I don't, I feel stronger because I think I will. Can't they leave that alone?"

We talked for about an hour more, and when I got up to leave, she grabbled my hand. "For God sake, Doc" she said. "You know that I know that I'll never get those guys. Don't write that in my chart or they'll be back at me again about my anger and how I have to let it out and let go of it. I just love fantasizing about what I'd do to them if I caught them. You know I'm devastated by this, but please tell them to cut me some slack. I doubt this hospital has seen many raped black British female cops who are football fullbacks, so I don't fancy that I fit too well into their idea of recov-ering. I'm afraid we Brits deal with our emotions a bit differently than you Yanks, any-way. I think we're a lot less public about them. You know, stiff upper lip and all that."

As I wrote this chapter, I tried to contact Sharon. After several failed attempts, I was finally able to speak with one her former football teammates. She told me she had lost contact with Sharon but had heard that she had returned to live in London and was recently remarried. She said, "You know Sharon. She's a very strong gal, and that attack only seemed to make her stronger. It was strange, though. When I think about it, she seemed to soften up a bit in a way after her attack. She stopped playing football and gave up her job as a cop. She went back to school to study art and then moved to England. I don't know what she's doing there, but I heard from one of her former teammates that she's . . . doing great and, of all things, is painting watercol-ors and really into art." Based on this report, it seems that Sharon was thriving.

Open-Minded Help

Many rape victims benefit greatly from various forms of counseling and learn-ing about the experiences and stages of adjustment from prior rape victims. However, thriving even through that or any other horrible trauma is a highly indi-vidualized process. Expecting a pre-established coping style based on pathogenic assumptions can restrict the individual's development of their own explanatory style and inhibit their search for their own sense of meaning and manageability.

While many victims of trauma become survivors or show remarkable resilience, less attention has been paid to the controversial possibility that some victims of sexual assault manage to thrive because of its horror. Without support groups, without therapy, without going through a predetermined set of pre-established stages to enter a lifelong state of recovery, some victims manage to thrive. They have more intimate and loving sexual relationships, and are able to love and be loved again at levels they may never have experienced before.

This in no way means that support groups and therapy are not crucial, vitally important, and sometimes essential processes for many victims of sexual assault. It does indicate, however, that thriving is one of the most uniquely personal of our human capacities. The best therapy for thriving is to help patients develop their own explanatory systems free of the therapists too-often pathogenically based biases.

Those offering help to my patient focused on what they had been taught by pathogenic psychology about surviving and recovering from sexual assault. Her rape counselor had told her that she herself was a rape survivor who would be in a state of recovery for the rest of her life. While this information and orientation might be extremely helpful to this woman and other victims, it can restrict the thriving of many others. Thriving can be the kind of long-term process to which her counselor was referring, but sometimes thriving happens instantaneously in the form of what psychologists William Miller and James C'deBaca refer to as a "quantum psychological change."[2]

Research on thriving reveals evidence of dramatic transformations that seem to take place from "out of nowhere" and in ways not yet fully understood. These are the true mysteries of thriving, times when for apparently no reason, we can suddenly feel enlivened, empowered, and strengthened because of a severe trauma.[3] In their eagerness to help us through our problems, those who counsel patients might consider being careful not to suppress this rare but unique quantum thriving response by imposing their concept of coping based exclusively on the pathogenically based goals of survival and recovery.

A Curriculum for Thriveology

Those trying to help the patient described above kept trying to deal with what their pathogenic training taught them would surely be depression due to her refusal or inability to face reality. They failed to see that it is often reality that saddens us so and that creative denial and calming self-delusion can help buy us time to begin work on altering and developing our explanatory systems. They were essentially well-trained pathogenisists, not thriveologists.

In the outpatient clinic I named the Problems of Daily Living Clinic (PDLC), we worked from a different perspective. We saw our clients' challenges as existing not inside them but in their interactions with others and their world. We related to those who came to us as clients, not patients. We saw ourselves as teachers, not therapists. We were concerned with learning, not "treatment," and were forever in search of their symptoms of well-being. It was only because the hospital insisted that I include the word "clinic" in the name of our program that the name was on our door and letterhead. "Clinic" derives from the Greek *klinike,* referring to "medical practice at the sickbed," and that was not at all our orientation. We were concerned with facilitating psychological health, not treating mental illness.

In the PDLC, we assumed that survival and recovery were not enough and that these adjustments overcame but failed to take psychological advantage of the transitional problems in our lives. Most therapists are trained to assess the signs of problems, surviving, and recovery. We are taught how to help a patient return to "normal" but not how to help them transcend normalcy. As an alternative, our clinic offered the choice for thriving through the problems of daily living.

There may be immediate life trauma for which survival itself would have to be the ultimate goal, and conditions for which lifelong recovery may be the only alternative. Just as we must avoid the dominance of the pathogenic model, we must also be careful to not convey a tyranny of thriving that makes those who intentionally and freely choose survival or recovery feel guilty or somehow "less" than those who are able to elect the thriving path. However, even for those who choose survival or recovery, it seems possible that some degree or form of the emotional, mental, or spiritual growth of thriving can still be possible and should be offered.

In order for a "thriving therapy" to evolve, therapists will have to abandon their nearly exclusive dependence on the pathogenic model. They must learn to identify, study, and help patients mobilize their natural human resilience, strengths, and virtues. One such psychologist is Dr. William Garmezy, a researcher at the Palo Alto Center for Advanced Studies in the Behavioral Sciences in Palo Alto, California. He directs a program dedicated to the study of resilient or "stress-resistant" children. Writing about the dominance of the pathogenic paradigm, he has stated that "health practitioners and researchers are predisposed by interest, investment, and training to seeing deviance, psychopathology, and weakness wherever they look."[4] A new therapy for thriving would look for common strengths, signs of health, and the power of our natural resilience to move us on to thriving. It would not only diagnose problems but analyze potential, and the first clinical question might be not "what's wrong?" but "what's right?"

Based on the thrivers I've studied, here is a preliminary curriculum for positive psychology and the training of thriveologists.

A Curriculum in Thriveology

- Students would read case studies not of the sick and troubled but of people like Izzie, Sharon, Mosha, Beethoven, and other thrivers like those you are reading about. Just as doctors have for so long tried to learn about health by examining case studies of the sickest among us, so "thriveologists" in training would try to learn about flourishing by studying the most thriving among us.

- Students would study how thrivers seem able to constantly broaden, modify, and strengthen their explanatory styles and "frame" life events in a growth-promoting way. This would include reading the works of the positive psychologists as presented in the Thrivers Manual in part 2.

- They would learn how so-called unhealthy psychological defenses might also help them be on the psychological offensive by serving as creative psychological strategies for transitioning through life's challenges.

- They would study ancient philosophies, cultural mythology, literature, poetry, plays, music, and the lives of those who created them. They would learn to look not only at the angst that often accompanies creativity but also for the ways highly creative people learn to thrive through their suffering.

- They would read about Buddha's Four Noble Truths as they apply to health and healing. Thriveology students would learn that suffering isn't sick but essential and natural, that we contribute to our own suffering through our unrealistic expectations of a life without suffering, that we have a choice as to how we will explain and find meaning in the world and our lives, and that there are ways we can exercise that choice to become more consciously creative.

- They would study the research being generated by the newly established Positive Psychology Network founded and coordinated by Dr. Martin Seligman and consisting of three centers: positive emotion, directed by psychologist Ed Diener; positive character or traits, directed by psychologist Mihaly Csikszentmihalyi; and positive institutions, directed by sociologist Kathleen Hall Jamieson.

- They would read extensively about the research in human consciousness, cognition, and the many theories of what consciousness is and how it seems to work at a level of much more than just one brain in one body.

- To help broaden their understanding of consciousness, they would study sound parapsychological research, including studies on the power of intent, presentience or "knowing ahead of time," and other "psi" phenomena, and quantum events such as nonlocality and the influence of observation and what is observed.

- They would be trained to recognize some of the constructive and instructive aspects of depression and in how to free us from our "happy-philia," our compulsive love of happiness and dread of sadness. It would teach how we can learn from our sadness to discover the true and deeper sources of our comfort and joy.

- Thriveology students would be required to take a series of intense courses in life appreciation. Classes in music (including a course in the Beethoven Factor), art, poetry, dance, and the gifts from various cultures past and present would focus on the ways in which people come to appreciate life to its fullest.

- They would take required counterpathogenic courses such Pre-Viagra Sexual Joy, Healthy Codependence, The Joy of Being Dysfunctional, Releasing Repressed Memories of a Great Childhood, and Gifts My Parents Gave Me.

- As mentioned earlier, they would do residencies on cancer units, at hospices, and other places where intense thriving is in progress.

- They would be taught how to interpret research findings from Aaron Antonovsky's "salutogenic" perspective described earlier, meaning they would learn how to look at the "strange percentage" in any study that don't seem to fit the dire predictions of the pathogenic approach.

- They would be taught to aim higher than teaching patients how to cope with or reduce stress and anxiety. Instead, they would be taught that these processes are essential motivators for and signs of growth. They would learn that, if we realize and actualize our unique human skill of controlling our own perceptions and constantly creating our own consciousness, we can be relatively free from the ravages of stress.

- Courses in world stress alleviation could be offered. Instead of teaching stress management, students would be taught to identify and address the root causes of stress and suffering in the world in general.

- Classes would be required in developing the sense of humor, including The Joy of Being Abnormal, He or She Who Laughs . . . Lasts, and The Art of Mirth-itation.

- All students would be required to write a dissertation on their own "thriving model," someone in their lives who helped them find meaning and joy in living.

- All students would be required to undergo personal in-depth thrive-analysis and a tracing of their own thriving history. Enhancement groups might be formed in which the students discussed their strengths, virtues, and thriving abilities throughout their lives and the lives of their families and friends. They would focus on how many things their parents did right and how they loved them in their unique if not always perfect ways, how their siblings were not always rivals, and how their strong and mature "inner adult" was just crying to be recognized and released. They might cry together about the wonder of how strongly resilient they are in spite of a less-than-perfect childhood. They might try to discover how they were benefactors and not victims of an essentially good life. The advanced group might even search for its members' deeply repressed memories of forgotten loving and healthy sexual intimacy that will help them love.

Perhaps this positive psychology curriculum would help free us from a passive waiting for good luck and freedom from suffering and allow us to realize that we are well made to not only survive but thrive through life's problems of daily living. It might awaken us to the truth that our capacity to thrive depends not on what we have or do but on how we choose to be and our ability to take charge of our own perceptions.

This thriveology curriculum would not be a psychology of mind over matter. Instead, it would train its students to put their minds on what matters most in leading a life of delight. They would be taught that it is what they choose to put on their minds that matters, their unique capacity to be the composers of their own consciousness and not mindless reactors to the outside world. It is in this way that students of thriveology might learn to search for the ordinary magic and thrill of thriving that would help their patients lead a life full of the joy that gives them goose bumps.

6 Conscious Acts of Creation

"It seems abundantly clear that consciousness-directed intention is a powerful force that must be incorporated into any new scientific paradigm."

—William A. Tiller, Ph.D., physicist and author of CONSCIOUS ACTS OF CREATION: THE EMERGENCE OF A NEW PHYSICS[1]

This Is Really Weird

"This is really weird," said a young medical student. She was talking to doctors outside my hospital room and didn't know I could hear her. She may not have known that those of us trying to thrive through our crises work very hard to collect as much information as we can and are ever vigilant of our surroundings. Even though the pathologically oriented have explained their view of our situation to us, declared their diagnosis, and clarified our symptoms of illness, we are forever busy trying to find our meaning in what has happened to us. We don't always trust, and certainly do not unconditionally accept, information that restricts our ability to comprehend and try to control our problems. In my case, it seemed that the more my physical body failed, the more my sense of hearing, smell, and vision became hypersensitive, so I could detect the whispers of doctors and nurses outside my hospital room.

"This guy is dying and looks so weak, yet he seems so strangely hale and hardy. It's weird because he's so frail and close to death, but at the same time he seems so energetic and alive. He seems to think he's invincible. I think

he's in some very serious denial and that we should order a psychiatric consult."

The above statement was made by a doctor-in-training working for the first
time on a cancer unit. I heard it when I was dying of cancer and just after I had
gone through several courses of chemotherapy, whole-body radiation, and a bone
marrow transplant for Stage IV lymphoma. I had heard the medical staff describe
some of my fellow patients in much this same way. We were puzzling to them
because they confused being hardy with being free from illness, and their pathogenic criterion for wellness was limited to not being near death. They looked for
sickness or its absence, not the mysterious presence of thriving. Until they had
worked a long time on the cancer unit, they were not prepared to deal with the
many invincible souls busy thriving there.

Invincible, But Not Inviolable

The meaning of the word "invincible" is to "not be overcome" or to be
"unconquerable."[2] It is not the same as being "inviolable," which is defined as
"being beyond violation."[3] I had never felt more violated than when cancer had
taken my body hostage. I was experiencing pain that I could never have imagined a human being could endure. Cancer had spread throughout my body and
was eating away my bones, and I was so physically weak that I could barely lift
my head. My sense of violation, however, changed but did not lessen my sense
of invincibility. I wasn't physically strong, but I remained in charge of how and
what I would think. I kept trying to figure out new ways to construe what was
happening to me, and refused to allow cancer to conquer my spirit. If necessary
now, my invincibility might have to include a way to frame and assign meaning
to my dying.

I could only hope the poisonous chemicals would stop the cancer from eating away at my body before they destroyed my body in the process, but I refused
to let cancer be the ultimate definer of my life. It might destroy what I was, but
never who I was. I would not let it ravish my identity or rob me of the one thing
I could still do—give my own meaning to my life.

Positive psychologists are learning that vulnerability and invincibility are
not mutually exclusive concepts. Because of the complex, mysterious, and
often subtle processes involved in thriving, the violation of our body and our
psyche does not have to result only in a struggle for survival. Invincibility is
possible because thriving represents much more than a return to equilibrium,
for that may not always be possible. It is going beyond survival and recovery to

a higher level of being alive before we die, what Yale psychologist Jeannette R. Ickovics and Miami psychologist Crystal L. Park call a "value-added" model of thriving.[4]

A Value-Added Approach to Adversity

Positive psychology's value-added orientation to dealing with adversity suggests that individuals and even whole societies and nations have the capacity to make the most severe challenges an impetus for growth. Sometimes our thriving starts from the catalyst of a trauma we only indirectly experience.

Many of those not directly touched by the September 11 terrorist attacks reported that it caused them to begin to reassess their lives, to look for a deeper meaning in life, and to cherish more the simple pleasure of being alive. While the governmental response of tightening security, offering assistance to those who lost loved ones, and pursuing those responsible for such cruelty may have helped in the survival and recovery process, thriving requires construing what happened in a way that allows us to appreciate life and the world even more because of what happened.

Ultimately, the degree of our triumph over terrorism and other senseless cruelty in the world will be less a matter of impermeable security and military action, and more a matter of an evolution of our consciousness. It will depend on focusing less on what was taken from us than the value we can learn to find in our lives because of it. We can only truly feel safe and even invincible again when we are able to comprehend what happened on that dreadful September day and at other times of horror, construe some constructive personal and national meaning from it, and think about it in ways that allow us to manage our lives with increasing joy, calmness, confidence, and love.

This creative construing of thriving through major events that indirectly affect millions of people was illustrated by Los Angeles Lakers basketball star Kobe Bryant's reaction to the terrorists' attack on the United States on September 11, 2001. He wrote," One of the things I have always believed is that no matter how bad something is, you can take something positive out of it. The one time I wasn't sure of that was on September 11."[5]

He goes on to say, however, that after a few weeks he began to see something good happening from the tragedy. He says he is more patient now and realizes, "Life is . . . too short to carry grudges and therefore I've become more forgiving and understanding. I've learned also that you can't take things for granted."[6] He says that he will particularly no longer take the phrase "see you later" for granted. Bryant found new meaning in his own life because of the tragedy of September 11. In a way, like many of us who still hurt from that terrible day, he became a little more invincible the day the Trade Center towers came tumbling down.

A Wave or a Ripple?

The January 2000 issue of the *American Psychologist*, the journal of the American Psychological Association, was dedicated entirely to the work of psychologists studying human strengths and our capacity to thrive. The 1998 *Journal of Social Issues* had contained articles focusing exclusively on the issue of thriving. Despite this increased interest in a more positive psychology, it remains to be seen if psychology is riding a new wave or experiencing just another ripple.

It is not only the pathogenic bias of many psychologists and other health care workers that blocks the full emergence of a positive psychology. Another major obstacle is the existence of the popular psychology that emerged as an alternative to the doom and gloom of scientific but negativistic psychology. Research-based positive psychology has to compete with a firmly entrenched popular positive psychology based primarily on opinion rather than empirical data.

Pioneering work in promoting a more positive psychology began in the 1950s and 1960s. The early humanistic psychologists such as Carl Rogers and Abraham Maslow offered a kinder, gentler, more optimistic alternative to the dominating clinical and behavioral orientations. At a time when psychology seemed more concerned with rats than people and with sick populations rather than healthy individuals, humanistic psychology's emphasis on individual strengths struck a welcome chord.

Although much less pathogenic and negative in their assumptions, humanistic psychologists tended to be more philosophical than scientific in their approach. Their emphasis on our personal strengths spawned myriad self-help movements that continue today. The development of a truly scientific positive psychology has to compete with hundreds of essentially nonscientific popular self-help books, psychology gurus, countless therapies and programs for self-enhancement, and a seductive "will it and it shall be done" philosophy. Dr. Seligman has written, "The 'psychology' section [in bookstores] contains at least ten shelves on crystal healing, aromatherapy, and reaching the inner child for every shelf of books that tries to uphold some scholarly standard."[7]

The research in positive psychology and its findings about resilience and thriving offer fascinating and encouraging news about us, but much remains to be learned. This young science must compete for attention with a self-help movement that offers appealing but essentially unresearched answers and programs right now. While it is likely we were never as weak and vulnerable as pathogenic psychology said, we may not be as individually all-powerful as most of the popular programs for self-improvement promise. Establishing a cumulative empirical base for this new science is crucial, but first we must realize that if we already think we know, we may never be able to know.

Where Did All These Sick People Come From?

Late one night, I was walking through the always-crowded waiting room for our emergency room at Sinai Hospital. I had just finished seeing several patients and was eager to get home. As I walked quickly by, a woman holding tissues to her nose and appearing feverish and congested grabbed my arm. "Doctor, I've been waiting for hours," she said between coughs. "Will someone please tell me where all these sick people are coming from? Isn't there anyone out there who is not sick? Doesn't anyone feel fine anymore?"

If you have ever spent what seemed like hours in a doctor's waiting room or at the emergency room, you may have experienced the feeling that almost everybody is sick, coming down with something, or worried about being ill. Research confirms your impression. At any one time, a near majority of the population of the modern industrial world is sick, meaning they feel or have been told that they exist in a morbid, pathological condition in need of some form of intervention or treatment.[8] We have become a society consumed with avoiding becoming sick, a frightened flock of worried well, failing to realize that being ill is as natural as it is inevitable and can be as life-enhancing as it is challenging. Instead of focusing on adding value to our lives, we seemed consumed with just trying to stay alive.

Thrivers don't tend to cluster in physicians' waiting rooms. They are at the opposite end of the health and well-being continuum from "the patients." They are often what researchers call the "statistical outliers," the ones who mess up our studies of illness by foiling predictions made by pathogenicists about the outcome of illness. Is this apparently invincible group a strange subset of genetically lucky people who somehow managed to avoid the stressors that get to most of us?

This explanation is not likely true, because stress in life is omnipresent. None of us escapes it, because stress is the toll we pay for traveling the path of life. There is something more that accounts for this invincible group, and that something is the thriving response. But we are not likely to learn about thriving by studying those consumed with surviving.

Positive psychology pioneer psychologist Aaron Antonovsky writes, "Barring stressors that directly destroy the organism, peoples' health outcomes are unpredictable. This is the mystery the salutogenic [positive psychology] orientation seeks to unravel."[9] Despite all of our medical and scientific advances, we can accurately and completely explain less than half of the variance of human illness and suffering. This means that despite our many remarkable medical and scientific discoveries, most of the reasons we get sick or suffer mental problems are not yet fully understood.

From a pathogenic research point of view, there are always those pesky thrivers who confound our studies by seeming to be invincible and refusing to react to adversity as our negative psychology might predict. As positive psychologists Dr. Martin Seligman and Mihaly Csikszentmihalyi point out, "Treatment is not just fixing what is broken; it is nurturing what is best."[10] It is an objective of positive psychology to learn from that mysterious percentage in almost every study that defies the all pathogenic odds.

A Broadening Definition of Thriving

The more psychologists study thriving, the broader their view of it becomes. They are beginning to see that we are capable of mobilizing significant resources to grow through almost any crisis and as a result, also enhance the total system in which we live. We seem to have a powerful capacity to add value to our own life while enhancing the lives of those around us in the process.

Epidemiologist Jeannette R. Ickovics and psychologist Crystal Park define thriving as "the effective mobilization of individual and social resources in response to risk or threat, leading to positive mental or physical outcomes and/or positive social outcomes."[11] Perhaps a significant difference between the popular psychology concept of thriving and the researched version is popular psychology's focus on the "us" as well as the "me."

One of the thrivers was a plumber. He had been buried alive at a job site and rescued just in time, and his words express the "systems" or "us" aspect of thriving. He said, "As I lay in the pitch black and choking on the dirt I kept breathing in, I didn't really think about making it through for me. Why go to all that trouble to fight to stay alive just for me? I thought that a chance to live again would be a chance to love again, and that's what I intended to do like I never did before. I want to make my family's life better than it ever was, and I want to do all I can to help others. Since God still saved me a place here on earth instead of under it, I'm going to try to make it a better place."

Creative Compartmentalizing

In addition to their "us" or "systems" orientation, another characteristic of those who thrive is that they do what most self-help books say not to do. They are good at compartmentalizing their lives. They can add value to their lives by seeing their problems as confined to a temporarily atypical and very strange time while still regarding their lives as on an upward psychological trajectory. They are able to see their crises, as one thriver put it, as "a very crazy time in my life," and maintain a sense of contrast between that time and what she called her "normal, ordinary life."

Particularly when it comes to memories of past adversities, thrivers establish a mental and emotional barrier between the experience of their crisis and their generally enjoyable life. This creative compartmentalizing may be why I found very few ruminators in my interviews of thrivers, and why future-oriented optimism more than past regrets also characterizes thrivers.

Thrivers concoct all sorts of mental tricks and ways of thinking their way through and out of trouble. Sometimes their explanatory styles are at the very least extremely creative and at their furthest ranges seemingly crazy or even schizophrenic-like as seen by pathogenically oriented psychologists and psychiatrists. Thrivers tend to be very creative construers who, as Izzie did, learn how to turn tragedy into opportunity by using humor and clever mental twists and takes on events in their lives, all of which serves to isolate and mentally encapsulate their traumatic times from the general upward flow of their lives.

Thriving's creative construing involves accepting objective facts while construing the implications of these facts for oneself. What will happen may not always be under our own control, but the meaning of what does and does not happen is always a matter of our own consciousness and what we elect to put into it.[12] The next time you are told, "Don't fool or delude yourself," consider the wisdom of the thrivers and consider that the opposite approach might be helpful, particularly at life's toughest times.

Laughing It Off

Our psychological immune system does what our physiological immune system does when it detects an antigen challenging our system. It tries to isolate and contain the invader. It offers up mental strategies that serve to compartmentalize and separate the bad times from the better and makes us immune to becoming "awfulizers" kindling or suffering our way through life.

Izzie was described by his family and clinic staff as "a real joker." As you will read in chapter 10, a sense of humor is a key component in thriving. Those who have it usually also have a highly creative consciousness. We had to be constantly on our toes to understand his double meanings and often paradoxical, funny, and highly creative way of thinking. We were often shocked by the frank, easy, direct, and even humorous way he spoke of the horror he had experienced. The fact that he had spoken of seeing some of his guards as friends was viewed by some of the psychiatrists in my clinic as clear evidence that he had "identified with the aggressor to defend against decompensation." But from the positive psychology point of view, Izzie had applied his natural thriver's talent for very creative construing.

Izzie told us that he had given funny names to his guards based on their individual quirks and even their special brand of cruelty. He called three of them the "three blind rats," naming them Hitting Harry, Whipping Willy, and Kicking Ken. Positive psychologists call this kind of creative construing "conscious cognitive strategizing," meaning that we can make up our own minds to assign meaning to whatever happens to us, even when our way seems very strange to others.

Quantum Thriving

Another way thrivers consciously create value for their lives at times of adversity is their ability to "let go." They are able to allow themselves to "go along" in happy denial or to intentionally continue to fool themselves to buy what Izzie called "a little mind time" to mentally accommodate to whatever is happening to them. This time for creative construing allows thrivers the opportunity to modify their explanatory system to a more adaptive way of construing the events in their lives. During these periods, they are able to fantasize and distort reality in ways those who feel they must constantly face reality are not able to do. Although as you read earlier, the thriving response can happen suddenly and spontaneously, most thrivers have the extraordinary ability to "wait things out" until they can construe their way through them.

It may be that the "quantum thriving" response is actually only a much accelerated version of the thriver's "patience with problems" that is currently beyond our ability to measure. Human consciousness is not constrained by time or space, so there may be things going on in the thriving response and in the consciousness of those who employ it that exceed our current grasp of "reality."

Some principles from quantum physics may play a role in sudden thriving. The quantum principle of nonlocality that allows for freedom from time and space, the uncertainty principle that explains the fact that the act of observing alters what is observed, and Einstein's theory of the relativity of space and time also offer some ways to begin to understand the instantaneous quantum kind of thriving. Even so-called parapsychological, or extrasensory "psi," phenomena may be at work. This is why I included study of "psi" and quantum concepts in my proposed curriculum for a positive psychology.

Whatever is going on in sudden thriving, most thrivers seem to be able to wait until they can see things as working out not only for the best but for the better. By compartmentalizing and allowing distortions of both their internal and external reality to go unchallenged until they have time to come up with a better or more effective explanatory system, thrivers are able to wait until the immediate severity and stress of a threat have passed before fully mentally grappling with their challenge. As a result, they can be more creative than reactive and more intuitive than impulsive. This allows them to experience what Izzie called "a crazy kind of control."

The Power of Pretending

Another feature of thrivers' creative consciousness is that they are great pretenders. They are able to use their imagination to help them protect and enhance their explanatory system. Their philosophy seems to be, "If life doesn't seem to have much value at the moment, I'll just pretend for a while that it does until I can do something to enhance its value."

Izzie said he intentionally engaged in distorting reality and that he gave some sense of value to the endless moments of his imprisonment by telling himself he heard rescuers coming. He said, "I think I really knew the chances of our rescue were slim, but it made it more bearable to let myself think I heard them coming or let myself believe the latest rumor of our rescue. In my mind, I would make the sound of an explosion way off in the distance into a sign that help was coming. I would sometimes look into the guards' eyes and try to see their fear that armies were coming for us.

"Sometimes, we would all be very still at night and sort of agree without saying it to pretend we heard help coming in a faint rumble of tanks way off in the distance. Some would say they felt it and would put their hand on the floor to feel the vibrations. We would all go along and take it very seriously, but deep down we knew we were just fantasizing much as children think they hear Santa Claus on the roof. When things become absurdly insane, making yourself a little nuts can really help you match up to the situation you're in."

Lawrence Langer offers a similar description to Izzie's intentional insanity in his book titled *Holocaust Testimonies*.[13] A death camp survivor is quoted as explaining how the human spirit can not only prevail but also prosper in the face of catastrophe. She said she managed to deal with the memories of the horror of her experience by making a "sort of schizophrenic division . . . a compartmentalization between [her] memories of the camp and [her] so-called normal life."[14] Most of the thrivers I interviewed used this cognizant craziness as a means of psychoimmune containment of their crisis. Positive psychologists sometimes refer to the above aspects of thriving as "enlightened denial" or "positive illusion."[15]

Steeling Ourselves

"I am much more able to roll with the punches now." These are the words of one of my fellow cancer patients who had gone through several remissions and recurrences of his cancer. They represent another conscious act of creation at times of deep suffering. Social psychologist Michael Rutter refers to repeatedly successfully growing through a series of prior challenges as emotionally "inoculating ourselves against the effects of stress."[16] As you read earlier, thrivers are constantly boosting their psychoimmunity and steeling themselves against stress by learning through their adversities.

One way to build our psychological immune system and become inoculated for crisis is to make ourselves available to help others through their adversities. Gaining experience with extraordinary problems even if they are not our own can provide a boost to our psychological immune system. Experiencing a kind of "surrogate stress" by becoming deeply involved in helping others through their traumas is not only a kind and loving thing to do. It also is a form of problem practice helpful for the development of insights that might come in handy later in our own life, a kind of "pretrauma testing" of our thriving talent.

Research from the field of psychoneuroimmunology shows clearly that regular doses of altruism can have positive effects on our physiological immune system. The same seems to be true for our psychological immune system. You will be reading about the specifics of our psychological immune system in chapter 7, and you have already read about some of its basic rules that guarantee that all emotions can be adaptive, no emotional state lasts, and the more down we are driven, the higher up we seem to bounce.

Psychological Offense

The Diagnostic and Statistical Manual of Mental Disorders of the American Psychiatric Association (note the pathogenic emphasis on "disorders" rather than "order") refers to many of the value-adding thriver's skills described above as "defenses." As you have read, from the point of view of positive psychology, these are less defenses than emotional offenses against relentless suffering of kindling or victimhood and the joyless fatigue of constantly trying to survive.[17] These defenses can be seen as proactive problem management strategies and ways of being on the emotional offensive in dealing with crises.

The Thriver's Manual offered in part 2 of this book describes many of the mental and emotional strategies that thrivers use to help them grow through stress. If the American Psychiatric Association published a counterpart to its diagnostic manual, an Optimistic Manual of Mental Strengths, it might include thriving components such as enlightened denial, aware self-delusion, intentional fixation, purposeful pretending, comic and calming regression, creative construing, fantasy framing, delightful dissociation, and the other skills that help us add value to our lives when life seems the most difficult.

Because thrivers tend be on the psychological offense, they can become a little uneasy when things seem to be going far too well for too long. They know life may not be nearly as terrible as it seems when things seem to be going badly, but that it is also not nearly as wonderful as it appears when things seem to be going splendidly. They are wise enough to keep the psychological immunity strong by continuing to mentally grow even when they are not being pressed by crisis. Rather than allowing themselves to become lulled into maintenance mode, they remain mentally on the offense and keep strengthening their psychoimmunity through their ongoing creative consciousness. They seem to build up a thriver's saving account to be used for life's stormy days.

Izzie discussed the psychological immune system vigilance and offensiveness described above when he said, "What goes up must come down, and that includes all of our lives. You enjoy both the ups and the downs because they go together like night and day. It's like driving. You shouldn't be less prepared just because the roads are dry or because you have never had an accident. You should always be working on being a better and better driver, not just a defensive one."

Lessons from Children in Paradise

"Yet there were others [children of deprived upbringing], also vulnerable ... who remained invincible and developed into competent and autonomous adults."

—Pioneer resilience researcher Emmy Werner

They should have been emotional wrecks. From the perspective of the pathogenic orientation of modern psychology and medicine, they were children who should have become depressed, promiscuous substance abusers who failed in school and were in constant legal trouble.

They were children rendered vulnerable by being born into poverty to parents who had little education, were often from troubled families, and often suffered from serious mental health or substance abuse problems. Many of these children were born to single mothers who were depressed or schizophrenic. If there was a father, he was seldom at home and was usually a semiskilled or unskilled laborer with a short temper who offered little comfort or guidance. Many of these children were born prematurely, and their mothers often smoked, drank, and generally neglected their prenatal care. Many had experienced difficult births and spent their early years in families plagued by an unrelenting series of conflicts.

This vulnerable group of 700 children grew up on the Hawaiian island of Kauai from the years 1955 to 1979. Although the islands of Hawaii are often seen as a paradise, this was a period of continual social change on Kauai. This island home had seen the influence of the arrival of hundreds of newcomers during the war in Southeast Asia. These were usually strangers with little understanding or concern for the culture they encountered. The burgeoning daily influx of tourists also disrupted these children's daily life, as did the increasing noise and the hectic pace of visitors coming and going. They had also seen the assassination of one president and the public disgrace and resignation of another.

The availability of contraceptive pills and mind-altering drugs presented them with temptations and choices not faced by earlier generations. Poor nutrition and neglect exposed them to a variety of illnesses, and many experienced severe forms of verbal and even physical abuse. They had every reason to feel miserable and messed up, to give up and act out; and many ended up as the pathogenic model predicted.[18]

As did many other psychologists, I considered the Emmy Werner and Ruth Smith work to be a pioneering study in the field of positive psychology.[19] It represented one of the earliest calls to look at "the others," the group that did well rather than those who "lived up" to pathogenic projections. It was one of the first studies to explore the concept of human resilience. However, I found few of my clinical colleagues who either knew about the study or considered it as groundbreaking as I did. Even though Werner and Smith themselves emphasized the resilience of a subset of these children, most of my colleagues still tended to see only the predicted pathology in the vulnerable children.

By their standards, the Kauai children were what pathogenic-oriented psychologists would call "highly at-risk children." Werner and Smith followed these children from a few months before their birth until they were in their early 20s. Each child was interviewed and given various questionnaires and examinations, and their health records were monitored closely. The researchers studied the impact of a life that most health care workers would have predicted would result in grievous lifelong debilitating developmental problems. What the researchers discovered is the factor that is the focus of this book. Some of the children thrived through their adversity.

Out of the 700, Werner and Smith identified 42 girls and 30 boys who, in their words, were children who "remained invincible and developed into competent and autonomous young adults."[20] They had found life value through their suffering to become confident, loving, responsible, achievement-oriented young people. They had remained invulnerable to challenges that would be expected in the pathogenic view to have devastating effects. They had somehow managed to mobilize their psychological immunity and thrived through their years of stress, and Werner and Smith set out to learn how. What they and now other pioneers in positive psychology learned is that we have the ability to be consciously creative people.

Making Up Your Mind to Thrive

John Milton wrote, "The mind is its own place, and in itself can make a heaven of hell, a hell of heaven." Researchers studying thriving are interested in why and how some of us are able to creatively construe our way through problems to happiness while others succumb to these same problems. They take the "person-focused" rather than "variable-focused" model of understanding the source of the hardy way of thinking that characterizes thrivers.

Positive psychologists look beyond the variables of good homes and model parents as explanations for why some children seem so invincible. Instead, they ask what it is about the thrivers themselves that allows them to persist in making a Heaven of their Hell. They look to personal consciousness rather than external circumstances for answers to why we thrive.

Abraham Lincoln is one the most famous thrivers in history. He certainly had more than his share of adversity. He experienced a devastating business failure in 1831, was defeated for the legislature in 1832, failed miserably again at business in 1833, and followed that in 1836 with what was then called a nervous breakdown. Trying to come back stronger than ever after this series of traumas, he was defeated for Speaker of the State of Illinois Legislature in 1838, and defeated yet again for the office of elector in 1840, congressman in 1843 and again in 1848. He was defeated for vice president of the United States in 1856 and again for the Senate in 1858.

Throughout these many trials, he also experienced the stress of personal and family illness. Then he was elected president in 1860 during one of our country's most difficult times. He had to hold the country together during the Civil War, and he became one of the most revered figures in American history. He was a highly sensitive man who became irritated, easily saddened, and angry when he saw injustice and cruelty. He often appeared sullen, depressed, and withdrawn. He was far from being a constantly upbeat person with an always positive attitude, but he did what all thrivers do. He was able to creatively construe the events in his life and become stronger and wiser for his pain. In words that capture the essence of thriving, he wrote, "Most people are about as happy as they make up their minds to be."[21]

Looking at Life Top-Side Down

The objectivist or Western-materialistic orientation tends to look at life from the "variable" or outside influence point of view. It sees us as essentially reactive to the "variables" that influence us and believes that those of us who are lucky enough or worked hard enough to arrange the "variables" in our favor will have the most advantages in life. This point of view relates to what psychologist Michael Lerner calls the "just world phenomenon."[22] This is the idea that whatever our life situation, we essentially had it coming. If we are suffering or flourishing, beautiful or ugly, healthy or impaired, we somehow and in some way must be getting our due. A comfortable income, good genes, absence of illness and particularly the absence of any severe emotional tragedy, trauma, loss, or severe mental stress or illness in life are seen as the foundation of a deserved good life. Positive psychologists are learning that this premise is wrong.

Research shows that the "event" aspects of our lives account for less than 8 to 15 percent of the variance in our reported happiness.[23] That means that 85 to 90 percent of how happy we are with our lives, how we deal with the crises and setbacks that happen to us, and our overall sense of well-being is due to the meaning we make of what happens to us. We have conscious control of the crucial pleasure percent, the average 90 percent of the joy of living that is a matter of how we choose to construe the events in our lives.

It's not good fortune or "doing" something that makes us feel calm, content, and joyfully connected with others and the world. It's what and how we think about our lives in our world. Choosing to construe our lives our way and to continue to develop and enhance the adaptability of our explanatory styles is what determines the content of our consciousness and therefore whether or not we lead value-added lives. Positive psychology is learning that there is nothing that life can throw at us that is beyond the adaptive capacity of our creative consciousness.

Dealing with life from the perspective of the person (the top) not being a passive victim of whatever the just world happened to hand us (the bottom) as our destiny takes plenty of time. It requires looking within our relationships and for our inner maturing and interacting adult instead of always within ourselves for our failures or in search of an unhappy and neglected inner child. It involves taking plenty of time for creative construing and even periodic elective intentional self-deception. It requires using the traumas in our lives as SIGs, or stress-induced growth, experiences that can boost our psychological immunity. It is a process of employing just enough modulated madness not only to cope with the chaos of life but to be able to dance gleefully within it.

Positive psychology shows that there is a range of mental skills that help us go beyond the hands we are dealt and the variables we were given. We have the innate talents like framing, evaluating, interpreting, mentally self-disputing against our own flawed self-degradation, contemplating rather than reacting, waiting and seeing, being our own memory maker by choosing what we will remember, having a good "forgettory" when we need one so we can give up and move on, and seeing strength as not only victory but sometimes enlightened giving up.[24]

Unlike other animals, we are not bottom-up reactors dragged instinctively though a set of circumstances. We are made to thrive because we are conscious beings with the capacity to make meaning, to frame the events in our lives and put them in a more positive, constructive light. The research is clear. We are invincible because we have the remarkable gift psychologists call "cognitive processing."[25]

Creating a Context for Our Lives

Cognitive processing is the technical name for "meaning-making." It refers to the fact that we not only live within contexts but also play a crucial role in creating them. We are not slaves to one possible world, but in many ways we constantly engage in conscious acts of creation.[26] Because we can choose to construe anything that happens to us in our own way, we have an infinite array of possible worlds.

An important part of cognitive processing is what positive psychology researchers call the "construal approach to happiness."[27] These four words offer another definition of thriving. In the invincible group of Kauai children, Werner and Smith discovered not only victims and irreparably damaged "inner children" doomed to a life of recovery. They saw children who tapped their natural but long-overlooked human power not only to bounce back in the face of adversity but also somehow to construe what happened to them in ways that allowed them to rise far above it to make life what they wanted it to be.[28]

You can see another example of our creative consciousness in the case of a patient I worked with a few years ago. She had just begun her career as a high school English literature teacher. She was a twenty-two-year-old woman who had been left pentaplegic (unable to move her arms, legs, or breathe on her own) by a drunk driver. She was unable to move any part of her body other than her head and lips. She was on a ventilator, so listening to her struggle to speak required time and patience. She worked hours a day at her computer, which was specially adapted to allow her to operate the keys with a stick held in her mouth. She was writing a book about her experience and had made many "chat room" friends around the world.

If you took the time, you could hear in her frail voice the unmistakable hardiness of her thriving spirit. With the humor you have read in many of the thrivers' stories, she joked, "You don't have to feel screwed. You can construe. Trust me, that one word has very special power. The dictionary says it means to discover and apply meaning, and what a power that is. It means your life is all in your mind. I am actually happier and more productive now than I have ever been. I sure have more friends and, as you can easily see, I am totally free from multitasking."

The effect of our point of view and how we mentally frame what happens to us can also be seen in a study of a group of Portuguese immigrants who came to Canada to seek a better life and more fulfilling job opportunities. The men who immigrated viewed the move as a wonderful opportunity for a new beginning in life, and their health significantly improved after they moved to Canada. However, their wives tended to feel involuntarily dragged along on their husbands' adventures.

In their minds, they construed the move to be a disruption of their highly valued family ties back in Portugal. Both were now living in the same conditions, but the disappointed wives were significantly more likely to become sick than their more optimistic husbands, the study showed.[29] Controlling for all other variables, the only difference between the husbands and wives found in the study was in the meaning each group assigned to their immigration.

By coincidence, I had the opportunity to interview one of the subjects of the study above. She had come to Sinai Hospital's cardiac unit after a severe heart attack and lengthy resuscitation. I was called to speak with her because of her highly depressed state, which the nurses and doctors thought was "complicating her recovery." We managed to find an interpreter, and we talked about her near-death and her life in general. When I asked her how she had viewed her move to Canada, she responded in tears. "For my husband, Canada was the beginning. For me, it was only an end. No more family for me. For him, nothing could change his mind about his new life. For me, nothing could change my mind about my lost life. It broke my heart, and I long every day for my family. I need that longing to keep me going."

Another of my patients, a psychology professor and son of Irish immigrants, spoke with me about the importance of how we cognitively frame the events in our lives. He had heard me use the example of the Portuguese women in a lecture to illustrate my point about the impact of mental framing on our well-being.

The professor said, "Before my family came here from Dublin, they were living in poverty and had been near starvation in their homeland. They came to a much better situation with good food and a clean place to live, but they died by the hundreds of tuberculosis. In fact, the death rate was 100 percent higher in those who came to America than in Dublin at the same time, even though the immigrants were now living in vastly more favorable conditions. I'm sure a major reason for this was that most of them didn't want to leave. They were transplanted against their will and devastated by the discrimination with which they now had to deal. It proves your point about how you look at things." The message from these examples seems to be if you don't have a healthy outlook, look out![30]

Taking the Long-Range View

Thriving, like happiness, seems to depend on our willingness to become consciously creative and maintain a life-long perspective of happiness. Positive psychologist Sara E. Snodgrass offered her personal account of her thriving through her metastasized breast cancer.[31] The fact that she shared her personal journey in a professional journal indicates her growth through her cancer and shows a spiritual strength that is so often characteristic of thrivers.

Snodgrass is aware of the research showing that the thriving response can occur automatically and spontaneously in the form of a quantum-like event, but her thriving experience came about gradually. She engaged in a lengthy process of learning about her disease, possible new treatments, appraising her resources, and developing a belief system and an adaptive and dynamic action plan. She writes, "Perhaps some of this growth has been automatic, such as my optimism and desire for control over my treatment; however, much of my growth has taken deliberate effort."[32] I suggest that this effort is the creative consciousness of the thriving response.

My own experience with cancer involved the same lengthy, reflective process of thriving described by Sara Snodgrass. I could not manage a consistent positive attitude, but I could manage to work toward one and benefit from an ever so slight upward psychological trajectory over time. During my months of cancer treatments, I often felt a "future free" sense of being totally in the moment that allowed me to thrive even as I suffered, a timeless reflection similar to Snodgrass's experience that seemed somehow to reduce at least the urgency of the pain. I realized more than ever before in my life that the future is quite unpredictable, so I focused more in the present and let the future take care of itself. I received very few sudden insights into the meaning of life and never felt I was becoming a "whole new person." Instead, my explanatory style seemed to be evolving and changing slowly over time. I was "up" one day and very "down" the next, but I made the decision to keep my general psychological trajectory on an upward course. I constantly worked to try not to get too sad about feeling sad.

A Trend, Not a Type

Writing about the qualitative aspects of learning about thriving and a long-term view of the process, psychologist and thriving response researcher Sean Massey and his coauthors offered a warning. They challenge the idea that thriving is fixed or static, or an immediate response to adversity. They wrote, "This suggestion [that thriving is an immediate or constant or fixed personal characteristic or response] stands in sharp contrast for us, because we view thriving as a process in which one experiences the inevitable ups and downs of life. If thriving is considered growth in the face of adversity, does a person's immediate state determine her or his level of thriving, or does the researcher need to consider the person's overall trajectory?"[33]

When I use the word "thriving" in this book, I am referring to a trend and not a type. I use it as a matter of shorthand convenience in summarizing the many complex and often contradictory aspects of thriving shown by various persons in various ways at certain times in their lives. While I call them "thrivers" or "invincibles," I am actually referring to people engaging in various manifestations of the thriving response, not personality types. The only consistent common thread I've found in my research on thrivers is that they are able to engage over time in conscious acts of creating their own context for their lives.

A Moment of Decision

I saw some of my fellow cancer patients engaging in one of the most difficult, dramatic, and sacred moments of thriving. I saw them preparing to give up when they heard the diagnosis of cancer. I saw them make a mental shift to preparing for death. That one single conscious decision—to decide to prepare to live or get ready to die—is a pivotal time in facing our mortality. But no matter what the decision, thriving is still possible. Death is of course unavoidable, but preparing to thrive through our dying requires becoming more alive before we die.

Psychologist Dr. Sara Snodgrass reflected on her own "moment" of decision when she discussed her own experience with cancer. She said she reflected about her diagnosis and asked herself, "Am I using this current moment in the best way possible? If I can really live each moment fully, think of what a wonderful life I will have lived whenever it ends."[34] Like other thrivers, Snodgrass remained the composer of her consciousness even as she faced her own death.

We can all learn to thrive in our own lives by remembering Snodgrass's question, "Am I using this current moment in the best possible way?" This question is the stimulus for the kind of creative consciousness that allows us to develop our thriveability. Even at such a frightening time in her life, Snodgrass consciously created the context of her confrontation with her mortality.

We are invincible not because we can elevate ourselves to superconsciousness status but because we have the capacity to wait, think, imagine, tolerate, forgive, learn, delude ourselves, change, grow through our ups and downs, and set our own psychological trajectory. In flying an airplane, the slightest moving of the stick can profoundly alter the flight of the aircraft, but the pilot can change course again by just a nudge of the controls in the desired direction. If you are thinking or feeling that your thriving response is not as strong as you wish it to be, all it takes is a little mental, emotional, and spiritual nudge to send you upward again. Asking yourself if you're using your moments in the best possible way helps you remember to take charge of the content and quality of your consciousness.

When Werner and Smith examined their data on the children of Kauai, they noticed something very significant. While the thriving group had gone on to grow through their stress, so had a majority of the group that had not originally seemed to be thrivers. The researchers found that a majority of the suffering, surviving, or recovering "non-thrivers" they had identified as their original maladaptive group eventually showed signs of thriving when they entered their adult years.[35] The psychological trajectory of many of their lives had been turned upward and they too, in their own way and in their time, were learning to thrive.

Werner's and Smith's finding, that many of those who seemed initially not to be so resilient turned out to be thrivers, gives hope for us all. It suggests that, if we will pay attention to it, there seems to be a momentum attracting us toward a thriving life. We all seem able to lead a value-added kind of life even when so many things can seem to rob it of its joy. We can all perform the ordinary magic of conscious acts of creation, and part 2 of this book offers a manual for the creative consciousness that gives this magic its power. It is an invitation to think about your life as if you just discovered for the first time your extremely good fortune to have one.

PART II
A Thriver's Manual

"In order to arrive at what you are not,
you must go through the way
in which you are not."

—T. S. Eliot, THE FOUR QUARTETS

7 Living a Thousand Times Over

"We underestimate how quickly our feelings are going to change in part because we underestimate our ability to change them."[1]
—*Daniel Gilbert, Ph. D., Harvard University*

Three Not-So-Little Words

"You have cancer." How do you think you would react if you heard these three words? Like most people, once I could only imagine the horror I would experience if I ever heard them, but when I did, something very strange happened. Instead of the terror and sad helplessness I thought I would feel upon receiving this news, I felt a strange calmness and a sense of a beginning to a new phase of my life. I had been in such severe pain for so long, and had received so many wrong diagnoses, that finally knowing what was destroying my life seemed to set into motion a series of mental and emotional events that—if I had not been studying the issue of thriving—I would never have imagined possible.

I knew that my physiological immune system was under severe stress and failing. Lymphoma is a peculiar kind of cancer because it can destroy the body's defense system designed to deal with attacks such as overgrowing cells. In effect, the very system you need to fight the cancer is the system that becomes increasingly weakened by it. I also knew, however, that I had another immune system ready to help me, and I decided upon hearing the three devastating words that I could prepare to become more alive even if I would die.

About ten years after my cure from cancer, I read a book written by ten professional women titled *Breast Cancer? Let Me Check My Schedule!*[2] Each woman described how she managed to thrive through her cancer not only by maintaining her professional life but also by finding new interests, meanings, and priorities in her life. I felt much the way these women did when I was diagnosed with Stage IV lymphoma. Cancer was terrible, but it was also immensely interesting.

One day on the bone marrow transplant unit, my wife and I set up an office in my hospital room. We put up a small table and chair near my bed and plugged in my laptop computer. I was receiving an intense course of chemotherapy doctors called the "scorch the Earth" approach, and whole-body radiation that soaked my body with toxic energy and left me in almost constant pain. In order to deal with the constant nausea and diarrhea caused by my treatments, we asked that a portable toilet be placed near my chair. I joked with my nurse that I could use a little "writer's block" or any kind of block if it would stop the constant diarrhea caused by my chemotherapy. I began work on a book titled *Making Miracles* (recently reissued under the title *Miracle in Maui*). If my cancer was going to spread, I decided it was going to have to outrun me, and I am still running today.

My wife took pictures of me as I received my bone marrow transplant, and I looked like a dead man. I was pale and skinny, and I could barely hold my eyes open. When I asked her why she was taking so many morbid pictures, she said, "Because someday you will be lecturing on how you thrived through your cancer and showing slides of these pictures to your audiences." My wife, Celest, has always been my co-thriver through a series of life traumas, and she continues in that role today. Like all the other co-thrivers I met on the cancer unit, she was able to continually construe even the most devastating events in ways that somehow made them more comprehensible and meaningful.

Some mental process seemed to kick in when we received the cancer diagnosis that started me thinking much more about living than dying. My wife and I cried bitterly, but even through our tears we began to talk of our future and began embracing even more than we had before every moment of our life together. Somehow I knew the shock and fear would not last, and I could feel my psychological immune system going to work for me. It's remarkable how the pain and shock of hearing the three terrible words, "You have cancer," can be reduced by the three words, "I love you." It's inspiring and comforting to be reminded by those who love us that our lives and theirs depends less on our circumstances than our consciousness.

Becoming Conscious of Our Consciousness

What if there was something you could do that might extend your life seven and one-half years? What if this something was more powerful than having low blood pressure, having low cholesterol, maintaining a healthy weight, abstaining from smoking, or exercising regularly? Researchers at Yale University have discovered that something: it is how we elect to think about aging and whether we consciously construe it in a positive way.[3] It is whether or not we elect to thrive or languish as we age.

Becca Levy, lead author of the Yale study and assistant professor of epidemiology and public health at Yale, has stated, "Individuals who reported more positive self-perceptions of aging demonstrated significantly longer survival rates than those who had negative self perceptions of aging."[4] In other words, how we elect to perceive the meaning and value of our later years strongly determines how many later years we will have. What's on our mind seems capable of influencing our physiology so strongly that can add, on average, one more year of life for every ten years that we live. A joyful perception of aging can result in a person who would have lived to age 70 earning a "senior savoring" bonus of seven years. Clearly, there is an immense power that comes from how we choose to construe our lives, and that choice is the creative core of psychological immunity.

The powerful influence of how we think about what happens to us has been slow to come to the attention of a modern medicine that for so long was certain that our consciousness had little if anything at all to do with our health. Until the emergence of a less pathogenic model of illness, sickness was seen as some externally caused or perhaps genetically precoded pathological wiggling of atoms and molecules that resonates bottom up through the body system to eventually make us ill. If it was acknowledged at all, our consciousness was seen as essentially the brain's reaction to whatever was happening to us. It was seen more as a reporter than an author of our lives. It could let us know we are sick, but not have any significant impact on making us well. It was not considered to have a role in changing the actual outcome of a "real" physical pathological event.

We know differently now. Scientists are learning that consciousness is much more than the firing of neurons in our head. While it doesn't agree on what consciousness is, modern medicine is slowly beginning to acknowledge that consciousness exists beyond a bundle of nerve fibers. It is seeing that we are capable of remarkable acts of conscious creation that profoundly affect our physiological state and even play a role in determining the length of our lives.

Mind Over Matter Doesn't Matter That Much

Unfortunately, there has been a negative side effect of recognizing the power of the mind or human consciousness. Because of the long domination of the dismal pessimistic orientation of the pathogenic view of the human experience, and the denial of the role of consciousness in health and healing, we overreacted to the evidence that consciousness may matter. When research seemed to be showing that our beliefs and thinking do in fact interact with our immune system and play a role in illness, healing, and even the length of our lives, there was a consciousness revolution. Instead of trying to learn more about the importance of consciousness and its complexities and paradoxes, an oversimplified "if we think it, it will happen" concept evolved.

The years of neglect of the role of consciousness in health and healing seemed to lead to an over-compensation. "Mind over matter" became a part of the self-help movement, but no matter what we've been told by pop psychologists and gurus, mind over matter is a myth. With the possible exception of interesting research on the very slight and subtle capacity of our intentions to alter physical systems, no matter how much we put our mind on outside matter, it doesn't matter much. What does matter is what we allow to matter to us, for this is what impacts our psychological and physiological immune systems.[5]

Physical reality is not significantly altered despite our most positive thinking. But by tuning in to the way our psychological immune system operates and learning about how it tends to work when under stress, we can assist and boost that system's capacity to help us thrive through any adversity. To the extent that this system works on its own and in harmony with unconscious processes, we can do our best not to get in its way by injecting our own obstructive thoughts.

Izzie, the death camp survivor, knew he could change his mind but not the physical constraints of the prison walls. His thriving was due not to his mentally moving mountains but to his learning to think about, explain, construe, and develop his own explanatory style as to what mountains, walls, cruel guards, and his imprisonment would mean for him. Izzie thrived because he remained the master of his mind. He knew when he was intentionally fooling himself or pretending to hear the deaf man's symphony or the distant sounds of approaching rescuers, and both his psychological and physiological immune systems seemed to respond to the meaning his mind kept creating. When matters seemed at their worst, Izzie made his mind matter more.

Thriving is based on knowing how our psychological immune system works and maximizing its efficiency by allowing it to work by its rules, not by clinging to the popular psychology myth that we can accomplish anything with sufficient mental will power. Izzie said, "I don't think we can do a lot about changing the actual outcome for most things, but I think we can do a hell of lot to decide the *income* and whatever happens to us inside our skin. I can never change what they did to my family and me, but I can control what I will allow it to mean to me."

Stress Can Be Good for Your Health

Stress is bad for your health. That statement is now accepted by the lay public, scientists, and doctors, and there can be no doubt that chronic stress can weaken the body's systems, resulting in hardening of the vessels around our heart, elevation of our blood pressure, and a weakening of our physical immune system.

Most research has been focused on demonstrating that negative emotions can lead to disease or at least increase our proneness to it, but less attention has been paid to how stress can result in our becoming stronger and healthier, not only psychologically but also physically. There is now evidence from research in positive psychology that indicates that even the most severe stressors can result in the individual's becoming stronger and healthier.[6]

Clinical intern Elissa S. Epel, neuroscientist Bruce S. McEwen, and epidemiologist Jeannette R. Ickovics wrote, "Under conditions of stress, one would expect a physically weakened system, but positive physiological changes can occur—often in the context of psychological thriving. In physiological terms, this translates into greater restorative. (i.e. anabolic) processes than destructive (i.e. catabolic) processes at work."[7] They point out that psychological thriving can lead to physical thriving through what they call a "toughening-up" process. In other words, mentally thriving through a crisis can become "embodied," or made a part of, our body's systems and strengthen them over time.

Our psychological immune system becomes stronger in much the same way our muscles do. To build stronger muscles, we must first stress and break them down, resulting over time in stronger, bigger muscles capable of lifting more weight. When we thrive through many traumas, we strengthen our psychological immune system and become better able to handle the weight of life's crises. Like our muscles, a broken spirit can become a much stronger one.

Fighting, Flowing, and Growing

It is beyond the scope of this book to go into detail about the neuroendocrine system's response to thriving and the physiological details of how repeatedly growing through stress enhances our physiological well-being and makes our body stronger. In simple terms, we have what are called "anabolic" (generally physically enhancing) and "catabolic" (physically stressful) neurohormones flowing through our entire body. The term "anabolic" refers to processes of maintenance, growth, building, creation, and those that strengthen our system. The term "catabolic" refers to processes of weakening, consuming, using up, and those that generally weaken our system.

When we experience stress or a highly alert emotional state, our sympathetic or nervous system causes catabolic hormones to be released. These are the same hormones that lead to the pilomotor erection response you read about in chapter 5. They are made for our short-term survival and for staying alive, but not in large and persistent doses for helping us enjoy and make sense of living. They are hormones designed for fighting back to save our lives, not lying back to reflect on its meaning. They are made for quick and intense reaction, and they prepare us to fight or take flight. In the long run, however, they put immense stress on our body systems. While thriving can be energizing, constantly *trying* to survive can lead to illness.

The parasympathetic or relaxing nervous system secretes "anabolic" or "building and restoring" hormones, which counter our aroused state caused by the catabolic or "burning and protecting" hormones. Anabolic hormones cause us to feel more like we are flowing than fighting. They help us settle down, heal, and become reenergized. Catabolic hormones burn energy while anabolic hormones save it.

Catabolic hormones include the cathecholamines such as adrenaline and noradrenaline and cortisol, the one that remains elevated for the longest period after we experience stress. Huge and prolonged secretions of cortisol can lead to serious damage to our body.[8] That's why the most devastating kind of stress is that which seems to have no end and no way out, and that's the kind of stress thrivers are best at dealing with. Their creative consciousness always eventually allows them to discover a way to thrive through their chronic stress.

Just as weight lifters strain their muscles every day for hours a time, chronic cortisol secretion puts immense strain on all the body systems. Anabolic hormones such as growth hormone, insulin, insulin-like growth factor (IGF-1), and sex steroids counter this effect. By striving through a series of stressors, we experience allostasis, our body's ability to adapt to our ever changing and challenging world. When allostasis improves, we become more fit. Because we have stretched our limits, our body becomes stronger and we are more able to physically thrive.

Psychological Bodybuilding

There are two ways we might be able to become physically stronger because we have psychologically thrived. One way is that our repeated mental and emotional dealing with acute or major trauma seems to steel or inoculate our nervous system against further stressors. When we thrive through acute adversity, we seem to become less catabolically reactive to such stressors in the future. Our brain seems to be a little calmer at the next calamity, and our entire body system becomes less stress-sensitive because it is not flooded with as large a dose of catabolic hormones. Our anabolic hormones increase faster, and the rate at which the catabolic hormones decrease also speeds up. In terms of dealing with stress, our body systems become stronger.

This first form of psychological "bodybuilding" is not effective if we merely survive and recover from stress. By construing a stressor in a constructive, growth-oriented way, we toughen our body even more by rendering it less sensitive and reactive over time to the damaging effects of the catabolic hormones like cortisol. Thus, mental thriving contributes to a more stress-resistant physical body. This may be one reason basic training in the military and particularly in elite special forces units includes not only rigorous physical training but also constant psychological pressure. To achieve victory in battle requires not only survival and resilience. It also requires warriors who can thrive through the worst scenarios to become both mentally and physically stronger.

Chronic, unrelenting stress or consistently making big deals of lots of little stressors does not seem to have the toughening effect, so the best mental exercise regimen for psychological bodybuilding is to try to thrive through many big problems over time. The trick seems to be to avoid getting caught up in making big deals of little hassles or becoming emotionally entrapped in one lifelong unrelenting stressful situation.

My interviews with thrivers indicate that they have the skill of breaking trauma apart into mini-traumas rather than viewing life as one constant crisis. One of the thrivers illustrated this process when she said, "My daughter will never be free of her emotional problems. I deal with this by taking it one problem at a time, and when that problem is over, it's over. I avoid seeing her as a permanently problematic child or my life as having to deal forever with a frustratingly difficult person. Instead, I see her as a child with problems that I'm helping her deal with one big aggravation at a time."

The second psychological bodybuilding technique is to be sure to "give it a rest" between each acute stressor. Exercise physiologists know that exercising our muscles every day without rest results in damaged, not stronger muscles. We need to have our psychological immune system stressed if it is to get stronger, and acute and intense problems from time to time seem to enhance our psychoimmunity. However, feeling under stress all the time by chronic stressors eventually destroys that immunity.

Our time spent in the toxic catabolic or burning energy state of our psychological and physiological immune systems is reduced when we find a way to rest or get away mentally from our stressors. One of the thrivers called this a "perception pause" that allowed her to "shut down and let my mind take a little power nap to get energized again."

Another way to "get away from it all" is the thriver's technique of being willing to "go a little crazy" when under duress. As you have read, thrivers often engage in some degree of self-delusion that at least temporarily isolates and compartmentalizes their stress. Doing so provides them with just enough escape from the reality of their situation so that the catabolic hormones can be reduced and the anabolic hormones have the chance to increase.

A Thriving Dying

If we view a trauma as any challenge to a psychological immune system designed to deal with it, we may feel more confident in our ability to grow through it. We can consider stress not to be gradually killing us but actually making us stronger. We can feel less intimidated by whatever life has in store for us. One thriver said, "When I felt stressed before, I used to say, 'Oh no, what's next?' Now I usually take a deep breath and say to myself, 'Okay, now let's try to figure this one out.'"

Even the process of dying can involve a degree of psychological bodybuilding and an opportunity to thrive. By following the two principles above and breaking this universal and inevitable life challenge into its parts, we can avoid seeing death as one big catastrophic event. We can consciously divide dying into its spiritual, emotional, physical, and social components, and focus on the one or two with which we still have the mental capacity to deal. We can use thriving's periods of fixation, regression, self-delusion, and enlightened denial to buy us time to get some mental rest.

In this way, the mind and even the body can become at least a little stronger for dealing with one of the most important times in our lives. One of my fellow cancer patients expressed this idea when he told me, "You know, I've learned one thing from this rotten cancer. Anyone can live reasonably well, but you have to be pretty damned strong to die well."

Of course death cannot be denied, but we can thrive through even this most traumatic aspect of life. We can use our minds to give our failing bodies at least a little more strength to fight and, when the time comes, to more easily, gracefully, comfortably, and meaningfully let go.

I was speaking one night with one of my fellow cancer patients. He knew he was dying, but I saw that he was researching the purchase of a new car. "Looking for a gift for your wife?" I asked. "Hell, no," he laughed. "I'm looking for myself. I've got every car catalogue I could get my hands on. Thinking about a new car gets me away for a while. I know I'll probably not ever really buy it, but who cares? People who aren't dying look for new cars they can't afford, so why should I let my dying deprive me of that simple pleasure? And you know what? After a few minutes of car shopping, I feel a little physically stronger, too."

The day he died, his nurse told me that she found a Mercedes-Benz catalogue beside him on his bed. She said, "I can't imagine what possessed him to waste his precious last moments shopping for a new car." I knew that he had not wasted a single moment, and that he had been a little stronger physically at the end because his thriving had made his moments in many ways more precious than those who take living for granted.

Psychological bodybuilding is a way of embodying the thriving response so that it becomes translated into tangible physiological benefits. When we mentally construe adversity into ways to grow, our body becomes more quickly habituated to the catabolic hormones, eventually reacting less intensely to them over time, and our anabolic hormones are freed to have a more immediate, prolonged, and protective effect. Reducing stress is a good idea, coping with stress can be helpful, but thriving through stress can be an excellent psychological and physical fitness program.

Failure to Thrive

Psychologists and physicians have long known about a condition called failure-to-thrive syndrome.[9] It is a cluster of symptoms found in premature babies, severely neglected children, and also very often in the elderly. There is significant loss of weight, the muscles become weaker, general life energy level diminishes, and overall weakness and vulnerability to illness result. It is the opposite of the physiological hardiness that can result from the kind of psychological bodybuilding I've been describing.

Psychologists have long known that the failure-to-thrive syndrome is related to overexposures to prolonged and unrelenting stress. The stress on our body's systems of entering the world too soon for the body's capacity to function, of living in a home characterized by constant turmoil, conflict, fear, or exploitation, or simply living many years eventually results in the catabolic hormones taking their toll. When we are in an almost constant catabolic state, thriving becomes extremely difficult, but even then there are those who still thrive. Werner and Smith's thriving Kauai children (discussed in chapter 6) are an example of the threat of failure to thrive being transformed to the thriving response.

The mind and body are one. To think of them as separate or to refer to the mind being over the body is destructive to our thriving response. It causes us to live our lives in an artificial dichotomy and with the false belief of separateness between our consciousness and our physical bodies. Spending hours in the gym while neglecting the mind does not lead to physical, emotional, mental, or spiritual thriving. Meditating, contemplating, or trying various mind-over-body exercises while failing to exercise and attend to the physical body also results in leading "half a life," a life in which we fail to thrive. The body and mind are in constant reciprocal dialogue. A sick or suffering body bothers and distracts the mind as much as a bothered and agitated brain disturbs its body.

Group Thriving

Positive psychology's assumption is that most of life's problems rest within relationships and not within individuals. For pathogenic medicine and psychology, the word "system" has tended to refer to an individual's body system or individual behavior. The new psychology sees a system as a total interactive process between persons relating in and with the world. Health and illness are viewed as "systems concepts," meaning everything we do and experience in life takes place within an interrelated collective context.

We do not live, get sick, get well, or die alone; and thriving depends on knowing and living with the recognition that nothing we do, say, or feel is isolated from everything else, and that includes our psychoimmunity. Our physical immune system is affected by the systems of those around us, their health, and their healing. Our hearts can sense the energy of other hearts around us.[10] Thriving is a total mind-body-others life system. It includes not only our mind and our body, but the minds and bodies of everyone around us.

Our psychological immune system is not independent, either. It not only influences our body but is influenced by it. By paying attention to our physical health, we are strengthening our mind and therefore our thriving response. We exercise our body not just to live longer but so that we can live well. We thrive not just to live more years but also to find more meaning in them. One of the best ways we can enhance our thriving response is to do moderate, enjoyable exercise with someone we know who seems to be a thriver.

Traumatic Ghosts

Evidence of our failure to capitalize on the power of our psychological immune system can be found in post-traumatic stress disorder. PTSD occurs when a life trauma becomes frozen in our memory, causing us to overreact to events only remotely related to the original stressor. After my father was shot and wounded in a robbery, he told me, "Every time a door slams, a firecracker goes off, or a car backfires, I begin to tremble and duck for cover. I dream about being shot and feel the burning in my hand whenever somebody on television shoots a gun."

PTSD is related to changes in the brain that in turn cause a catabolic hormone reaction. In an unnecessary and overreactive preparation for a threat that no longer exists, two neurochemicals called catecholamines (adrenaline and noradrenaline) are secreted to get the body ready to deal with an extreme emergency, even though it exists only in our memory. We can end up depleting our thriving resources by constantly automatically mobilizing them in response to mental false alarms.

In spite of his thriving, Izzie still described having moments of PTSD. He said, "Sometimes when someone quickly raises his arm over his head, I flinch and duck. I don't even have to think about it, but an image of a prison guard with a night stick hitting me again and again flashes through my mind and my body reacts before I have time to stop the thought."

Persons suffering from PTSD can sometimes be very "flappable," meaning that they can show the kindling response whenever an event happens that reminds them of a past trauma. Author Daniel Goleman wrote that researchers once thought that anyone who was extremely "unflappable" was in a state of denial or even repression.[11] My own interviews and research on the thriving response show that it is the thrivers' way of adaptively construing what has happened and is happening that makes them seem "unflappable."

The Value of Tempered Temper Tantrums

Goleman wrote that unflappable people "become so adept at buffering themselves against negative feelings, it seems, that they are not even aware of the negativity. Rather than calling them repressors . . . a more apt term might be 'unflappable.'"[12] The thrivers I interviewed, however, could be just as flappable as anyone else. They were not any more consistently laid-back, naturally calm, or imperturbable than the rest of us. In fact, they seemed to be able to intentionally allow themselves to, as one thriver put it, "go a little nuts for a while," then rein their emotions back in, and begin again to work on developing a more effective explanatory style.

Unlike those who kindle and ruminate about their problems, thrivers were able to distract themselves from the chain of sadness or anxiety-maintaining thinking. While kindlers and often survivors and recoverers seemed to try to distract themselves from their present sad thoughts by coming up with other sad and fearful thoughts, thrivers managed to find "mood shifters." They were able to enhance and promote their psychological immune system's tendency to avoid becoming stuck in one emotional state.

Thrivers sometimes scream, swear, have angry outbursts, have a hard cry, sulk, or withdraw. But whatever they think during these times seems different from what is on their mind regarding the bigger problem disrupting their lives. It seems that they could intentionally allow themselves to "lose it" over a meaningless hassle such as being short-changed at the grocery store. One of my fellow cancer patients used what she called her "somewhat tempered temper tantrums" as a way to distract herself from becoming overwhelmed by her anxiety over her next chemotherapy treatment.

Thrivers sometimes use their overreactivity as a kind of self-administered ECT, electroconvulsive therapy often called "shock therapy." They employ it to allow them a temporary respite from their big problem, and that helps them forget that problem for at least a while.

The difference between helpless chronic flappability and intentional flappability seems to be whether or not we are in the process of expanding our explanatory style and not just stuck with what Goleman calls "a set of bad mood thoughts" that keep recycling in the same explanatory system. Thrivers seemed to have a keen awareness of their agitation when their psychological immune system mistakes a past memory for a present threat, and when they inhibit their own thriveability by what one thriver called "getting stuck in the same old mental mud."

The thriving response involves our ability to intentionally and selectively delude ourselves away from our bad mood makers. When my mother was feeling very down about yet another bout of life-threatening pneumonia, she accidentally dropped one of her small oxygen tanks on her ankle. It caused a small but not dangerous wound. She cried bitterly and became very angry with those she thought responsible for not safely storing her tanks. When I tried to comfort her, she said, "Wait. Not yet. This little temper tantrum I'm having is getting my mind off my breathing problem. Let me enjoy it for a few more minutes."

By engaging in periods of intentional flappability, we can prevent our potentially catabolic-state-inducing memories from dominating and weakening our psychological immunity. This intentional distraction is not "venting," which goes on and on for the purpose of "getting something off our chest." It is first and foremost a necessary distraction to buy time to work on our explanatory system.

Intentionally distracting ourselves allows the compartmentalization of a toxic memory so our psychological immune system can work more freely with real and present stressors. It allows us to maintain a generally upward psychological trajectory, and the result of this psychology is a healthier physiology. We experience less catabolic and more anabolic hormones, and our body becomes more ready for growth through—and not just survival of—adversity. Because they do not allow the ghosts of past trauma to become frozen in their minds, thrivers often appear calm under stress. In fact, they are actually just as flappable as anyone else, but always extremely mentally active in dealing with real and present problems.

The Crisis Chain Reaction

You have read that we tend to deal with severe crises in our lives with subtle conscious or sometimes unconscious decisions. We decide if we will engage in kindling, survival, recovery, resilience, or thriving. Our psychological immune system functions in different ways during each phase of this crisis chain reaction.

Fighting It: The first stage is kindling, a kind of emotional and mental flailing about that does little to help our situation. Unless we are able to keep our primitive brain centers in check, most of us "lose it" for at least a little while when a trauma first occurs. Instead of putting out the emotional fire, we cause it to flare up by trying to fight or flee our situation. This kindling only worsens the impact of the crisis and lessens our ability to deal with it effectively. Our psychological immune system immediately and reactively goes into its catabolic defense mode. As a result, we become agitated, unreasonable, irrational, and eventually drained and exhausted from dealing with a fire we ourselves are fueling.

One of my patients illustrated the kindling response when he was suddenly and unexpectedly fired from a job he had held for 20 years. He said, "I went ballistic. I made everything worse for my family and me by yelling and cursing. I threatened to sue and even wrote a letter to my boss threatening to sue him. If my wife hadn't told me to cool it and let it go, I don't know what would have happened."

Facing It: The second stage is the survival response. Unless we become fixated in this confrontational stage for too long, the anabolic hormones now begin to counterbalance the catabolic hormones. We become a little more settled and calm, but we are not yet "back to normal." Because we have less of the catabolic and agitating neurohormones flowing through our brain and body, we can become more rational and reflective. The man who lost his job described his entry into this phase when he said, "I guess you can fight reality for only so long.

You either burn out or you settle down and face the facts. Eventually, you have to start thinking about what you can do to survive."

Accepting It: The third stage is the recovery phase. The anabolic aspect of our psychological immune system becomes more dominant, and we begin to experience short spurts of more physical and emotional strength. We might be able to feel our psychological immune system kicking in as we emotionally bounce back up from being down. As if we have been knocked down by a punch to our face, we manage to get to our feet and walk, but we're still a little mentally groggy. We can do much of what we did before the trauma, but we sense that we are not far from relapse to survivor mode.

With less mental effort than is involved in the survival stage, we manage to put the adversity in the background of our consciousness, but it is always there ready to send us back to the "fight it" or "face it" stages. As he entered this stage of crisis management, the man quoted above said, "It took more than a year or more for me to recover from the shock of what those uncaring bastards did to me. No thanks to them, I got another job and I am getting on with my life, but I think I'll be recovering from what happened for a very long, long time."

Getting Past It: This is the resilience stage. When we feel emotionally stressed, we sometimes say or others tell us that we are "bent out of shape." Using the example of bending metal, in the "fight it" phase we become angry because someone or some event bent us emotionally out of shape. We may try to struggle angrily to force ourselves back into shape or surrender and mope over the shape in which we find ourselves. In the "face it" stage, we look at the "metal," acknowledge that it doesn't matter much who bent it or why, and try to do our best to work with the metal in its bent condition. In the "getting past it" stage, we manage to bend the metal back to almost its original shape, but we can still become frustrated and let it spring back to where it was originally.

Resilience, as I am using the word here, does not just mean returning to normal but to a more consistent normalcy with less threat of regression back to an earlier crisis management state. During this phase, our psychological immune system is characterized by a dominance of anabolic neurohormones. Because of this reduced agitated state, we become less sensitive to new stressors and memories of the one that set off the crisis chain reaction in the first place. To the outside world, we seem none the worse for wear, and some may say that the "old us" is back. However, deep in our own private consciousness where we do most of the construing and framing of the events of our lives, we easily recall the trauma. Our psychological immune system is still vulnerable to the symptoms of PTSD and slipping back down through the above stages.

When he seemed to be in the "getting past it" stage, the man who lost his job said, "People say they can't tell I ever went through that hell. I think I'm at peace with it now, but from time to time it all flashes through my mind and I get that rush you call the catabolic reaction like I'm totally reliving the whole thing in every cell in my body."

Growing Because of It: This is the thriving stage. Anabolic neurohormones are now dominant, and we are able to voluntarily construe what happened in such a way that it continues to be a stimulus for new emotional, mental, spiritual, interpersonal, and even physical growth. We have managed to compartmentalize the memory so it does not spill over to flood the corridors of our mind. We feel closer to those around us and value our time spent with them more than we did pretrauma.

During this phase, the trauma demands much less of our emotional time and our "emotional metal" seems stronger because it was bent out of shape. Instead of bordering on PTSD, we enter what might be called PTTR, post-trauma thriving reaction. We feel our psychological trajectory going and staying back up, and new stressors elicit a lower degree of catabolic response.

Thrivers report that they never forget their trauma and don't really want to. They are able, however, to frame it in such a way that it is seen as an essential and even necessary part of who and how they chose to become. At his three-year clinic follow-up session, the man quoted above said, "I know I'm stronger in all ways now than before I went through the termination. I'm not telling you I don't remember it, and I guess I can't or don't want to forget what happened. But it seems like it happened in another lifetime."

Another example of the interaction between our psychological and physical immune systems comes from findings about PTSD. A study of survivors of Nazi death camps showed that about three of every four of those who survived had symptoms of PTSD a half century after their experience. Looking at this research from the salutogenic or thriving point of view, we note that one of every four who had reported symptoms of PTSD no longer had them. They had managed to thrive despite the terror they had experienced and even though—and I would suggest because—they had reported symptoms of PTSD in the past.[13]

There was also evidence in the death camp study that indicates how the emotional immune process of psychological thriving can become embodied into our physical immune system. The concentration camp survivors who still had symptoms of PTSD showed the higher levels of catabolic hormones in their brains that are usually associated with PTSD. Those who had managed to psychologically thrive past their PTSD showed no evidence of the elevated catecholamine-like neurohormones such as adrenaline, noradrenaline, and cortisol. Their thriving had become embodied in their physical system.

A Daily Plan for Psychoimmunity Enhancement

As with our physiological immune system, if we neglect our psychological immunity or think in ways that get in the way of its basic rules of operation, it can fail us when we need it the most. Living a daily life that embraces the seven basic psychoimmunity rules may help protect and strengthen that system. Here's the daily plan for psychoimmunity enhancement I developed from my interviews with thrivers. I share it with my patients as a summary of the seven rules of psychological immunity.

- *Let it go.* Don't spend $100 worth of psychological energy on a 10-cent problem. Don't burden your psychoimmunity by needlessly squandering its resources on daily hassles. Remember, no one upsets you. You upset yourself.

- *Have faith.* Don't get emotional about being emotional. Stop aggravating yourself. Unless you cling to them, all emotional states pass. Trust your inborn mental resiliency.

- *Calm down.* Don't be a thrill seeker. Extreme highs can be as stressful to your psychological and physiological immunity as severe lows. What goes up must come down. Living your life with the intensity that was known to our ancestors only at times of battle eventually exhausts your entire line of defense against stress.

- *Wait a while.* Don't despair over sadness. Stop ruminating. Even if it seems impossible at your darkest moments, you will someday and some time feel as happy as you are now sad.

- *Suffer humbly.* Don't be a martyr. Everyone suffers. Suffering is as natural and necessary as it is difficult. It is essential to a truly authentic, deeply meaningful, and joyfully shared life.

- *If necessary, give it up.* While giving up has a bad reputation in Western thought, it is essential to a strong psychological immune system. Despite the adage, "Winners never quit," thriving through a crisis often involves intentional and considered disengagement from failed efforts or scaling back to a lesser goal in the same domain. This can allow the psychological immune system to "reboot" and focus its efforts more efficiently and effectively.

• *Cheer up.* You're much stronger than you feel and think. You were made not only to endure but to flourish through your pain. Until we personally come to know just how bad things can get, we often fail to see how powerfully resilient we are.

The above recommendations are examples of how thrivers think about their daily life. One of my patients was a single mother living in a poor and crime-ridden area of Detroit. In a six-year period, she had seen three of her sons killed in gang-related slayings. She summed up her thriver's way of thinking when she said, "I stopped counting the number of times I've been devastated. I'm a very religious person, but I began to think that life is pointless. Then, when I heard the talk about Mr. Beethoven's thriving, I began to think that just existing is point enough. Everything else is a bonus. I find so much joy in my other children. I've had to learn to let the bad times do what they do and wait them out. Somehow, you come back stronger than ever. I don't mean you're not sad forever, because you are. I have anger and sadness scars all over my heart. But somehow your sadness and grief helps you find the bonuses in living that others may not find. I guess that's what your Mr. Beethoven did. You become more immune to the pain and more sensitive to the joy."

Living a Thousand Times Over

As you have read, Beethoven's psychological immune system seemed to strengthen as his hearing failed. Despite the traumas of his life, he managed to thrive until his death. He went through periods of panic, self-doubt and recrimination, anger, envy, and profound depression and despair. His psychological trajectory dipped and rose throughout his life, but it seemed to remain sufficiently generally upward to allow his creativity to flourish. The power of his psychoimmunity is reflected in his music's capacity to awaken within us a sense of our own thriving spirit.

I have used Beethoven as a role model for thriving, not just because he was such an extraordinary talent but also because he thrived as an ordinary flawed and far less than perfect man. He was far from the image of the always joyful and contented person we might think a thriver is. He was an iconoclastic misfit and driven workaholic; he paid little attention to his appearance, and felt constantly nagged and pressured by his feeling that "fate was knocking on my door." He ignored most established conventions and frequently lost his temper. Far from being a people person, he once said, "I love a tree more than a man."

Beethoven did not confront his deafness with unrelenting grace and calmness, but somehow he climbed to remarkable creative heights at least in part because of it. Despite this picture of an often troubled and frustrated genius, Beethoven remained consciously creative. Something within him allowed him to be sufficiently psychologically immune to be able to express a love of life and nature that resonates in our souls whenever we hear one of his symphonies.

As a summary of what you have read so far about thriving and the psychological immune system, consider again the thriving I described as the Beethoven Factor. It would have been amazing if Beethoven had been born deaf and still managed to compose remarkable music. His amazing feat would have shown that he could overcome one of the most terrible of disadvantages a musician could face. It is perhaps even more amazing and characteristic of thriving, however, that Beethoven had been able to hear, lost that gift, and still was able to vividly recall his memories of those lost sounds.

If you have lost someone dear to you, try now to hear the sound of that person's voice. If you're like most people, you will probably have difficulty hearing that voice again, and that uniquely wonderful sound may seem lost to you forever. Even if an audio- or videotape is available, most of us feel that we can't really seem to hear the exact tone, special inflection, and unique resonance we had so often taken for granted.

To thrive through the trauma of my father's sudden premature death, I have often tried to hear my deceased father's voice. If I take plenty of time and try to listen with my heart and not my ears, it sometimes seems that I can hear his childish laugh. I can hear him say one of his favorite words, one that he loved to drag out for emphasis. Even when he was severely weakened by chronic heart failure, he would describe events in his life as "beee-uuu-tee-full." Perhaps the way I try to listen for my dad's voice is in some very small way similar to how Beethoven listened through his deafness. Perhaps it was this way of thriving that allowed him to set the silent sounds to music.

We can imagine Beethoven walking through the woods listening through his deafness for the sounds he once heard. We can imagine that a smile might have come to his face as he heard from somewhere inside him the chirping of the birds, the rippling of the streams, and the rustling of leaves. He wrote, "No one can love the country as I do. My bad hearing does not trouble me here. In the country, every tree seems to speak to me, saying 'Holy! Holy!' In the woods, there is enchantment which expresses all things." This intense thriving in and with nature is expressed in Beethoven's Sixth Symphony, "The Pastoral." It is this profound awakening to and embracing of life that is characteristic of those who have learned how to thrive.

If you will take some time to listen to Beethoven's music or the work of a composer that seems to stimulate your own creative consciousness, you might hear what Mosha, the piano teacher tortured by the Nazis, heard. Perhaps you will feel inspired to thrive no matter what life has offered you. Perhaps you will experience the thriving expressed by Beethoven as he approached his death and wrote, "I will seize Fate by the throat. It will not wholly conquer me. Oh, how beautiful it is to live—and to live a thousand times over." Perhaps that's the ultimate definition of thriving, to be able to seize whatever fate has in store for us and because of it, to be able to live a thousand times over.

8 Testing Your Thriveability

"After a time of decay comes the turning point. The powerful light that has been banished returns."

—I Ching, The Book of Changes

The Choice of a Lifetime

Beethoven, Izzie, Mosha, and the other thrivers you have read about all did it. Somewhere in the midst of their suffering came a turning point when they made the choice of their lifetime. They elected to go beyond surviving and recovering and opted to thrive through their challenges. They could have elected to remain in suffering with their pain, struggle to survive it, or try to recover or return to their prestress state. They chose instead to try to become stronger, wiser, and more fully and authentically alive because of their problems. They didn't just cope with their problems; they used them to learn how to relish the moments of their lives that were free of the stress, grief, and pain of the events that led them to their turning point.

If we choose to thrive, we have to make the choice to become conscious that we are conscious. We can elect to do what other animals can't. We can choose to become observers of our thoughts and how we are thinking, reflect on our inner mental processes, and try to know that and how we know. Author Julian Huxley wrote, "Man is nothing but evolution becoming conscious of itself." In a way, that's what thriving is—becoming conscious of how we are evolving in our world.

We don't have to wait for a catastrophe in our lives to decide to engage in the creative consciousness that characterizes thriving. We can decide now to do some extensive mental work, tune in to our psychological immune system, and go beyond languishing through life. We can decide to try to grow because of our problems and not just recover from them and live with a consciousness that more openly, freely, and regularly discovers the full gift of life. We can make the conscious effort to extend the lessons of our suffering into a more adaptive and life-enchanting philosophy of living. In other words, we can elect to flourish.

In what seems to be an increasingly fast-paced, hectic, distracted, and cynical world, taking the time to reflect about the point of it all can seem a waste of valuable time. Survival and recovery take much less mental and emotional time and energy than trying to learn to thrive because of a life trauma. Getting back to normal is easier and quicker than reflecting about whether we really want to go there again. Persons who have developed their "thriveability" use times of challenge as times for questioning what "normal" has become for them. They use them to develop and refine their explanatory system and strengthen their psychological immunity.

The Chicken Broth Disaster

Those of us who have known major trauma in our lives are sometimes amused by what some people consider a crisis. "Oh, my God," said a woman to a confused stock boy in the grocery store. "This ruins absolutely everything for the party. I needed chicken broth for my recipe and you tell me you're out of it? The party is tonight, and now I have to fight the traffic again to find another store. I don't have the time for this. If they don't have it, everything will be ruined. Do you know what a mess this makes of my life?" As the bewildered stock boy searched the shelves frantically, the woman kept talking out loud to herself. "It's supposed to rain, they've chopped up the damn street in front of our house so no one will be able to park, and half the people haven't even had the common courtesy to RSVP."

Knocking a few cans to the floor as the woman repeated, "Come on, come on," the relieved clerk said, "Oh, here they are," and handed her his peace offering of a can of chicken noodle soup. "For God's sake," sighed the increasingly disgusted woman, "You don't even know the difference between chicken noodle and chicken broth? Just forget it. This is becoming a worse disaster. This is the last time I'll ever shop here."

While it may seem that this woman was joking, she clearly was not. She slammed her grocery cart into a shelf and, with tears in her eyes, stalked angrily out of the store. I walked over to comfort the dismayed clerk, but he refused to stop looking for the chicken broth. "There!" he almost yelled holding up a can of chicken broth. "If she could have waited one more minute, it was right in front of her all the time."

I had seen less intense reactions than this woman's in my fellow cancer patients when they received bad news about a necessary painful procedure. I had seen the "tempered temper tantrums" they used to escape for a few moments from their pain or worries about a coming treatment, but their tantrums were modulated and purposeful, not helplessly reactive. When I heard the angry woman complain about the traffic, I remembered how often I had looked outside my hospital room window and longed to have another chance to get stuck in traffic. If we are the ones constantly making mountains out of molehills, we end up living in a perpetual state of survival. One thriver said, "You can't thrive through your problems if you're the problem."

On my way home from the store, I saw a car resting on the front lawn of a home. I could smell burned rubber and torn-up sod. The neighbors had gathered around a little girl sitting on her bike. When I stopped to offer assistance, the girl's mother said her daughter was frightened but not injured. She said, "That crazy woman over there almost killed her."

I saw the chicken broth hunter sitting on the curb crying. She seemed to recognize me from the market and looked up. She said, "I just wasn't thinking. I almost killed her. I was in such a damned hurry and so distracted that I just didn't see her. I can't stop shaking." At that moment, the police arrived and began questioning her. I had to leave, but I've always wondered if this stressed and distracted woman would see that day in her life as a turning point. I wondered if she would survive or recover from her accident or maybe even wake up in time to become more conscious of what really matters in life.

Unfortunately, many of us don't recognize our full thriveability until something as drastic as the car accident above occurs. Until something major imposes a significant turning point, we aren't usually able to calm down to be conscious of our consciousness or to think about how we have come to think. I hope the lessons in this thriver's manual will provide you with some ideas for thriving right now, and before something happens that forces your hand.

Reading Your Lifeline

To help my patients understand the idea of turning points in their lives that can lead to the choice to thrive, I asked them to draw their lifeline. I asked them to draw a timeline from the year of their birth to the date of their death, which we set at an arbitrary 90 years. I then asked them to place on that line the events they felt had caused them to become somehow more alive, wiser, and stronger. I asked them to include those times when they found new meaning in their lives and asked them to forecast and add similar events in their future. Most of my patients filled their lines not only with what seemed like positive events but also with the negative traumas of their lives.

As I stated in part 1, I am using the word "trauma" as anything that messes up our life plans and shakes up our explanatory system. For the woman above, the silliness and life-wasting nature of the missing chicken broth could have served as a call to draw her attention to her failure to thrive in her life. Hopefully, the near killing of a child by her trance-like tenseness and almost unconscious way of living will have served as a hammer to her consciousness that helped her find her turning point toward thriving.

A trauma in the way I am using the word refers to any event that offers a sufficient threat to our explanatory system to set off the crisis coping chain reaction of worsening, suffering, surviving, recovering, and potentially thriving. A key ingredient for thriving often seems to be a profound sense of life disequilibrium. Trauma in this sense may not be bad. It could range from a desired but unexpected pregnancy to the sudden death of a parent. Both of these events can be traumatic in their capacity to act as antigens or stimulants to our psychological immune system. If we let them, they can cause us to seek new meanings about living that we might not have sought without becoming traumatized.

While most of my patients placed several events that are generally seen as desirable happenings on their lifelines, all of them included more "negative traumas" as significant turning points. Death, the loss of a loved one, the end of a long-term relationship, a severe career crisis, and serious or life-threatening illness were considered turning points at least as often and usually more often than events such as a birth, a wedding, or the experience of sudden good fortune or high-level success.

When I asked my patients to discuss their turning points, they inevitably spoke at more length and with more reflection and emotion about the "negative" traumatic events. It is a principle of the functioning of our psychological immunity that we often seem to find more happiness and contentment in reflecting on past negative events than on present or future positive events. One of my patients said, "I looked at the lifeline exercise from the point of view of things that would really cause me to rethink my life, not just things that made me happy. There's something about thinking about how bad things were that helps you realize how great things can be."

To begin your evaluation of your thriveability, I suggest you draw your lifeline. Place past and anticipated trauma in your life along the line. Take some time to reflect on the events that seem to be turning points and consciousness crossroads. If possible, discuss these turning points with someone you love who may have thrived or will thrive through them with you. As you think about events that turned your life around, you will probably notice what one of my patients did. She said, "When you said a trauma was anything that caused you to see your life differently, I put meeting my husband, our wedding, getting my medical degree, and the birth of our twins on my lifeline. But the more I thought about it, the more I started putting things like the death of my dad and my mom's stroke as the really major turning points."

To paraphrase a well-known statement, life's most enlightening turning points seem to be the times that try men's and women's souls, the events when our psychological immune system is put to the test and we are forced to think or sink.

Sixteen Questions

As you look at your lifeline from the perspective of the above moments of decision, here are some questions to ask yourself as you consider your turning point entries.

• What did I learn because of this traumatic turning point?

• How was I changed emotionally by what happened?

• How was I changed mentally by what happened?

• How was I changed spiritually by what happened?

• How was I changed physically by what happened?

• What bad came from the trauma?

• What good came from the trauma?

• How were those I love affected by what happened?

• How was my view of family life affected by what happened?

- How might my life be different now if that traumatic turning point had never happened?

- Are there ways in which I seemed to need this trauma in order grow and become more alive?

- What did the trauma take out of me?

- What did the trauma add to my life?

- What did the trauma add to my family's life?

- How were my faith, beliefs, and general life explanatory system affected by my trauma?

- Were there ways in which I may have had to have that trauma to teach me how to be more alive?

Your answers to the above questions don't matter as much as the mental process of reflecting about these traumatic turning points in your life. To contemplate these questions is to engage in the act of creative construing that is essential to thriving. Thriving is not coming up with the right answers to life, but learning to keep asking new questions about living.

Noah's Thrivers

Although this chapter focuses on helping you assess your own thriving ability, it is important to remember the systems context of thriving. When we feel we are thriving, we may actually be experiencing the growing strength of the entire system in which we live. Families, communities, and even nations have the ability to thrive.

Just as individuals do, countries also come to their own traumatic turning points that offer the opportunity for them to raise their consciousness in order to thrive. One of the thrivers I interviewed provided an example of both the personal and the collective thriving response. She was an 82-year-old Armenian woman who had suffered from severe diabetes and kidney failure. She was on dialysis and had had one leg amputated due to a diabetes-related infection. She embodied the hardiness, happiness, healing, and hope you will read about in the next four chapters of this manual on thriving. Her sense of her own identity and mental power to employ a constructive, optimistic, and creative explanatory system had been strengthened not only by her own life traumas, but by the adversities and resultant diaspora of the people of Armenia.

Diaspora occurs when a country's population becomes scattered throughout the world. Because of the many traumas imposed on Armenia, less than half of the Armenian population still lives in their home country. Despite that fact, this woman still felt the pain of her country's many tragic turning points. As a result of her enduring identification with her homeland, her fellow Armenians' national thriving had also become a part of her own. She seemed to merge her own consciousness with the collective consciousness of her country.

Armenia has been referred to as the "cradle of civilization."[1] Whether or not the people of Armenia actually share a history with Noah, they have known the stress of being threatened by immense natural, political, and military crises that threatened to drown their own culture. The people of Armenia have endured adversity for centuries. They have known genocide, religious persecution, the terror of Stalinism, catastrophic earthquakes, and most recently the economic stress of the difficult transition from a totalitarian political system to a democratic free-market economic system. According to positive psychologist Meline Karakashian, despite and because of these traumatic turning points, there seems to be a thriving nature to the Armenian people. I sensed that invincibility in the Armenian woman I interviewed.

Karakashian wrote, "In the Armenian experience, thriving is achieved through individuals' unconscious motivation to progress and make up for the nation's past losses, to defy the odds, and prove to the world that this nation is as permanent as Mount Ararat."[2] The Armenian woman revealed this same invincibility. She said, "Like my country, I've seen so much suffering. It's been made up of one tragedy after another with periods in between where I guess God expects me to take it easy for a while, enjoy life while I can, and think about what it all means to get ready for the next crisis. We Armenians thrive because it is our nature. What you call thriving is what we call *dobal*, which means to become stronger no matter what problems you face. That is me, that is my life, that is my country."

Individuals thrive because of the four general styles of consciousness you will read about in the following chapters and as measured by the test at the end of this chapter. Countries thrive by the collective manifestation of these same capacities. Through their religious systems, preservation of their languages, arts, literature, sports, and various forms of cultural networking, they remain consciously engaged with and thrive through their traumatic turning points.

As it is with the terrors faced by individual thrivers, no catastrophe or threat of terrorism can prevent a nation willing to thrive through its traumatic turning points from becoming stronger because of its suffering.[3] The thriving of the United States in the aftermath of one of its most horrible traumatic turning points, the September 11, 2001 terrorist attacks, is also evidence of the *dobal* the Armenian woman described. Because of the sudden trauma of September 11, people around the country report re-examining their life priorities, treasuring moments with their families, and trying to appreciate more the simple pleasures of life. They are reflecting on the meaning of life and death and the importance of not waiting until something is gone to fully celebrate what they have.

The Power of the Piper

We will all face terrible crises in our lives. Because we have been given the gift of life, we must also be willing to accept the challenge of the inevitable crises that come with the chaotic nature of living, and some of them may cause us major-league suffering. When your next life trauma comes, where will you start? What is the degree of your thriving resource from which you will begin to deal with your adversity? The Thriveability Test offers one way to at least estimate the degree of "thriveability" you will be able to draw upon the next time you are faced with a traumatic turning point.

Even though I offer you the Thriveability Test, none us may ever truly know the true nature and extent of our thriving resources until they are put to their most severe challenge. The best we can hope for is to be able to estimate our starting point, and I hope the test may help in that process.

I learned more about thriving when I met a member of the New York City Fire Department Bagpipers. I heard him talking to someone months after the collapse of New York City's World Trade Center towers. He was speaking to some guests waiting to go on the same television show on which I had just appeared to discuss thriving through terrorism. He spoke quickly and with a pronounced Irish accent, but I eavesdropped and managed to write down his words. He said, "I would have never thought I had it in me. You think you're a pretty strong guy, but then you learn what strength is. I played for three or four funerals for firemen every day for weeks after the towers went down. I knew most of those guys personally, and we always pipe 'Amazing Grace' as the widow and children enter the church. It breaks your heart every time, but this time it tore my heart out.

"The other day, we played for one of our own pipers crushed trying to save people in one of the Towers. You think you will never recover from something like that, but you play again a few hours later for the next funeral. I guess you have this inner strength you never knew you had until you really have to rely on it, and that's when you know how strong you really are and that you can deal with anything."

Before taking the Thriveability Test, remember that thriving is, as the bagpiper said, actually a way of dealing with yourself and your private thoughts and emotions, not the event itself. Once they occur, none of us can change the traumas that happen to us, but we can elect to be meaning-makers and assign our own significance to our traumas, what they will come to signify for our future living, and what we learn about ourselves from our suffering.

One of the thrivers I interviewed told me of her struggle to deal with the abduction of her daughter. I met the young mother at a lecture I gave on thriving several years ago. She spoke with me after my talk and tearfully described her continued agony in dealing with the kidnapping and the endless years of not knowing her daughter's fate. She said, "Where do you start with something like that? People tell me how heroic it is of me to keep going, but I don't understand what option they think a person has. They ask me how I can be so brave, but I'm not brave. They ask me how I'm dealing with it, and I can't really explain to them how I'm really not. Nobody could. I can't deal with it, but I can try to deal with me and how I feel and think about what happened.

"I'm doing my best to deal with my emotions and thoughts. That's why I came to hear you speak about thriving through crisis. I was angry when I saw the title of your talk because I thought you meant that you get over it and that what happened was actually a good thing for you. But I hear you saying now that, even if it is something as horrible as having your child suddenly taken from you by some animal, you still have the ability to keep growing and getting stronger. You don't actually get stronger because something terrible happened to you but because of how you learned to think and feel about life and yourself because it happened.

"I see now what you mean by thriving. Just like you said that Beethoven never really accepted his deafness but grew through and because of it, I guess you grow because of the new meanings you find in life, not the bad thing itself. That is a very important distinction to make. When you get hit in the heart like I was, you finally ask yourself, 'Where do I go from here?' At least that much is up to you."

Reliable Sources

Based on resilience and thriving research and my interviews of my patients and other thrivers, I designed the following Thriveability Test as a tool to help those interested in learning more about their thriving response and to provide a source of insight into their "stress stamina." I have since given this test to over

1,000 persons around the world and base the scoring on their patterns of response as related to interviews I conducted with many of them. I present it here not as a definitive way of measuring your thriveability but as a starting point for your self-study of the status of your psychological immune system before you read the rest of this Thriver's Manual.

I based each of the following questions on the groundbreaking research of some of the pioneers in the field of positive psychology. Suzanne Ouellette Kobasa, Mihaly Csikszentmihalyi, Aaron Antonovsky, and Martin E. P. Seligman were among the first psychologists to focus their attention on our human strengths rather than vulnerabilities, and most positive psychologists consider them to be major contributors to their emerging science.

Kobasa's research has been in the area of mental hardiness, a kind of stress-resistant mental toughness. Csikszentmihalyi's focus has been on the happiness that results from a sense of flow or total involvement in life. Antonovsky's work has dealt with the process of finding a sense of coherence in our lives; a meaning, comprehensibility, and manageability that help us grow through adversity. Finally, Seligman's writings and research have dealt primarily with how we learn an optimistic framing of life events, a creative construing of events that leads to a consistently upward psychological trajectory.

I have also used the work of these four psychologists as an outline for this Thriver's Manual. I did so because their concepts of psychological hardiness, mental flowing, a sense of coherence, and a generally upward psychological trajectory capture the characteristics of the thrivers I studied. All four of these leading positive psychologists and their many research colleagues are working hard to learn about the amazing strength of the human psyche. It is this pioneering group of scientists that has established the foundations of positive psychology.

I also designed the Thriveability Test based on my own interviews of the invincibles, the thriving superstars you are reading about. These interviews were conducted not only in my clinic at Sinai Hospital, but in many countries where I lectured on thriving, including Germany, England, Russia, Spain, Italy, Japan, and the Netherlands. I spoke with people from these places about their scores on the Thriveability Test, the turning points in their lives and their progression through the five phases of crisis management.

The four parts of the test—hardiness, happiness, healing, and hope—constitute the cornerstones of the Thriver's Manual. I hope you will take this test before continuing on in the Thriver's Manual, and once again when you finish this book.

The Thriveability Test

Using the following scale, score yourself on the items below. It is important to also have someone who knows you very well score you. My research shows that many of us either do not know our own strengths or, because of lack of full understanding of the principles of the psychological immune system, tend to over- or underestimate them.

5 = That's Me Always
4 = That's Me Almost Always
3 = That's Me Most of the Time
2 = That's Me Often
1 = That's Rarely Me
0 = That's Not Me At All

Hardiness

1. ____ I will stick with a problem, work it out in my mind, and easily change my mind and my life philosophy.

2. ____ I mentally focus on one thing at a time and never multitask.

3. ____ I'm the strong one with the cool head whom everyone turns to when things go wrong.

4. ____ I can tell when its time to just go with the flow and can easily give up trying to stay in control.

5. ____ I see problems as challenges, not threats.

_____ Total Hardiness Score

Happiness

6. ____ I get so into the flow and involved in things I enjoy that I lose all sense of myself, where I am, and time.

7. ____ My family thinks I'm a real joy and great fun to be with all the time.

8. ____ I easily put work and family problems out of my mind, don't ruminate about them, and easily get absorbed in the task at hand.

9. _____ I laugh hard and long more than 20 times a day, never smirk in disgust, and frequently "squile." (A squile is a broad tooth-bearing smile accompanied by squinting eyes.)

10. _____ I don't compare my luck or happiness with that of other people.

_____ Total Happiness Score

Healing

11. _____ I have a strong but adaptable belief system that helps me understand the evil in the world.

12. _____ I think things happen for a reason and that they work out for the best if we figure out how to make the best of them.

13. _____ I have had a major crisis in my life that I have come through being much stronger than before.

14. _____ I easily and openly show my fears and vulnerability and can reach out for help and support when I need it.

15. _____ I never ask "why me" and have no resentment for any of the negative events in my life.

_____ Total Healing Score

Hope

16. _____ I never take things personally and easily forgive others.

17. _____ I don't generalize about people or events.

18. _____ When something negative is over, it's over. I don't carry a grudge and do not keep revisiting past problems or injustices.

19. _____ I am not judgmental or prejudiced and easily give everyone the benefit of the doubt.

20. _____ When it comes to my life and what has or might happen, I see the glass as half-full, not half-empty.

_____ Total Hope Score

_____ Total of All Your Four Invincibility Scores

Interpreting Your Thriveability Test Score

As stated above, I have given various forms of the Thriveability Test to more than 1,000 people around the world. Various parts of it have been translated into Japanese, German, and Spanish. There was a variance in the scores of individuals in regards to which category or categories were their strongest aspect of thriving. For example, some people made up for a comparatively low score in hardiness by a higher score in hope. Thriving is a uniquely individual skill and shows itself in varying ways and with different combinations of the four factors of hardiness, happiness, healing, and hope.

Here is a scale you can use to get a general idea of your level of thriveability at this time in your life.

90–100 = Thriving *(flourishing)*
80–89 = Resilient *(in recovery)*
60–79 = Surviving *(languishing)*
59–50 = Suffering *(in victim mode)*
49 and below = Kindling *(worsening your problems)*

Remember, you have a strong psychological immune system and your own unique way of thriving, so this test is only intended to cause you to reflect on how you have or will deal with the turning points in your life. If the score you gave yourself is lower than you think it should be, be sure to have someone who knows you well score you. If that score is comparable to your own low scoring, chances are it's accurate. If that person scores you higher, you are probably being too hard on yourself. If that person scores you significantly lower than you did yourself, you may not be thinking hard enough about how you are thinking. After one wife had scored her husband 40 points lower than he did himself, she said, "That's the problem. I don't think he's conscious enough to know how unconscious he is." Thriving requires hard mental work and vigilance for what we are putting on our mind.

Your actual score on the Thriveability Test means much less than your willingness to learn about thriving and its potential in your life and the life of those you love. If you scored lower than you thought you would on the test and became angry, challenged the test, or even ridiculed it, chances are that your low score was accurate. If you laughed and took a low score as a challenge and with the idea that you can think in new ways that might improve it, your psychological immune system is stronger than you think and ready to work for you.

No matter what your total score, it is important to look at your score on each of the individual four categories of the test—hardiness, happiness, healing, and hope. What were your strong areas and what categories offer the possibility of learning more about thriving?

There is another way to take the Thriveability Test that I have found helpful with those I counsel about thriving. Try taking the test "group style." Answer each item on the test as a group with your family or friends. Spend plenty of time discussing each item and come up with a score that you feel collectively represents the thriveability of your group as a whole. If you are married, score the test as a twosome and determine your marital thriveability, a factor I called "intimate invincibility."

The idea of learning from the inventory is to talk about and learn more about thriving, not to compete for the highest score. And remember, no matter what your score is, first of all do nothing at all. Let the meaning of the score sink in and reflect on it occasionally for a while. You may notice that, over time and without doing much at all, just becoming aware of the components of the thriving response might raise your score and make it a little easier for you to come through your next major turning point with an upward psychological trajectory.

A *Thriving Reminder List*

Based on the research that was the basis of the Thriveability Test, here is a list of the traits of those people who have learned to tap into the power of the psychological immune system to maximize their thriving. You have all of the following thriving talents, but you may not be using them to their fullest.

You will read about each of these traits in the following four chapters, but I suggest you copy them down and keep them close at hand as your read as a reminder and just in case you need them when your turning point and moment of decision come up. Next to each trait, I have placed a quote from one of the thrivers that illustrates the nature of the thriving response.

Twelve Thriver's Traits

Hardiness

1. Challenged—"Things happen for a reason, but it's up to us to figure out the reason."

2. Committed—"I'm in this for the long haul and will never give up."

3. Controlled—"I'll either deal with this or know when to give up and move on."

Happiness

4. Selfless—"I'll just lose myself in what I'm doing."

5. Involved—"I get really absorbed and lost in what I'm doing."

6. Free—"Sometimes I get so enthralled in something that I lose all sense of time and place."

Healing

7. Integrator—"It is just going to take some time to figure this out."

8. Meaning-Maker—"I'll make sense of this in my own way."

9. Manager—"I always know that somehow I'll come up with a way to deal with whatever is getting to me. I just have to take some time to figure things out."

Hope

10. Externalizer—"Life is rough for everyone. I don't have any problems everyone else doesn't have."

11. Calm—"All bad things must come to an end."

12. Contained—"One bad apple does not spoil the bunch."

By reviewing these characteristics of thriving, looking for them in your own and others' lives, and in the stories of the invincibles you have been reading, you may find that your own thriving threshold may become lowered simply because you have become more conscious of what it takes to thrive.

9 Hardiness through the Hard Times

"All suffering prepares the soul for vision."

—Martin Buber

An Emotional Audit

The afternoon I had just received the news I was dying of cancer, I walked slowly and dejectedly to our mailbox. I felt lost and helpless, so it seemed that taking my daily ritual of a walk for the mail was at least a small step to regaining some sense of order in the chaos into which my life had been cast. I was living in Michigan at the time, and the beautiful bright spring day seemed in harsh contrast to my dark mood. It was Good Friday, and the meaning of that day and signs of nature's awakening all around me made me feel isolated from the universal celebration of new life. Everything seemed to be coming to life just when I was losing mine, but I was in for an awakening I did not anticipate.

As I walked up the long driveway from our home, I noticed all the buds on the trees ready to burst forth with new life, the healthy kind of growth that contrasted with the toxic growth of cells going on in my own body. I could smell the wet freshness of the just-past thaw, and when I heard the birds chirping and saw several robins building nests, I could walk no further. I began to cry in envy of their new beginnings all around me when it seemed that I was facing my painful end. I sat down on one of the large boulders that lined our drive, but the ache of the cancer eating away at my hips caused me to jump up and groan. I wiped the tears from my eyes and while trying to shut out the energy of spring, I proceeded to the mailbox.

After pulling a stack of envelopes from the box, I began my slow walk down the tree-lined drive back to my home. In an effort to distract myself from the sounds, sights, and smells of spring, I began to sort through the envelopes. I noticed an enveloped marked "Urgent. Internal Revenue Service." I opened it as I walked, but stopped suddenly when I read the words. "You have been selected for a random compliance audit of all of your State and Federal tax records for the previous three years." As I placed the notice back in its envelope, I began to laugh harder than I had for months.

After having just received the devastating news of my cancer, I was amused at the irony of the notice's words "not to be alarmed or concerned in any way." The notice said that all my prior tax fillings were "entirely in order and appropriate," but that a few taxpayers from every state were being randomly selected by a Social Security number lottery draw for "an extraordinarily thorough and complete total audit and review of all related files and documents." I had apparently "won" the IRS lottery and been selected for its rare if dubious honor on the very day I was told that I had contracted an extremely rare type of cancer that randomly and suddenly strikes young and healthy people at the prime of their lives. I thought, "How bizarre. I have never won a thing, but today I'm two for two in having my number come up."

When I entered our home, my wife saw me laughing. While my family had tried their best not to cry in front of me that bad Good Friday, her eyes and the eyes of my two sons eyes were red from sobbing. She looked at me as if I had finally given in or even lost my mind. "What in the world is so funny?" she asked, as if hoping that I had brought news from the mailbox that my cancer was all a terrible mistake. My answer revealed a hardiness that I never knew I had, the hardiness that is one of the four crucial components of thriving through crisis.

"We're in luck," I said. "We won the IRS lottery. We've been selected for a random audit."

"You think that's funny, Dad?' asked my son Scott, who also seemed sure his father had been pushed over the emotional edge by the barrage of bad news. "Yes, son, I do," answered. "This whole day is funny in a way. I keep getting bad news on Good Friday. Come and sit down with me and I'll tell you why I'm laughing."

Scott, my older son Roger, and my wife, Celest, sat with me on the deck overlooking an acre of grass that seemed to be getting greener by the minute from the energy of the spring sun. Because my hips had become so sore from my walk, my wife had to help me sit down in one of the chairs. I told my family that for some reason I did not yet fully understand, the IRS letter had been a strange kind of turning point that caused me to feel energized and to put my problems in a different perspective. I still felt sick, weak, and more frightened than I had ever been in my life, but something about the timing of the absurdities, contrasts, and oddities of that traumatic spring day seemed to cause me to make up my mind to begin to deal with our crisis in a more constructive manner.

As I discovered in my interviews of thrivers, there came a time in my coping with cancer that I had to make up my mind about how I would deal with my adversity. You read in chapter 9 about the points of decision in the crisis chain reaction, and the IRS letter had seemed to help me in a most peculiar way to realize such a point. Somehow, it caused me to reflect more deeply on my feelings and thoughts about my trauma rather than give in to reacting helplessly to it. In the form of a bizarrely timed cosmic joke, I became aware that it was time for me to do a serious emotional audit of my own way of thinking about my predicament.

Because of my slow and sick stroll to the mailbox and the contrasts and ironies it brought to my mind, everything that was happening to me seemed to shift slightly from an insurmountable problem to an immensely difficult challenge. It was as if the cosmos was tapping on my shoulder to tell me to pay attention and get the point that life is full of chaos and pain, but also continued adventures and challenges in discovering new beginnings.

I wrote about my Good Friday emotional audit in a journal I kept about what I called the "cancering phase of my life." I reflected on the many meanings regarding suffering and rebirth that are represented by Good Friday as I wrote, "This seems at the same time to be the best and worst of my 47 Good Fridays. This one has made me more afraid than I have ever been, but also more awake. I am sicker, weaker, and in more pain than I fear I can bear for much longer. I can either give in to this crisis or get into it. I can engage and embrace this time of my life. What has happened to me is not my choice. What I will make of it must be."

As I sat with my family on the warm spring Good Friday, I made up my mind to allow the fresh new energy of spring all around me to revive my spirit and "remind" or awaken my consciousness to grapple with the strange synchronicity of the diagnosis of my cancer juxtaposed with a sacred day and the comparably silly IRS audit. It all seemed to be an introspective-inspiring example of the necessary local pain we must suffer for the privilege of being alive in a world that itself is constantly dying and being reborn. I had left for the mailbox as a weak and vulnerable man, but returned a hardier soul.

A Stroll through the Stages of Trauma

When I was told I would likely die, I became as angry and resentful as I was frightened. I became a "kindler" by fueling the fire of my predicament with emotions that only made matters worse for my family and me. I blamed doctors for not finding my cancer earlier before it had gone to Stage IV, spread throughout my entire body, and began to eat away my bones. I was resentful of those who seemed to be violating all the health rules I had always followed but did not have cancer. I thought I tried to be a good person who did not deserve what was happening to me and immaturely thought of others who it seemed should be more deserving of cancer than I.

By the time I took my trip to the mailbox, I walked as a victim. I felt pity for my family and myself and focused on my suffering. I felt jealous of springtime and all it could mean for those who were not suffering as I was. I saw the new life all around me as reminders of my final spring rather than invitations to come to back to life. I was even jealous of the trees and flowers for their opportunity to be reborn and the birds for their joyful chirping for their new beginnings.

Until I realized that I was forgetting to celebrate the spring I was in, I cried because of the springs I thought I would no longer see. Until I realized that I could choose to remember and relish the seasons I had experienced in ways I never did before, I felt sorry for myself that I would never again be able to smell the burning leaves of fall, feel the cool wetness of snowflakes on my cheek, or hear the insects singing on a warm summer night.

By the time I began my walk back down our long driveway with the IRS letter in hand, my consciousness had changed. I had become distracted from my suffering just long enough to start thinking about where my tax records were and how I could help my family find them and, if they had to, face the audit without me. When I felt that I had to survive long enough to not let my family down, I went from worsening my problem, suffering as victim of it, to being concerned about surviving.

When I entered my home laughing, I had recovered enough to talk with my family not as a victim or survivor but as someone intent on recovering and just maybe, thriving through this terrible time in my life. I was still dying, but I felt more resilient and alive than before I had begun my walk. Something about the insistence of spring and the realities, responsibilities, and challenges of living in the often absurd world as represented by the IRS letter seemed to boost my psychological immune system.

Crisis coping is circular, not linear or hierarchical. Like other thrivers I have interviewed, I would recycle countless times through the kindling, suffering, surviving, recovery, and thriving phases of coping with my trauma, but I made up my mind to keep the general trajectory of my consciousness spiraling upward. One reason for my awakening was the power of the first of the four general characteristics of thriving to be discussed in this Thriver's Manual, our psychological immune system's capacity to keep us mentally hardy at life's most difficult times.

Stress Kills—But Not Always

Hardiness is a matter of consciousness. It's how we elect to process what happens to us. It is not the result of good luck or strong genes but of learning how to assign our own meaning to whatever happens to us. Put simply, hardiness is making up your mind to figure out ways to thrive through stress.

Suzanne Ouellette Kobasa has spent years studying the effects of stress. At a time when her colleagues were identifying stress as a key agent in disease, she was among the first to look at what Louis Pasteur called the terrain. She did not accept the idea the stress invariably makes us sick, and suggested that how we thought about life and its challenges was as important as what happened to us. She thought that a civilization smart enough to create the complex world that stresses us so must have people smart enough to deal with the stress in a life-enhancing way.

In a series of groundbreaking studies conducted in the mid 1970s that helped establish the new field of positive psychology, Kobasa and her colleagues at the University of Chicago first presented their concept of hardiness. At a time when so many of her pathogenically oriented colleagues were proving again and again how vulnerable we are to the pressures in our lives, she was studying our natural capacity to thrive because of them.

Kobasa defines hardiness as "a set of beliefs about oneself, the world, and how they interact. It takes shape as a sense of personal commitment to what you are doing, a sense of control over your life, and a feeling of challenge."[1] These three C's of commitment, control, and challenge have been known for years by researchers in positive psychology, but in the context of human thriving, they represent much more than a simplistic formula for coping with stress. They serve as a template for a highly adaptive and hardy consciousness.

I went through the "three C's of hardiness" several times during my bout with cancer, and I learned that the hardiness of the thriving response is not a goal but a lifelong process. Our hardiness cannot be judged based on conquering a problem or surviving a serious illness. It is most accurately viewed as what we choose to put on our minds when we are going through adversity.

Sometimes I saw my pain as a challenge, but I would often relapse, trying to bear it or even feeling like surrendering to it by dying just to escape it. I remained committed not just to staying alive but also to my family and to continuing to learn through my experience. Sometimes when I was at my physically weakest, that commitment wavered and the mental effort did not seem worth it. There were times that I felt in control of my destiny, but other times I felt totally victimized and helpless.

I learned through the evolving and continuing process of hardiness that, if we are patient, remain engaged with our adversity no matter how tempting it is to give in, and remember that the meaning we give to what is happening to us is the fuel for our psychological immune system, that system seldom fails us.

A Hardiness Imprint

One of my thriving patients was diagnosed with leukemia. She described herself as having been a very "resilient and hardy person," but she was having trouble dealing with the stressful ups and downs of her physical and mental condition. She came to our clinic for help for what she called her "terrible mood swings in reaction to the good news and bad news times." The course of leukemia can be charted by counting the patient's red blood cells. The more red blood cells, the more vigorously the body is fighting against the cancer. Her treatment took place over several years, and she had finally become extremely frightened and depressed by the swings in her blood count. She said, "I'm terrorized every time the doctor's office calls. I feel totally out of control. I vacillate from thinking I'm going to die to thinking that I'm going to live, but the swings are exhausting me. I've got to get some control over this because it's ruining whatever life I have left."

The words of this cancer patient reflect her innate mental hardiness. Instead of surrendering to whatever prognosis was given her and remaining captive to her latest laboratory results, she was seeking ways to control her situation. I discussed with her the hardiness research from positive psychology, and we looked together for examples in her life when she had felt the commitment, challenge, and control she now longed for.

In working with patients to awaken their natural resilience, I have found it helpful for them to match the research on hardiness with their own "hardiness memory imprint," a time in their lives where they or someone close to them seemed to have experienced Kobasa's three C's of hardiness. After thinking awhile, she said, "I guess the closest I can come to being hardy was when my husband cheated on me and left me and the kids. I was devastated, but something in me kept me going. I guess I did it for the kids. I was really committed to remaining a good parent for them. After feeling depressed, I sort of got pissed off and took what happened to me as a challenge to be a great parent and have a good life despite what happened. I remember feeling getting back in control again. It wasn't easy, but we made it."

I asked her to reflect back on what she had just told me and to try to identify the catalyst, the stimulus that would change her from reacting and surviving to a more hardy orientation to her life. Without pause, she said, "It was always for the kids. No doubt about it, but they're pretty much grown up now and they don't need me like they did before." I didn't respond and just waited for her to reconsider what she had just said. "Oh, I get it," she said smiling. "I guess you think I should be thinking about the kids and their welfare." My answer surprised her.

"No, not really," I said. "I think you will find it helpful to reflect on how you felt at the times when you were the hardiest, and for you it seemed to be when you thought about your children and their needs. To remain hardy through the ups and downs of your cancer, you will have to trust in your psychological immune system. To help it along, you will have to remember how you felt, what you were thinking, and the meanings of life that tended to make you feel the hardiest. Don't think about events or other people, think about how you were thinking at times when you felt your hardiest."

As I continued my invitation to find her hardiness imprint, she said, "That's tough, because I'm an up and down kind of gal. I'm hardy one day and weak the next." I answered, "Thriving is a little like riding a roller coaster. You first have to make up your mind to get on for the ride, and once you do you must stay on and ride the ups and downs. Don't get down on yourself at the down times. Go ahead and be sad and worried, but remember that your psychological immune system will see to it that you will always have your up times.

"Thriving is learning through hardship and not necessarily always overcoming it. It's not always getting better but always doing better no matter what happens. Your kids mattered most to you when things were the toughest for you, so you found your hardiness by thinking like a loving parent. That was where you found hardiness and your sense of commitment, challenge, and your desire to take control. Maybe they need you in a different way now, maybe someone else needs you, or maybe you have different needs. Maybe the meaning you gave to your life then has changed, but the point is to look back at how you felt when you felt hardy and ready to deal with your problem. Try to retrieve that feeling now, reflect on it, and let it come back to you as it did years ago. Your hardiness is still within you."

We talked for several more minutes and after a long, quiet pause she suddenly exclaimed, "I need me! I know the kids still love me, my husband needs me, but I need me. I missed out on a lot and I want to experience more of life. I want to commit to holding on to my life. I want to beat this thing for as long as I can and I want to be in control, not just reacting to the latest blood test. I want to be hardy for me for a change."

I suggested to her that we conduct an experiment to see how her hardiness was progressing. I asked if she would agree to have her blood test results sent to me at the clinic over the next year. I suggested that instead of just receiving the results, I would talk with her oncologist and call her when the results came. Instead of giving her the count, I would first ask her to guess at it. I would ask how she was doing on the three Cs of commitment, challenge, and control. She answered, "That's a great idea, but if I'm going to be the one in control, I think I should get the results, not open them, call you and make my guess and then talk about them." Her hardiness was already showing, and we agreed on her terms.

Over the next several years, her medical test results varied greatly. Her guesses were almost always accurate, and she said she could correlate them with the degree to which she "felt hardy." She said she was "more right on" when she could construe what was happening to her to create a sense of challenge, commitment and control. Her second marriage had also failed and during that time, her red blood cell count went significantly down. When she rebounded and began a new career as a legal assistant, her count went up. Then something surprising happened.

Her oldest daughter was diagnosed with breast cancer and her own blood count went significantly up. I asked why she thought this was the case when the stress of the news of her daughter's illness had been so devastating for her. She answered immediately, "That's a no-brainer. When Sally found out about her breast cancer, I went right into my hardiness mode. I wasn't going to let it take her. I was committed to helping her and we worked together to take control of her treatment. We called around the country for the best advice and looked into alternative treatments. I never felt sadder, but I never felt stronger."

As of this writing, my patient is still doing fine and her leukemia has remained in remission. After three years, her blood count has stabilized within a more narrow range. No doubt good medical care, a skilled and sensitive oncologist willing to go along with our plan, strong genes, and just plain good luck played a role in her health, but the immune system is also enhanced by the hardiness component of thriving.

The Hardiness of Job

Hardiness does not mean being emotionally perfect and balanced at all times. Being hardy offers no guarantee of freedom from suffering. Hardy people can have very difficult lives, but they seem to find the patience to be able to take their time to find meaning and a source of growth through their stress regardless of the degree of their adversity. Hardiness is a way of thinking about life, not an impermeable emotional state guaranteeing a stress-free life.

In Judeo-Christian thinking, the story of Job teaches lessons about hardiness. Job was leading a healthy, wonderful, bountiful life—then suddenly, everything changed. Job went from being on top of the world to suffering from a painful, disfiguring disease. His wealth quickly evaporated and worst of all, he lost his seven sons. Through it all, however, his enduring patience and unshakable faith carried him through. Nothing that happened to him changed how hardy he was or how he thought about the meaning of life. Perhaps the patience of Job could also be seen as the hardiness of Job.

One of my hardy and thriving patients was a highly successful investment banker. He owned homes in three countries and a yacht, and enjoyed perfect health. He woke up one morning with no feeling on his left side, and today is lucky to be alive. He suffered a severe stroke that makes it difficult for him to walk, and his speech is slow and labored. He heard my lecture about the lessons from the story of Job as they relate to remaining hardy and resilient.

He said, "It's funny that Job and the word 'job' are spelled the same. You have to realize that life is always a job even when it seems so easy. I try now never to take the 'bear market' times in my life for granted. That's when you have to heavily invest your emotional capital and build up your spiritual equity. It's the same principle as the stock market. It's easy when it's up. The challenge and the even the fun for me is when it was down. That's when what you call hardiness is really tested."

Another of my hardy patients illustrates the many faces of hardiness. She experienced three bouts of breast cancer. She was far from the quiet, reserved person we might think of as having the patience of Job. She had been a highly aggressive, ornery, competitive, cynical woman who considered her success as a software salesperson to be due to her drive and what she called her "take no prisoners" attitude. I spoke with her many times during her various treatments, and she knew I was researching a book on the hardiness and the thriving capacity of the human spirit. She had struggled through years of chemotherapy and surgeries, and was known as one of the most difficult patients on the cancer unit, earning the nickname "Ms. Grinch."

She wanted me to be sure I included her view of thriving and hardiness in my book. In her typical challenging way, she said, "I'll bet you'll never put my words in there. You probably want stories of people who were strong and hardy souls transformed by their cancer to become kinder, more loving people who cherish every moment. Well, that's crap. I really hate those stories of the ungrateful, mean person who got cancer, survived, and was transformed to became a whole new person who loved every moment of living. I don't buy it. I'm exactly the same pain in the ass I was before I had cancer. I wasn't transformed by it, I transformed it.

"Cancer didn't change my life. I was strong enough to go through it and stay who I am and see life my way. I certainly didn't embrace my cancer. I hated it. I was a miserable person when I hurt. I'll never be one of those quiet, gentle people strumming their guitar and singing while they die. I'm going to shout, scream, and holler. It's my death. I'll die my way, thank you. I'll bet you'll never write that a very hardy person can be bitchy and not just blissful. I don't have the patience of Job, but I've got his guts."

I understood this uniquely hardy woman's views very well. When I almost died from cancer, I never felt I became a "whole new person" because of my experience. Any hardiness I showed was related to my efforts to try to remain the same person I had always been and protecting the continuity of my identity. I struggled to remain who I was and to keep finding meaning in life my way through my eyes, and I refused to let cancer dominate my consciousness.

I saw many other cancer patients doing the same thing, and I do not remember seeing any who said they were completely transformed by their suffering. They learned more about themselves because of it, but hardiness is not about abandoning an old identity for a new one. It is maintaining a consistent sense of who we are no matter what happens to us. As one of my fellow patients said, "I don't want to be transformed by my cancer. I want to stay who I've always been despite my cancer."

Thriver's Intolerance

Another important point about hardiness became clear as I talked to hundreds of thrivers. Persons who have grown through severe trauma, particularly serial trauma, often feel and occasionally show impatience with those who fail to recognize their own hardiness. The more severe and repeated their traumas, the more impatient and even intolerant these thrivers seem to become with those who appear to be taking their good luck for granted. They can become very impatient with persons, like the woman distressed in her search for chicken broth, who complain about comparatively small concerns.

One of my patients had gone through a series of miscarriages. She was emotionally crushed when she was eventually told she would never be able to carry a child to term. She had grown stronger through each disappointment and even at the news of her sterility, but said, "I can't help myself. If I hear another woman complaining about their kids, I'm going to throw up. I'd give anything to have the problems they think they have."

Another one of my hardy patients described her increasing intolerance for those who seem to take their good fortune for granted. She was a Vietnamese woman who had lost her daughter, her son-in-law, and their three children in one terrible night. Her son-in-law had worked late on Christmas Eve and was robbed and murdered while walking home to celebrate Christmas with his young family. The three robbers took his keys and, using his driver's license to find his address, went to his home, raped and killed his wife, and murdered their three children. They opened and stole the Christmas gifts and, before they left, sat down to eat the family's holiday dinner. This frail old woman who barely spoke English had received a call on Christmas Eve that is almost beyond comprehension in its horror. She had already suffered terribly for years in her own homeland, helped her family build a new and successful life in America, and then lost everyone she loved.

Despite her suffering, the quiet Vietnamese woman still remained calm, laughed often, and showed the same kind of thriving spirit I had seen in Izzie. I never saw her angry or impatient until one evening when a fellow patient in the waiting room had been crying and complaining about his wife, their pending divorce, and how his wife had failed to understand his needs and love him the way he wanted to be loved. By the time she came into my office, she was shaking and I could see rage in her eyes. "That terrible man," she said. "I hate him. He is wasting his wonderful life. He has healthy children, a chance at grandchildren, and still he complains. Most of his problems are of his own making, yet he is crying out there as hard as I cried when they killed my family. It raises such anger in my heart that I do not want there, but it is there. He is so weak with no reason."

I told thrivers like the woman above that some discomfort with those who have not yet realized their thriveability seems to be a side effect of stress-induced awakening to a more authentic kind of life full of appreciation for those things so many others may take for granted. Eventually our thriving can be stopped if we fail to realize that thriving is like any other human talent. Some realize, treasure, and develop it, while others may never fully realize they have it. To keep enhancing our thriveability, we must avoid as much as possible getting into a mental thriving contest. We maintain our own thriving momentum and hardiness if we use what seems to be the unappreciative nature of others to remind us to appreciate our lives even more. If we hope to thrive, we also must thrive through our experiences with those who don't.

Based on my interviews with those who have known severe tragedy, I have detected various levels of underlying resentment for those who fail to relish their lives. I try to help them realize their anger and see that suffering is always relative. I explain that hardiness cannot be measured by the magnitude of the trauma but by the content of one's consciousness. I warn them that their hardiness can help diminish anger's sometimes subtle but still damaging effects on both their physiological and psychological immune systems, but that their lingering resentment can eventually weaken their own psychoimmunity.

To mistake hardiness for the absence of negative feelings or resentment is to fail to appreciate the unique kind of strength that comes with hardiness. One of my fellow cancer patients was an often gruff former police officer. Even though he did not survive his cancer, he showed the sense of challenge, commitment, and control of hardiness throughout his last days. He said, "I think I kind of get a kick out of getting pissed off at the doctors around here. I feel in some ways better at living my life than they are. The difference between me and them is that I know I'm dying and they don't know they're barely alive. They are so consumed with their little battles and bullshit that they're forgetting to live. I'm in the battle for my life and they're busy battling their lives. As weak and sick as I am, I feel so much stronger than they are."

Stress Buffers

Although a good attitude cannot turn water to wine, research in the hardiness component of thriving shows that there is a "stress-buffering effect" experienced by those who assign meaning to their lives from the perspective of Kobasa's hardiness concepts of a sense of challenge, commitment, and control. This research shows that it is how we construe stressful situations that creates significant protection against the impact of stress on our physical health.[2] Here are just some of the findings about stress buffering.

A study of 157 attorneys showed no correlation between stressful life events and physical illness. It found instead a powerful correlation between physical health and attitudes and beliefs that reflected the hardy perspective in assigning meaning to life's challenges. Another positive psychology study looked at 100 gynecology outpatients who reported a significant amount of stress in their lives. As pathogenic psychology would expect, 60 of the women became sick, but positive psychology researchers were interested in the 40 percent who remained healthy. The women who stayed well showed Kobasa's hardiness traits of being mentally challenged, committed, and in control.

In another positive psychology study of hardiness, a group of 259 executives was followed for five years. Those who possessed the hardiness triad had stronger physical immune systems and had only half of the illness experienced by the executives who did not have these traits.[3]

What is the nature of a hardy consciousness? How does it help buffer us against the toxicity of our increasingly stressful lives? How do the hardy think that allows them to be so resilient and even thrive? The answers to these questions are the focus of the remainder of this chapter.

The Nature of Hardiness

Here is a list of the hardiness factors that emerge from a review of the studies of hardy people and my own interviews of thrivers who showed Kobasa's hardiness factors. Different researchers in positive psychology assign different names to these factors, but their findings confirm a very similar configuration of a hardy consciousness.

• *A Nonparental Hardiness Role Model:* Most hardy people who manage to thrive through adversity report having one very influential adult in their lives who provided a role model of hardiness. While it is obvious that having one or two hardy parents is a big advantage when it comes to being a hardy adult, research also shows that a nonparental, especially admired adult is also important. It seems that hardiness can be learned.

The invincible Kauai children you read about in part 1 almost always seemed to have had a strong adult figure other than a parent who they felt was important to their development. Psychologist Ann Masten studied more than 200 adults who showed the hardiness component of thriving. She reports that these thrivers found their inner resilience through bonds they had developed with a neighbor, family friend, teacher, minister, or other respected adult other than their parents.[4] As you consider your own hardiness factor, reflect back on the one important adult in your life other than your parents who seemed to influence your explanatory style and may have helped set your psychological trajectory upward.

• *Cautious Optimism:* Research on hardiness indicates that being a consistently upbeat and always cheerful optimist is not a necessary part of hardiness. Being hardy is not the same as being foolhardy. In fact, studies show that persistently highly cheerful, upbeat, optimistic children tend to die younger than their more timid, reserved, pessimistic peers. It may be that their excessive optimism exposes them to taking unrealistic risks that their more cautiously optimistic peers avoid.

You will read more in chapter 12 about the nature of a thriver's kind of true adaptive optimism, but hardiness does not always mean having an unqualified positive attitude. Cautious, concerned, reluctant, careful, and even frightened people can be mentally hardy, too. More important for hardiness is being able to construe life events from a perspective of the three C's of challenge, commitment, and control.[5]

• *Problem-Commitment:* Hardy people show persistent curiosity and involvement in whatever happens to them. Above all, they remain mentally and emotionally engaged in their problems and seldom throw in the towel. If they do, they've usually done a lot of thinking about it first and have construed their situation in such a way that surrender become a constructive way of dealing with their problem. For the hardy, a crisis is like being assigned very difficult but fascinating and challenging homework. Instead of complaining about it, they get right to work. Instead of saying, "Now look what I have to try to do," they say, "Look what I'm getting the chance to try." They may not like it, but they stick with it and do it. The less hardy look for excuses to get out of their assigned challenge or blame the people or events that gave them their assignment for its excessive and unfair level of difficulty. Hardiness is taking life's assignments seriously and responsibly, remaining absorbed in one's problems, and as a result, eventually becoming more absorbed in life in general.

• *Social Commitment:* When trauma strikes, hardy people maintain a deep, abiding commitment to family and friends. Those who fail to show the hardiness necessary for thriving often withdraw from family members just when they need them the most. Their kindling makes it difficult for them to capitalize on the thriving resources within their support system, but hardy thinkers trust in and value those around them.

- *Challenge:* Hardy people are in a constant state of discovery. They seem to have a drive to live to the fullest tempered by a deep sense of commitment to a goal in life much greater than an individual objective. They remain challenged by their problems and constantly look for new ways to comprehend and assign meaning to whatever happens to them. They never forget that they can never really thrive alone and that their goals are inextricably related to the lives of others. Whether by an enduring love, altruistic caring for others, or as in Beethoven's case through the sharing of one's talents and gifts, hardy people are far more than rugged individualists. Their thriving always seems to involve some way to figure out a strategy that allows them an enhanced connection with others and the world.

- *Control:* Hardy people believe they can eventually come up with a way of figuring their way through their adversity. Because they retain control of the content of their consciousness and are continually expanding and modifying their explanatory system, they feel emotionally and mentally competent to handle any problem.

- *Knowing When to Give Up Control:* Hardy people are also enlightened quitters. They know when no amount of thinking, feeling, and doing will change the course of events or improve their situation or feelings. They are able to focus on what they can control, ignore and intentionally deny the rest, and move on to other goals. They are like a person in a tug-of-war who seems to know when and how hard to struggle and pull and just when to let go to prevent unproductive and damaging straining.

   They are not bound by the Western world's negative view of giving up. They know that strength is not always about overcoming, but is sometimes about allowing oneself to be overcome. They know that strength is not always measured by victory over the outside world, but sometimes by changes in our inside world. They know that elective disengagement and moving on are also a form of strength. As psychologists Charles S. Carver and Michael R. Scheier point out based on their study of control and strength, the hardy know that persevering can turn out to be glorious stupidity and that giving up at the wrong time can turn out to be a tragic loss. They have learned that choosing wisely between these options is also an important human strength.[6]

Learning to Be Hardy

It may be that some of us are born hardier than others, but all of us can learn to be hardy. We don't have to go through the tribulations of the thrivers you have read about in order to begin thinking about our lives from their perspective of challenge, commitment, and control.

In their study of the invincible children of Kauai, researchers Werner and Smith found that these thriving young people showed signs of a hardy personality from the time of their birth and that they retained that hardiness into adulthood.[7] Summarizing the results of their Kauai study of hardy children, Werner and Smith wrote, "There seems to be a group of children who temperamentally and probably constitutionally have a better chance of making lemonade out of lemons."[8] But they also point out that even those children who did not seem to show early signs of emotional hardiness still managed to rally later in their lives. Over the years, they too seemed to have learned some of the hardiness skills of their more naturally hardy peers.

The good news is that all of us can learn to make lemonade from lemons. We can copy the thinking styles of the thrivers for whom hardiness seems to come more naturally. By reflecting on the above profile of hardiness, we can find guides for our own life that help us see challenges where others see hassles. We can try to remain committed, even when so much seems to be distracting us from our own way of finding meaning in our lives. We can try to exert control when we can, and learn to gracefully give in and go with the flow when we can't.

Hardiness is a form of mental resilience. Psychologist Ann S. Masten defines resilience as "a class of phenomena characterized by good outcome in spite of serious threat to adaptation or development."[9] I suggest that it is also a highly creative kind of consciousness that allows us to have good outcomes in life no matter what phenomena impinge upon it. Thrivers have good outcomes in their lives because they are good at construing crises in such a way that they focus on what they are already good at doing instead of what they cannot do. All of us can learn from that creative "lemonade-making" mentality so that we can thrive in our daily life regardless of how stressful it is.

Because they have such adaptive explanatory systems, thrivers tend to be good at intrapersonal comparative thinking. They are able to reflect upon their own lives, look for case scenarios that were even worse than their current problem and through which they managed to grow, and gain confidence through the comparison that they will be up to their current challenge. If they begin telling themselves that they can't possibly deal with their current problem, they are good at disputing their own view of their ability. As if they were arguing with another person telling them that they can't possibly succeed, they are able to argue themselves out of their pessimism. By doing so, they are able to find some comparative advantage, however small it may be, in their current situation.

As opposed to the "this is the worst thing possible" orientation of non-thrivers, the hardiers' "it could be so much worse" way of construing events in their own lives helps them remain mentally in the game and avoid what psychologists call catastrophizing. One of my patients was a high school journalism teacher. She said, "You know that the word 'hale' means free of illness or disease. I've been sick for most my life and I can barely walk, but I've taken it all in stride, if you will excuse the pun. I've learned that you don't have to be hale to be hardy."

Another one of the thrivers I interviewed was a mentally impaired young man who had been blinded by scalding oil splashed into his eyes while working at a fast-food restaurant. His statement captures the creativity of consciousness that underlies Kobasa's concept of hardiness. He said, "I know I look terrible, but I think it could have been much worse. It could have killed me, you know. It's kind of funny how becoming blind helps me look at life kind of different. Do you get it? I look different now because my eyes will not see for me anymore. I was always way better with my hands than my brain anyway. I can see with them, you know. I have very good fingers that make very good eyes. I can read what other people cannot read, so maybe I'm smarter than a lot of people know. Do your fingers see? I bet they don't, but if I learned to see with mine, I bet you could too. You would if someone splashed hot oil in your eyes, so why don't you try anyway?"

This very smart retarded man's words summarize the idea of the first component of thriving, a hardy explanatory style. His encouragement to keep trying anyway is the essence of hardiness.

10 Happiness for the Sad Times

Happiness: "A psychological construct the meaning of which everybody knows but the definition of which nobody can give."

—*H. M. Jones*[1]

Going with the Flow

Seriously ill, weak, and totally deaf, Beethoven stood with his eyes closed, conducting his "Ode to Joy." He was so caught up in the flow of conducting an orchestra and chorus he could not hear that he had lost all sense of self, time, and place. He kept on flailing his arms even after his Ninth Symphony had ended and the musicians finished playing. He was so happy and engrossed in what he was doing that a singer had to turn him toward his audience to see the applause and cheering.

For more than two decades, psychologist Mihaly Csikszentmihalyi has been studying what it is that causes people like Beethoven to be able to become so totally and joyfully involved in their lives even when their lives are full of challenges. Csikszentmihalyi was one of the first researchers to focus on optimum human functioning and to study why one of our happiest times is when we get so into the flow of living that we lose all sense of the problems in our lives.

Formerly professor and chairman of the Department of Psychology at the University of Chicago and now at Claremont Graduate University, Csikszentmihalyi is one of the most articulate and respected advocates for the emerging field of positive psychology. Along with Suzanne Ouellette Kobasa and Drs.

Antonovsky and Seligman, whose work you will read about in the following two chapters, he is considered by many psychologists to be a founder of the field of positive psychology.

Csikszentmihalyi is interested in what makes one moment seem so much more pleasurable than another and how despite the stresses of life, there are those who find happiness in their daily living. His work explores the second component of thriving, how to make ourselves happy no matter how hard life is on us. He sees a primary source of happiness to be related to what he calls flow, a state of concentration so focused that it amounts to absolute absorption in whatever we are doing. His work shows that what people really mean when they say they are happy is that they are in the state of flow similar to Beethoven's total involvement in his symphony.

My studies of thrivers indicate that their happiness despite their pain relates to their ability to concentrate and be consciously creative enough to become lost in the present joy of being alive. While their circumstances may be miserable, the joyful way in which they construe their world helps them thrive. As Csikszentmihalyi's research shows, thrivers' happiness is not dependent on external factors or life circumstances alone. It derives from their chosen state of consciousness and ability to cheer themselves up when things are looking down.

Beethoven showed all the characteristics of someone who could enter a state of flowing. His composing of his music was his form of a highly creative consciousness that allowed him to construe whatever happened to him in such a way that he could become totally unaware of himself and his problems. He wrote to a friend, "I live only in music, frequently working on three or four pieces simultaneously." His deep despair over losing his hearing seemed to be overwhelmed by his ability to get into the flow, to find total consuming happiness in his creative work.

Even in the early stages of hearing loss and when his career as a virtuoso pianist was ending, Beethoven wrote to another friend (and this quote is worth seeing again), "You must think of me as being as happy as it is possible to be on this earth— not unhappy." Why is it that thrivers like Beethoven who suffer so deeply are able to make themselves as happy as their lives are hard? The answer seems to be their capacity to flow joyfully rather than flail desperately at times of severe challenge.

Lessons from Lincoln, Izzie, Mosha, and Other Happy Souls

Another historical figure known for his ability to find happiness through his misery was Abraham Lincoln. As you have read, he endured a series of traumas in his life and experienced repeated bouts of depression and melancholy, yet he was known for maintaining his sense of humor, joking, and easy laughter. He wrote, "With the strain that is on me night and day, if I did not laugh, I should die."[2] Beethoven, Lincoln, and thrivers like Izzie and Mosha are distinguishable by their ability to think themselves happy even through an often terribly sad life. In fact, one of the most striking characteristics of thrivers is their ability to cheer themselves up.

Psychology has long assumed that happiness is a result of doing and feeling well, but positive psychology suggests another possibility: positive emotions themselves may come first and lead to feelings of flourishing. We may be happy when we feel that our lives are going well, but research now shows that we also feel happy because we first assign some positive, growth-oriented meaning to whatever happens to us. In terms of thriving, happiness is as much a means as an end.

No matter the event, construing it in a positive and happy light can lead to personal growth. Positive psychology researcher Barbara L. Fredrickson wrote, "The take-home message is that positive emotions are worth cultivating, not just as end states in themselves but also as a means to achieving psychological growth and improved well-being over time."[3] Fredrickson's research indicates that the experience of positive emotions broadens our consciousness and allows us to consider a wider set of meanings in life, expanding what she calls our "momentary thought-action repertoires [explanatory styles or creative consciousness]."[4] Beginning by finding some degree of happiness independent of our circumstances helps build what Fredrickson describes as our "enduring personal resources" and what I am calling the thriving response. As Izzie stated, "If you want to be happier, you have to begin by telling yourself happier stories about your life. You can't wait for them to happen to you."

Fredrickson calls her theory of happiness the "broaden-and-build" model, and it is central to understanding the happiness component of thriving. Her theory suggests that happiness is much more than a nice way to feel as a result of hard work or good fortune. Based on her research, happiness and its associated emotions of joy, interest, contentment, pride, and love are not just the result of a thriving orientation. They are the building blocks of it.

Thrivers are happy people not just by nature or luck of the draw. In fact, most of the thrivers I interviewed were distinguishable by the degree of their misfortune. They intentionally sought to make themselves happy by construing these negative events in the most positive light possible. Whether by enlightened denial, self-delusion, enlightened quitting, compartmentalization, or even temporary dissociation and getting lost in the flow, they managed to make themselves reasonably happy because they reasoned their lives that way. They seemed able to intentionally elevate their spirits and emotions.

Another thriver was a nine-year-old boy with a very serious physical immune disorder and diabetes. He was constantly sick and had to be tutored at home. He longed for friends and social contact, but was forced to spend much of his time either alone or with his single mother when she returned from work. Prospects for a long life for him were slim, but I never saw him when he did not seem happier than many of the people I saw in the cars next to me in traffic jams.

He described the "happiness first" principle when he said, "I don't see anybody around me who's going to make me happy. They seem sad when they see how I am. If I'm going to be happy, I have to do it. If I want to have a happy life, I will have to make it myself. All I have to do to make myself happy is watch Umu [the family golden retriever]. She knows how to make herself happy. She'll just suddenly get up and go get a toy. For her own dog reasons, she'll throw it all around, play with it, and wag her tail like crazy. No one has to play with her. Sometimes, she just starts wagging her tail like she gave herself a happy thought. Mom says she's a natural clown who is constantly entertaining herself, and that's what I try to do."

The Joy of an "Awe-Full" Life

We can't have a wonderful life if we lose our sense of wonder for life. We can't thrive if we allow life to lead us and become circumstantially delight dependent. Thrivers certainly don't show the happiness they do because they have lucked out and had a wonderful life. They make their lives wonderful because they have the ability to flow with their lives and construe simple but enduring happiness in their lives irrespective of what happens to them. I believe that this kind of flowing explains why I discovered so many happy people busy trying to heal on the cancer unit with me.

I often tell people that I have had an "awe-full" life. I explain that my suffering and pain have resulted in my finding more awe for living, and one way other thrivers and I do that is by being constantly on the lookout for ludicrous, silly, and funny aspects of daily life. The IRS audit letter I received that you read about in chapter 9 and its ironic juxtaposition with the diagnosis of my cancer seemed to strike a surprise blow directly to my funny bone. I had been so consumed with my fear and so distracted by my pain that I almost missed all the signals around me that should have made my life "awe-full."

I was laughing when one of my colleagues called to offer his sympathy for my cancer. When I told him about the IRS letter, he asked, "This has be the worst time for this to happen to you. How can you find an IRS audit funny, particularly now?" I answered, "I think this is perfect timing. I needed something to jar me out of my lethargic surrender. They say the only certain things in life are death and taxes, so I was hit with both at once on the same day. That's a real tragedy, but it's also really comical if you stop and think of the irony of the whole thing."

To Die Laughing

During my bone marrow transplant, visitors and medical students new to the cancer unit would often ask how the other cancer patients and I could laugh when things seemed so dismal for us. While going through my cancer, I published a book titled *Super Joy* and later released an audiotape series titled *The Pleasure Principle*. Both of these works described the role of humor and happiness in healing, but a pathologically oriented doctor I call a "pathogenisist" asked me, "How could someone going through what you were going through and so near death come out with such joyful material? My answer was, "I was just trying to copy Beethoven." One of my favorite "mirth mantras" during my cancer was, "If you don't keep your sense of humor, you're left only with your sense of horror. Silliness softens suffering." If you are going to thrive, there are two things you should never lose: your temper and your sense of humor.

For the last few days before her death, a young woman suffering from pancreatic cancer occupied the room next to mine on the oncology unit. I would listen late at night for Anne's unique and contagious giggle. I knew she had died when, just before sunrise one morning, the laughter suddenly stopped. It seemed as if someone had unplugged a wonderful music that resonated through the hospital walls. Every morning was a cause for celebration for those of us facing death, a sign that we were given at least one more beginning, but this morning was silent and sad without the sound of Anne's laughter.

Anne had watched hours of tapes of comedians that her husband had made for her, and I could hear her laughing most of the day and late into the night. I noticed that nurses coming from her room to mine would almost always have a smile on their faces. On my first visit to Anne's room, she saw me looking at her high stack of videotapes. "Those are my pain killers," she said. "When I laugh, my pain is much less. You know what people say when they are laughing really hard, 'Stop it. You're killing me'? Well, for me, it's the reverse. If I stop laughing, it will kill me. The pain is much worse when I'm not laughing." Research in positive psychology clearly shows that a hardy laugh does have pain-reducing and immune-enhancing capacities.

A few hours after Anne's laughter had stopped, one of the nurses came to my room with tears in her eyes. "Anne died early this morning," she said, busying herself by moving things around in my room in an effort to disguise her crying. "I swear that woman was invincible. She kept laughing up to the end. She really did die laughing. Just thinking about that goofy laugh of hers makes me smile again. I wish we had a tape of it to play to remind us of how it lightened the hearts that always seem so heavy around here."

A "Hardy" Laugh

When we refer to a "hardy laugh," we are accurately describing Kobasa's concept of hardiness and Csikszentmihalyi's idea of flow. Perhaps no other activity helps us lose our sense of self and awareness of our stress than a good, long guffaw. We can't laugh very hard for very long and still maintain a sense of time, place, and person. When we laugh really hard, we often say that we "lose it." What is lost is our sense of the press of outside demands. What is gained for at least a while is a sense of total joyful involvement in the present moment. We stop fighting, cease our attempts to flee, and start flowing.

When we laugh, the brain releases its natural opiates called endorphins, and as a result, our pain can be reduced.[5] Laughter also raises our pain threshold. Research subjects listening to comedienne Lily Tomlin joking about Alexander Graham Bell (her "one ringy dingy, two ringy dingy" comedy skit) showed significantly less sensitivity to pain than those who listened to a dull lecture.[6]

There is new evidence from positive psychology that our physiological immune system is also enhanced by laughter. Research subjects who watched a videotape of comedian Richard Pryor experienced an increase in the levels of the antibodies in their saliva that help the body fight off colds and other infections.[7] There is no doubt that, from a purely physical point of view, laughter exerts an anabolic or positive healing influence at any time in our lives, but it is being able to laugh easily at tough times that is most significant in understanding the thriving response.

Psychologist Lee S. Berk's research shows that the stress-induced hormone cortisol (a catabolic hormone) is significantly reduced when we feel very happy and laugh. As you learned in chapter 7, cortisol is released when we are in the catabolic, or "burning energy," state, and it has an immune-suppressing effect. Berk's research shows that laughter results in an increase of S-IgA (salivary immunoglobulin A), which helps fight infection. It also shows that there is an increase in our physiological immune system's natural killer cells that seek out and destroy abnormal cells and that these increases persist for a period of time after a hardy laugh. The level of plasma cytokine gamma interferon, another anabolic substance that strengthens our immune system, doubles when we laugh long and hard, and the increase lasts well into the next day.[8] If a single pill were discovered that could accomplish all these miraculous effects, it would be headline news.

Nine-year-old Patsy, another neighbor of mine in the bone marrow transplant unit, laughed and giggled every day. She showed me a get-well card someone had sent her that had a picture of a fairy flying over treetops. Inside, it said, "Lighten up. Fairies can fly because they are light-hearted." When we manage to "lighten up" and find some source of happiness at the stressful times in our lives, we also "lighten" our hearts. The relaxing, anabolic state of happiness and laughter helps prevent potential damage to the arteries that feed the heart and the heart muscle itself caused by the catabolic or "fight or flight" response.

Taking Tragedy Seriously but Lightly

Tragedy hits us hard, but a sense of humor can soften the blow. Hardiness, the first component of the thriving response, helps us deal mentally with our tragedies, but it is the second component of thriving, happiness, that helps us cope with it emotionally. Finding humor in trauma does not change the fact of the adversity or diminish its significance, but it can temporarily help us escape some of its pain and provide us time to find new meanings in whatever has disrupted our explanatory system.

Positive psychologist Dr. Joseph W. Meeker wrote, "When disruptions or threats to living processes occur, the comic way is to restore normalcy if possible."[9] In the easy times of our lives, comedy helps us find even more joy, but at the sad times it can also help us find at least a temporary sense of relief from the stress of our situation. When we keep our sense of humor when we suffer, we are also maintaining at least some sense of who we were before our trauma. Our laughter reflects how we see the world, and laughing when our world seems turned upside down is one way to hang on to that vision. It allows us to be able to lessen the immediate burden of our trauma by providing a less depressing context for what is happening to us until a newer, better, and perhaps more rational and adaptive meaning comes to mind.

Meeker wrote, "The comic way is not heroic or idealistic; rather, it is a strategy for survival."[10] By seeking humor, we are able to remain in charge rather than be victimized. Because we are setting the emotional tone of the event rather than just reacting to it, we are able to accept some of the unavoidable limitations imposed by our crisis. At least while we are looking for the comedy in what has happened, we are not consumed by looking at the negatives and not compelled to immediately transcend our problems.

Meeker pointed out, "Both tragedy and comedy arise from experience of misfortune."[11] Most tragedies portrayed on stage, in literature, or in the movies end with death. Tragic heroes and heroines almost always struggle valiantly yet fruitlessly against their problems and eventually succumb. They are very often "kindlers," unknowingly sabotaging themselves or victims and continuing to suffer no matter how hard they try to succeed.

On the other hand, most comedies end with some form of reconciliation. While tragic figures never seem to know when to quit, comic heroes usually end up giving in to those things they cannot change. They exert the thriver's kind of control that includes knowing when not to keep seeking it. At the end of a comedy, everyone seems somehow stronger, happier, and wiser after their crisis than before, and this is the ultimate definition of thriving.

Comic Contemplation

When we laugh in the face of adversity, it may appear that we are losing our minds. In fact, we are actually in the process of trying to make a new one. We are trying to construe what happened, and finding humor is one way to approach the problem. Humor doesn't require us to solve our problem. It gives us a moment of escape and sometimes offers creative if ridiculous ways to figure out what happened to us and why.

Joseph Meeker pointed out, "Comedy demonstrates that humans are durable, although they may be weak, stupid, and undignified."[12] Crises can cause us to feel vulnerable, dumb, and inappropriate in our reaction, but all of the thrivers I interviewed seemed able to use humor to help them flow through the worst times of their lives. It appeared to be their way of holding on to their identity and even mocking themselves and their situation long enough to hold it at arm's length, examine it, and begin to adjust their explanatory system.

Laughing in the face of tragedy does not diminish its agony or reflect a casual or cavalier reaction. It's not that we don't care that we are suffering, but that we are strong enough to keep laughing and to keep becoming more aware and alive because we are suffering. It is the result of a highly creative explanatory style that allows us to tell ourselves happy stories about our lives even when our lives aren't going so well.

Many people who approach adversity from the comic orientation do not necessarily laugh loud and hard. Instead, they reflect privately on what happens to them in a way that allows them to be free of endless fighting against their problems and more open to flowing with them. They may use sarcasm or quick wit, or just look at things from a silly point of view that brings a gentle smile to an otherwise tortured face.

To put hardiness, the first component of the thriving response, to work for us, we have to put our minds to it and learn to construe events in a challenging, committed, controlled way. To activate happiness as the second component of thriving, we have to be willing to comply with the common expression, "Just go with the flow."

Happiness is not an involuntary response. It is an intentional and conscious choice to frame events in our lives in a humorous light. To take the comic approach to crisis, we have to make the conscious choice to do so. We can't wait for someone to make us laugh, particularly at the most grim times. When it comes to thriving, it is less important that other people can make us laugh than that we can make ourselves laugh.

Taking an Oxygen Shower

If we are going to think clearly under stress, our brain needs all the fuel it can get, and oxygen is that fuel. When my cancer made me too weak to leave my bed, I began to notice what my wife referred to as my "occasional ins and outs." I wasn't getting up or exercising, and my blood oxygen level was measuring dangerously low. I would vacillate from being alert to distracted to almost oblivious to things and people around me. The room appeared to be getting darker and darker, even though the lights were on or the sun was shining through the window. I learned that I could brighten things up by smiling and laughing, because doing so "oxygenated" me.

Here's another simple science experiment you can try to see the effect of giving your brain an oxygen shower. When we smile and the facial muscles around our mouths contract, we experience an increase of blood flow to our brains. Put a wooden pencil between your teeth so that the ends touch each side of your mouth. Keep biting down as you continue to read and until you feel some discomfort in your facial muscles. You're probably more used to frowning, so your smile muscles will likely tire out quickly. After a few minutes of pencil biting, you will feel a slight warm sensation in your face and head, signifying that you have just poured an additional dose of oxygen into your brain to help you think a little clearer. It seems that one of the best ways to "clear our heads" might be to laugh our heads off.

In one of my simple science experiments, I had my psychology students bite down on a pencil as they wrote a one-page story. The next day, I asked them to write a story without the pencils in their mouths. When the class read their stories, they noted that the ones they had written while doing the pencil-induced smiling were generally happier and more upbeat than the nonpencil stories. I can't say the pencil-biting stories were any more well written, but the extra oxygen from forced smiling seemed to impact their explanatory style.

Mirth-itation

One definition of the word "silly" is "happy, blessed, innocent . . . needing compassion or sympathy."[13] When we are willing to be a little silly at times of adversity, we manage to some degree to diminish the importance and significance of our problems not only for us but for those who love and care for us. Our own laughter can be a powerful pain reducer for those who suffer with and for us. It can be a welcome signal that we are trying to thrive through our problems and an encouraging gift we can give even at our most frail and vulnerable moments.

After a very hard laugh that tenses our muscles and causes our body system to pulsate, we finally relax. I told my embarrassed nurses that the laughter they often heard on our cancer unit was our secret way of having sex. I told them that like sex, our laughter allowed us to get emotionally aroused, tense up, convulse in laugher, and then relax and sigh. When I told one of my nurses that I had figured out a way to have regular "laugh-gasms" on the oncology unit, she said, "Yes, but be very careful. Humor is a comically communicable condition."

Looking for humor when we are under stress can serve as a form of "mirth-itation." Just as meditation can free the mind of all consuming and distracting thoughts and allow an experience of total mental balance and focus, the kind of consciousness that helps us find the ludicrous and silly in adversity can help us change our mental gears and become more creative in our approach to dealing with our challenges.

Just as meditation allows us to free our minds from distraction, mirth-itation allows us to be free of the pressure of the moment so we can find the happiness, humor, and ability to laugh that allows us to temporarily forget our problems, our situation, and even ourselves. Just as we cannot effectively meditate and worry at the same time, it is also impossible to laugh and worry at the same time. We can, however, laugh and cry at the same time, so sadness does not prevent laughter. In fact, some of our healthiest laughing results in tears. Comedienne Lily Tomlin pointed out that when she laughs she sometimes cries, but that when she cries she doesn't laugh. She said she found value in the tears of laughter because it meant she was getting two benefits from one behavior.

How to Be a Gelontologist

The saying, "Laugh and the world laughs with you," reflects the fact that we are drawn to those who laugh easily and heartily. We are drawn not just to their laughter but also by our often unconscious interest and fascination with the point of view they have taken that is causing them to find humor where we may not yet see it. We wonder, "What is it that they see that makes them seem so happy? Maybe if I could see it, I'd be as happy as they seem to be." By finding some sense of happiness during the tough times in life, we are, as the definition of silly indicates, putting our troubles in new and creative perspectives. At the same time, we are acting in a way that attracts the social support we so desperately need when we are suffering. As a result, we can become twice-blessed.

Anne, the woman who watched the comedy tapes to decrease her pain, referred to the seductive nature of silliness. She said, "Do you notice how many more times nurses and doctors come to my room than most other rooms? I'm not really all that much sicker than the rest of you, but I think the silliness attracts them. They stay longer, too, because they start watching the tapes and laughing with me. Face it; most people aren't too comfortable with us dying folks. I really think they sometimes even hate us for our dying because it reminds them of their own death. Cancer repels, but happiness attracts." My own experience during my cancer supports Anne's view. I found sincere and soulful laughter to be the ultimate form of seduction.

Gelontology (from the Greek word for laughter, *gelos*) is the study of the salutary effects of laughter. Research in this important subfield of positive psychology indicates that we make our own happiness and we make ourselves laugh. We do so by construing or finding meaning in our lives and problems in a way that reflects not only our serious, rational adult approach to problems but also our inborn childlike playful thinking and pretending.

Anthropologist Ashley Montagu referred to our innate childish silliness as "neoteny,"[14] referring to a happy, innocent, childlike quality. All of the thrivers I interviewed for this book showed their own unique form of neoteny. Despite the horror of his imprisonment in the death camp, Izzie maintained what those who knew him well described as his playful, devilish nature. Describing how his neoteny had helped him thrive through his adversity, he said, "If you didn't laugh sometimes, the total horror of what was happening could overwhelm you. You had to pretend certain things were not as they were. Pretending was a way of temporary, undetected escape for me. You had to sort of clown around if you could. I remember hearing in the camp that Mosha would conduct small groups of prisoners. They would all laugh with her when she would point to one of them and say that their imaginary violin was out of tune. She would walk over and take the invisible violin away saying every time, "For heaven's sake, has your Jewish soul been cursed with a German ear?"

Emotional Deep Breathing

The happiness component of thriving is like emotional deep breathing. We tend to inhale when we experience negative emotions and thoughts ("Oh no! Now what? What next?") and we exhale when we experience positive ones ("Ah! Oh yes! I see!"). Researchers in positive psychology refer to this emotional broadening and balancing as our "thought-action repertoire," another name for the creative consciousness of thriving.

When we focus on seeking a happy meaning nestled somewhere in the misery of our adversity, our positive emotional state creates the urge to try to "play around" with options, push the limits, and be creatively receptive to several new options. All of these events are characteristics of the thriving response.[15]

In her book, *The Bad Stuff Is the Good Stuff,* psychologist Barbara T. Yanowski wrote of the role of a happy orientation to the saddest times in our lives. She experienced the adversity of alcoholism, divorce, cancer, and many other traumas in her life, and described how she managed to make the "bad stuff" in life turn out "good." She wrote, "In 1997 the doctor told me that I had cancer, like it was a bad thing. So it seemed at the time, but later, it proved to be an immeasurable lesson that led to a greater life than I ever imagined."[16] These are words of someone who has clearly learned to how to flow through her series of life traumas.

Research in positive psychology indicates that intentionally trying to construe a happier meaning when crisis strikes also results in the urge to explore, take in new information and experience, and expand the self.[17] When our negative emotions take hold, we are mentally and emotionally eager to get out of the present situation that seems to be making us so miserable. Quick escape might lead to survival, but thriving requires full mental, emotional, and spiritual engagement.

Developing our creative consciousness takes time. When we look on the bright side, or at least engage in the process of searching for it, we are more likely to want to remain right where we are, take in our surroundings, and savor and learn what we can in our current life situation. As a result, we have the time to think about what we are experiencing and look not only for Kobasa's three C's of challenge, commitment, and control but also a fourth C, a sense of the comical. The result can be a much more adaptive explanatory style.

The Real Pleasure Principles

Positive psychologists have shown that thrivers have happier and more flowing lives because they have become very good construers.[18] They mentally engage their problem, develop and adapt their explanatory style to their situation, and become more psychologically immune to future stressors. Research in positive psychology indicates that happy individuals construe naturally occurring life events, as well as contrived situations in the laboratory that present scientists' versions of what is funny to elicit the humor response, in ways that seem to maintain and promote their happiness, pride, and love for life and others.

Individuals who are less "happiness talented" tend to construe laboratory experiments and life problems in ways that seem to reinforce their unhappy, negative self-views.[19] To a large extent it is true that we get what we are looking for. No matter how wonderful or terrible life is, whether we thrive happily through it or merely survive or recover from its setbacks depends in large measure on how we choose to construe what happens to us.

This chapter ends with a set of findings about the flowing kind of happiness that characterizes the thriving response. They are derived from the research from the field of positive psychology, and each of them illustrates the importance of a central hypothesis regarding the thriving response and human invincibility; happiness is, after all, a state of mind.

Pleasure Principle 1: Don't Let Yourself Get Distracted from Delight

Psychologists have long embraced the concept of what they call "the pleasure principle." In its simplest version, it asserts that people spend their lives seeking pleasure and trying to avoid pain. This is sometimes referred to as an "approach-avoidance" orientation to daily living that focuses on trying to have a pleasurable life by seeking the avoidance of painful experiences.

Positive psychologists, however, are questioning this exclusively preventive orientation and suggesting that pleasure and happiness are much more than just the absence of pain. They are challenging the exclusive prevention and survival mentality of modern psychology and medicine, and focusing on a more "promotional" or positive motivation of concerning oneself with hopes and aspirations beyond the mere absence of adversity. They are finding that suffering does not exclude experiencing happiness and personal growth, and may in some important ways promote these positive states.

Sigmund Freud was the first person who wrote about the "pathology" view of the pleasure principle and to see the pursuit of pleasure as essentially a way of avoiding pain. He saw pain and pleasure as opposite ends of the same continuum, not as distinct entities. He wrote, "It seems that our entire psychical activity is bent upon procuring pleasure and avoiding pain, that it is automatically regulated by the pleasure principle."[20] Even when he wrote about what he called the "reality principle" and living "beyond the pleasure principle," his focus was still on the assumption that the ego or self "at the bottom also seeks pleasure—although a delayed and diminished pleasure."[21]

Pathogenic psychology embraces Freud's "pain verses pleasure" distinction. It fails to see that even those in severe pain can discover some degree of pleasure in some way or form within their trying circumstances. You have read the stories of thrivers that illustrate what research in positive psychology is showing; that humor and pleasure are not prevented by severe pain, and often help us withstand the debilitating effects of pain and the fear associated with it.[22]

Positive psychologist researcher E. Tory Higgins has discussed the differences between a pain prevention orientation and a pleasure promotion view of life. He suggested that pleasure can result from more than just success at avoiding pain. He proposes what he calls a "regulatory" view, which incorporates the possibility that life is not governed exclusively by the "no pain = pleasure" principle.[23]

Higgins identified the prevention motivation as dealing with strong ought-to's, sensitivity to the absence of negative outcomes and avoiding agitating emotions. In contrast, he says that a promotional life focus is more sensitive for positive outcomes. As one of the thrivers pointed out, "You can see more options with a positive outlook than a negative one. When you get so focused on the bad stuff, you sort of become distracted from the good stuff and lose your sensitivity for the simple delights in life."

Pleasure Principle 2: Get Off the Hedonistic Treadmill

Positive psychologist Edward Diener refers to happiness as "subjective well being."[24] He refers to the danger of leading our lives on a hedonistic treadmill, seeking more accomplishments and trying to get more things and more money, leading eventually to ever increasing expectations. As soon as we get the things we thought we wanted and achieve the happiness we hoped for, we quickly get used to what we have. Positive psychologists call this "habituating" to the new level we worked so hard to achieve. No matter how much we earn or achieve, we don't seem to stay happy for long. Another "have to have" or "must do" seems to always eventually pop up.

This form of quick boredom means that we get used to whatever state in which we find ourselves, and that includes both happiness and sadness. We are unhappy when we first encounter misfortune, but we soon get used to even the worst of circumstances, and what would have seemed to lead us to a certain life of misery no longer makes us totally unhappy. We might be very happy when fortune smiles upon us, but sooner or later it is "no big deal."

Diener points out that research on happiness indicates that we are destined to hedonistic neutrality in the long run no matter what happens to us. As one of the rules of our psycho-immunity asserts, we are built to be not too high or too low for too long. Thrivers seem well aware of the hedonistic neutrality principle. They seem to sense that they can eventually accommodate any degree of unhappiness and are not seduced by the hope for final and total pleasure. They are free of what has become the thoughtless hedonism of much of the modern world and its dominating ideology of materialism. They do not subscribe to the idea of just "doing one's thing" regardless of the long-term consequences, or that whatever feels good at the moment must be worth doing.[25] They have learned through their suffering that it is not only life that is short. Unless we choose to cling to them, all emotional states are also short lived.

The hedonistic neutrality principle asserts that reaching a goal guarantees that we won't be satisfied with that goal for too long. We may have thought we would have "finally arrived," but we are destined to be constant travelers moving through life at our own individual "satisfaction set points" no matter how successful we may become in terms of external rewards. We keep trying to move up, but once there, something spurs us on to go higher. Once we arrive again, it's not too long before we're ready to try to go higher than our preset neutral point. No matter where we think we can go to find more pleasure, we will always be there, and most of how happy we are is up to how we think, more than what we get.

One of the thrivers described his awareness of the hedonistic neutrality principle when he said, "I can guarantee you one thing about your goals. As soon as you reach them, they will go up. It's like a carrot on a stick in front of mule."

Pleasure Principle 3: Don't Think of Time as Money

"Time is money" has become a mantra of modern life. Research on happiness shows that this belief is a myth. As our income or amount of money in our bank account increases, we begin to increasingly assign a dollar amount to the value of our time. As a result, it becomes less and less rational for us to spend our time doing anything other than those things that make us money or in spending it conspicuously to announce just how happy we must be.[26]

One of the problems with the "time is money" approach to happiness is that the more of our time we spend investing time to get money to buy material things, the less of it is left for us to engage in what really makes us feel like we are thriving: growing, becoming, loving, and flowing. I cannot remember a single thriver talking much about money. Instead, they spoke of becoming more and more alive in order to enjoy the wealth of opportunities in the simple, ordinary magic of daily living.

My own study of highly successful people revealed that those who agreed with the "time is money" mantra were the unhappiest in their personal and interpersonal lives. They were also the ones stuck on the hedonistic treadmill and most prone to illness and depression.[27] Thrivers have learned that, beyond a certain minimum and in consideration of the suffering they experienced, any amount of comfort, material reward, fame, health, or good luck becomes irrelevant to being happy.[28] They have discovered that enduring contentment derives from remaining fully engaged in all that life offers.

Pleasure Principle 4: Don't Compare Your Happiness

Another aspect of the happiness component of thriving is the fact that happiness ultimately depends upon freedom from comparisons and competition. Those who engage in the kindling or victim responses to adversity often compare their situation with others, but thrivers seem immune to such comparisons. The positive psychology principle of "relative deprivation" states that being happy is easy, but being as happy or happier than other people is impossible because we assume others to be much happier than they really are.[29]

Because the world's resources are unevenly distributed, we tend to evaluate our happiness not in terms of what we have or need to live comfortably but in comparison with those who seem to have the most of what we think we want. We seem driven to keep up with the Joneses, but they are trying hard to keep up with us. One thriver pointed out, "I stopped trying to keep up with the Joneses a long time ago when I discovered they were a bunch of liars. They were doing what I was. They were saying they were much happier than they actually were and they had their own Joneses they were trying to keep up with."

Recently 52,000 readers of *Psychology Today* were asked what happiness meant to them. The authors of the survey concluded that happiness "comes from tending one's own garden instead of coveting one's neighbor's. . . . Happiness, in short, turns out to be more a matter of how you regard your circumstances than of what the circumstances are."[30] This simple but important concept of happiness being a matter of how we look at the world is central to the talent for thriving.

Evolutionary psychologist Steven Pinker used the German word *schaden-freude* to describe the comparative view of happiness. There is no equivalent word in the English language for *schadenfreude*, so I suggested that my patients learn it as a reminder not to seek their happiness comparatively. It means being happy only if someone else seems unhappier than we feel, a kind of glee derived by seeing others as more miserable than we are.[31]

Ambrose Bierce facetiously defined happiness as "an agreeable sensation arising from contemplating the misery of others."[32] As Beethoven seemed to do, thrivers are able to find their happiness by being energized by the happiness of others. They contemplate and construe their own misery in ways that bring a measure of happiness not only to themselves but also to those who care for them and are going through their adversity with them. The Hawaiian word for this is *aloha*. The word *aloha* has many meanings, but one of its most important is to find joy and contentment by sharing the sacred breath of life with others. Whether we lead a life based on *schadenfreude* or *aloha* plays a major role in determining whether we survive or thrive.

Pleasure Principle 5: Flowing is Enjoying

As you have read, Mihaly Csikszentmihalyi's concept of flowing is at the root of happiness and thriving.[33] We feel we are "flowing" when we become so fully engaged, engrossed, absorbed, and enjoyably immersed in what we are doing that we lose our sense of self, time, and even place. Csikszentmihalyi refers to these kinds of engrossing activities as "autotelic," meaning they become worth doing for their own sake regardless of any payoff or favorable consequences that may result from doing them.

When I asked Izzie how he managed to endure the endless days imprisoned in the death camp, he answered, "That's just it. The days were endless. They had no time to them. You just got so lost in your own mind that time eventually ceased to exist. Those who had the most problems were those who tried to keep track of time. You have to give a new meaning to time and fall into your own flow that fits your life that does not rely on a clock or calendar."

Another thriver told me, "When I was a patient on the bone marrow trans-plant unit, I was so busy trying to stay alive that I didn't have time to think about how much time I had left to live. I was too busy trying to figure out how to live my moments to have any time to worry about months and years."[34] I felt much the same way when I was on that same unit. I still remember the sense of being so completely into being alive that I seldom seemed to have the time to think about how long I would stay that way.

Pleasure Principle 6: Enjoy the Afterglow of Adversity

My interviews of thrivers revealed that, as we would expect, thinking about pleasurable present events makes us happy. You learned earlier that thinking about good past events makes us almost as happy as thinking about present ones, and thinking about a present and new bad event makes us the unhappiest. What was not expected from my interviews of these invincible people was the fact that, in every case, what made thrivers the happiest was thinking about negative past events.

Izzie provided an example of the impact of reflecting back on unhappy times. He said, "I know this will be hard to accept or understand, but when I think back on the terrible things I've gone through, it makes me feel happy. Maybe it's the idea that I made it and life is so much more valuable, meaningful, and enjoyable to me now, but thinking back actually cheers me up when I'm feeling a little blue."

Pleasure Principle 7: Find Your Feminine Funny Bone

Psychologist Herbert M. Lefcourt is credited with launching the humor and health movement. He was one of the first positive psychologists who showed how humor helps us thrive through stress. He found, however, that there is a difference in how men and women employ the thriver's technique of "comic construing."

Lefcourt's research showed that when men laugh, their systolic blood pressure tends to go up, but when women laugh, it tends to go down. He hypothesizes that this difference is due to the fact that women more often construe what is happening in such a way that they themselves are the target of the humor and laughter. Because of this humble-style humor, their laughter tends to restore social closeness. Men, on the other hand, tend to laugh in an attempt to enhance their position in the social hierarchy.[35] This results in a sense of competitive pressure, and as a result, men's blood pressure reflects that tension.

My interviews of thrivers indicate that regardless of their gender, their laughter is almost always of the feminine kind and at themselves. It seems to convey a humble modesty and vulnerability that attracts social support. Thrivers laugh hardest when they construe what is happening in the context of the feminine "Just look at what a foolish thing I did" rather than the male "Look at what a fool I made of you."

Another of my simple science experiments illustrated how the female-humor factor creates a thriving advantage. I placed chalk dust on the seats of the desks in the classroom of one of my college introductory psychology courses. I set up a video camera to record what happened when students began to arrive. When I showed the tape to the class, they saw the female sense of humor in action. As the women students entered, sat down, and noticed the chalk on their slacks and skirts, they got up, laughed, kept brushing it off until it was gone, and said things like, "How could I have done such a silly thing," or "Oh my, now look at what I did just did." Many of the women began to help other coeds brush the chalk away. When the men began sitting down, it was a different story.

As the men entered the classroom and sat down, they jumped up quickly when they saw the dust rise. Many of them seemed angry that they had been made the butt of a joke. They made only a few cursory attempts at brushing the chalk away before focusing their attention on finding out who played this trick on them. They often swore and said things like, "I'm going to kick somebody's ass," or "Who in the hell put that stuff there?" They also laughed, but usually while pointing at a fellow male student's pants and announcing to the rest of the class how much worse someone else's seat-chalking had been. The women recovered quickly from the prank, smiled, and began to prepare for class, but the men kept trying to find out the identity of the trickster or mocking the person who had the most chalk on their pants. They seem bothered, agitated, and inattentive during my lecture until, after several minutes, I told the class about my informal humor experiment.

As I showed the videotape to the class, they all laughed, but again the women were laughing at themselves and the men would shout out the name of other men they thought "really looked stupid" or who "really got chalked bad." However minor, the men's prolonged agitation and distraction seemed to interfere with their ability to get back to the task of learning.

The results of my simple science experiment seem to verify Lefcourt's hypothesis about the differences between the reason and purpose behind male and female laughter. It reveals the social and personal performance effects of the kind of humor we find in what happens to us and the importance not just of laughing but of why we laugh. It seems that, when it comes to thriving, a sense of humor is not enough. What is needed is a woman's sense of silliness.

Pleasure Principle 8: Laugh to Surrender, Not Control

Laughter can serve many purposes and derive from different ways of construing what happens to us. Psychologist Robert R. Provine's research on laughter shows that our laughter can also be a signal of submission and the giving up of control. Laughter can be a signal that we are willing to submit and as you learned in chapter 9, the control factor of hardiness includes the ability to gracefully give in.

Provine's research shows that laughter indicates mirth but also sometimes submission and surrender. Sometimes it indicates all three of these emotional states at once. For example, we often groan and laugh at what we call a "terrible pun." We may do this because we are showing our deference to the punster's clever trick, giving in and asking that we not be punned again, or sometimes just because the pun is funny.[36] We often laugh automatically at seemingly humorless times, such as when we stand up to say, "I have to go now." The average speaker laughs almost twice as much as the person to whom she or he is talking. We laugh in these ways to smooth social transitions, set a positive emotional tone, and to enhance feelings of group belonging, all of which are also important thriving skills.

The Two Ways to Wisdom

So far in this thriver's manual, you have read about the first two components of the thriving response. You have learned that hardiness and happiness are intentional ways of construing our lives that lead to invincibility and are not the result of it. The next two chapters discuss the final two keys to enhancing our thriving talent, healing and hope. For all four of these aspects of thriving, it is important to remember the central tenet of this book: if we choose to make it so, adversity can actually add to our lives. It can make us hardier and happier than we might have been without it. If we wish to thrive right now and without working our way through the kinds of crises the thrivers you have been reading about experienced, we have to apply these same strategies to our daily lives.

Mythologist Joseph Campbell pointed out that we become wise in two ways, by a sudden epiphany or by suffering.[37] If we learn to employ our thriving talents of hardiness and happiness, we make ourselves more available for an epiphany and the quantum kind of thriving associated with it. By remaining mentally challenged, committed, and in control and flowing by emotionally dealing with our problems from the comic point of view, it becomes more likely that we will find the unique wisdom and strength that comes from knowing how to grow through and find meaning in our misery.

Izzie discussed the role of hardiness and happiness in thriving. He said, "If you want to thrive through your problems, you have to have a very strong mind, a hardy soul, and an extremely sensitive funny bone. When you laugh really, really hard, you usually shed tears, so you can see that there isn't really much distance between the comedies and tragedies of life. They all mean you are living fully, and I think that this is how you learn to thrive."

11 Healing through the Horrible Times

"Above all, we should resist equating healing with feeling good. This is a difficult lesson for healers."[1]

—*Larry Dossey, M.D.*

The Gift of Sickness

Sickness is good for us and we can't learn to thrive without it. Some of the most horribly sick times in our lives can be the most important to the improved quality of our living. Sickness is our body's essential first and fastest response to anything that challenges our well-being. The sickness response is a set of physiological, emotional, mental, and behavioral changes that tell us that we are actually getting ready to thrive. Although the pathogenic model sees sickness as an enemy, it's really our evolved human system designed to give us the energy to deal with injury, infection, and psychological stress. It's a built-in energy saver that signals us to slow down and take it easy so the body can use its energy to deal with its illness.

In the positive psychology model, the process of healing from physical or emotional stress is essential to a full and healthy life. Healing in this view is turning even the most horrible times in our lives into an opportunity to learn to deal with our lives in new and more enlightened ways that can allow us to thrive. Dealing with severe illness can awaken us from our languishing and help us realize just how much of life we have forgotten to savor. It can involve discovering how to integrate events in our lives and use them to form a more congruent and inclusive explanatory style. It can help us modify our beliefs, values, and the story we tell ourselves about our lives so that we feel more connected with life as a response to our illness which caused us to feel so disconnected from it.

Healing does not necessarily involve curing or fixing, but it always involves what the integrative feeling medical sociologist and positive psychologist Aaron Antonovsky has called a "sense of coherence."[2] He identified this sense as including being able to comprehend what is happening to us (our explanatory style), find meaning in it (framing), and mentally manage it (creative consciousness). This healing component of thriving is what Antonovsky described as consciously composing a more coherent life, one that somehow now seems more logical because something caused it to seem so illogical.

Antonovsky did much of his research as a professor at the Department of the Sociology of Health at Ben Gurion University of Negev in Beersheba, Israel. He was one of the first researchers to focus on the difference between a pathogenic approach to understanding human functioning and what he called a salutogenic orientation, looking for what's right with us rather than what's wrong and how we can find meaning in the madness of our lives.

Remaining the Composers of Our Consciousness

Antonovsky's salutogenesis refers to our natural human strengths and virtues and our capacity to develop an increasingly adaptive explanatory system. It focuses on our ability to heal as Beethoven did, by remaining the composers of the content of our consciousness no matter what external events impinge upon it. From out of the painful humming din of his hearing loss, Beethoven found and conveyed through his music a sense of coherence that moves our souls. Even as he became sicker and his hearing worsened, his healing progressed to allow him to find meaning and manageability through his suffering. Somehow, he made sense of the senselessness of a deafness imposed upon a musical genius.

Similar to Kobasa's theory of hardiness and Csikszentmihalyi's concept of flow, Antonovsky's "sense of coherence" views what happens in the outside world as less important than what we choose to mentally construct as our inside world. When we confront a trauma in our lives and say we are "trying to pull ourselves together" or "get it together," we are referring to putting our lives back together again to achieve the kind of life lucidity that Antonovsky called a sense of coherence.

Antonovsky has referred to our capacity to thrive as a set of GRRs, generalized resistance resources. Instead of studying pathogenic factors such as external chronic stressors, acute life changes, and daily hassles, Antonovsky studied our remarkable ability to heal and become stronger through our natural adaptive resources such as maintaining control of our own consciousness, framing events in more meaningful and manageable ways, and responding to challenges where others feel helpless. He contrasted the healing and thriveability of our generalized resistance with what he called GRDs, generalized resistance deficits.

GRDs have been the primary focus of pathogenic psychology. They are the stressors in our lives and the frailties in our character. Antonovsky has suggested that for those who thrive, even these deficits seem to serve as stimuli toward a new and stronger sense of coherence. For thrivers, chronic stress, acute and sudden life changes, and daily life hassles become grist for the mill of their ever developing consciousness.

Like Beethoven, they are able to remain in creative control of their own consciousness even at the times of the most dreadful disappointments. They heal by composing a more fully developed, adaptive, and creative way of viewing themselves, their lives, and the world. Thrivers don't surrender mental control to their external world or allow their internal life to be dominated and disheveled by outside events. In other words, they are skilled healers able to make their lives whole again.

As you have read, Kobasa was among the first researchers to study hardiness and how we can become stronger because of the stressors in our lives. Csikszentmihalyi was a pioneer in examining our state of consciousness rather than external factors as the ultimate source of our happy flowing through the trials of our lives. Antonovsky's questioning of the almost exclusive pathogenic point of view played a major role in the evolution of positive psychology. All three of these positive psychologists assert the importance of remaining the composers of our consciousness as the key to thriving.

Thrivers tend to be hardy souls made stronger through their stress and able to become joyfully immersed in and flow with life. They also are miraculous healers whose explanatory systems work in tandem with their psychological immune systems to allow them to become a stronger whole than before their stress.

Emotional and Mental Healing

The field of psychoneuroimmunology has clearly established that our physiological immune system's cells (T-cells, B-cells, antibodies, etc.) are affected by what is on our mind. What we choose to believe about our world and life ultimately becomes our biology, and prolonged periods of stress or depression are known to suppress immune function. As you have read, research in positive psychology has established that we also have a psychological immune system. Research from this field shows that stress and adversity can result in forms of "psychoinfection" that elicit the sickness response in much the same way that an antigen causes our physiological immune system to make us feel sick while it does its work.

Psychologist Steven Maier's research shows that we have a built-in "sickness circuit" in the form of an immune-brain loop.[3] It seems that any form of stress, from being cold to hearing terrible news, taps into the same immune-brain loop that triggers the sickness response. When we are stressed, our brain (particularly a part called the hypothalamus) signals the body to go into its automatic sickness mode. Within an hour or two, we begin to feel that we are "coming down with something" or are "under the weather." We might develop a fever, the sign that energy is being spent by our body to fight off an invasion of some kind. To save energy, we lose interest in food, sex, and exploring and doing things.

Then to charge us up, the "sickness loop" causes us to feel anxious or agitated, and the catabolic, or energy-burning, hormone cortisol you read about in chapter 7 is secreted in large amounts. Even though doctors have long mocked the idea that going out in frigid temperatures without a jacket can increase our chances of catching cold, the discovery of the sickness loop between the immune and nervous system shows that our mothers were right when they said, "Wear your jacket or you'll catch cold." Just the emotionally induced stress of feeling cold can activate our immune systems which in turn can cause us to become sick.

In describing the nature of the sickness loop, Dr. Maier stated, "In a real, true sense, stress makes you physically sick. In addition, many of the changes over time in mood and cognition from day to day are driven by events in the immune system of which we are unaware."[4] The brain is constantly sending its messages to our immune system. The psychological immune system is also a participant in the constant chatter between our immune system and our brain. Dr. Maier pointed out that we have "a complete, bi-directional immune-to-brain circuit."[5] Stress makes us sick because both our physiological and psychological immune systems are in effect making us sick in order to make us well.

The Benefit Finders

My interviews with thrivers indicate that they are good at resisting illness and, if they do become ill, they are talented at learning through their sickness and finding benefit within it. Life presents all of us with turning points and serious illness can be one of those points, but only for those who choose to turn.

Thrivers make that choice. They embrace and engage rather than deny their sickness. They accept sickness as a necessary part of living and growing and weave it into their evolving life story. Instead of feeling inconvenienced by their sickness response, they use it as a consciousness catalyst for modifying their explanatory system.

Thrivers are what positive psychologists call "benefit finders." Psychologist David McAdams has suggested that thrivers treat their trauma as opportunities to re-create their life narrative and to structure a life story with more coherence and meaning than before their challenge.[6]

An emerging positive psychology literature on posttraumatic growth or SIG (stress-induced growth), indicates that benefit finding is one of the key characteristics of the thriving response.[7] It is not just changing our mind about our lives, but also is manifested in a new way of interacting with others and the world in general.[8] The families of the thrivers I interviewed reported that these benefit finders showed clearly positive changes in how they related to their spouses and children. At its simplest level, the Beethoven Factor is essentially benefit finding at times of the most severe life challenges.

Survival of the Sickest

What is sickness for? Why does disease exist at all? Why is there stress in our lives? If these things are not essential, why hasn't evolution gotten rid of them? If the severe stressors of heart disease, cancer, serious mental illnesses such as depression and schizophrenia are not necessary for life, why haven't the laws of Darwin's theory of natural selection done away with them?

These are questions being asked by the fascinating field of Darwinian medicine that is related to positive psychology. The answer seems to be that sickness is a built-in evolutionary experience essential for our long-term well-being.[9] We get sick so we can learn to heal, and by learning to become whole again, we learn to thrive. To be strong and get stronger, we need to be sick and learn how to thrive through our suffering. None of us escapes illness, but each of us has the opportunity to heal and thrive because of it.

Without the discomfort associated with fighting off infection and other challenges to our physical and psychological immune systems, the healing component essential for thriving is absent. When I lost control of my bowels and vomited dozens of times a day during my several rounds of chemotherapy and whole-body radiation, I had hours of negative thoughts and feelings. I seemed to need these as a way of purging some of the pain of my cancer, and I eventually came to see these mental and emotional symptoms as essential to my healing.

Once I realized that my suffering was an important part of my healing, I was able to get ever so slightly stronger and began to tolerate my treatments with more ease. Izzie said, "I think the reason some people haven't learned how to thrive is that they've been so interested in staying healthy that they haven't been sick enough yet to learn how to heal."

Patsy's Lessons from Sadness

I cried every day during my cancer treatment. I was already working on this book about thriving by interviewing thrivers on my cancer unit, but I began to question how my deep and pervasive sadness about my cancer could play any role in my being able to thrive my way out of my predicament. I kept asking myself, how can this sadness be useful? Why do I have it? Why do all of us on this cancer unit have it? What possible role in healing could such a bothersome feeling play?

I understood how feeling and showing happiness cause us to be more out-going and socially more appealing, and give us more initiative and perseverance, but my sadness often seemed to push people away or make them uncomfortable. I understood why my physical systems caused me to vomit in response to the toxins being injected into my system, but why did I have these distressing, sad emotions? How could they possibly be of any help to me?

As I delved deeper into my study of the thriving response, I began to think that sadness is as essential to healing as happiness. It would not have survived as an emotion if it did not serve some evolutionary purpose. One out of ten of us will experience serious depression in our lives, so it must have some adaptive reason to persist in the human psyche. As she had done so many times for us, the little girl in the room next to mine in the bone marrow transplant unit helped me crystallize my thinking about the thriving role of sadness.

Patsy was only nine years old, but her cancer had caused her to know more pain, suffering, and sadness than anyone should have to endure. She visited with me several times during her stay on the unit, and she was the poster child for thriving. She wheeled herself into my room one day while I was crying. I tried to quickly dry my eyes and compose myself, but she said, "It's okay, Dr. Pearsall. I cry all the time too. My minister says we need to be sad because this is a sad time for us. Being sad is only bad for us if we are sad because we are sad and we are never happy at all. When I cry, I think of all the happy things I miss, and then I remember them more, and then I sometimes feel happy again. It's like the big teeter-totter at school. It's not fun to always be down, but it's okay if you know you can go up again."

As you have read, Patsy often served as our cancer unit philosopher, and when she died, the patients and staff cried for days. All of us will never forget her. We never saw her feeling sorry for herself. Except immediately after a harsh dose of chemotherapy, we never saw her without a boundless childish energy that seemed to exceed that of healthy children. Her lesson about the naturalness of sadness and how it can get our attention to the happy times helped all of us in our healing.

Priming Our Psychoimmunity

Dr. Maier's research shows that our negative feelings such as sadness and other stressors can enhance our psychoimmunity. As you read in chapter 7, we seem to enhance our psychoimmunity by gaining trauma-adapting experience. Dr. Maier pointed out that "stress is another form of infection. And the consequences of stress are mediated by the activation of circuits that actually evolved to defend against infections."[10] If we think of the trauma and tragedies in our lives as emotional antigens, and understand that illness is a message from both our psychological and physiological immune systems to slow down, think, and find new meanings in life through the sickness response being offered us, we are better able to thrive.

To heal is not just to get or feel better. It means using our sickness to instruct us in new and deeper meanings about who we are and how we are choosing to construe our lives. By learning through and from our sicknesses, we can discover what it means to more fully appreciate our times of wellness. We often don't fully pay attention to the daily delight of just feeling good until we feel very sick. When sickness passes, we too quickly forget about the deep longing we felt for the days of ordinary wellness and the promises we made to ourselves about how we would not take our health for granted.

Like all thrivers, I will never again take one single healthy day for granted. My hope in offering this book is that those who have not yet suffered deeply will begin to enhance their sense of hardiness, happy flowing, and coherence before they are forced to do so. I have learned to relish the ordinary magic of wanting to eat, being able to eat and hold food down, being able to take a full breath on my own, wanting to make love again. Every time I experience the sickness response of a cold or the flu, I use these times as reminders that I am lucky to be alive to be sick, just how wonderful and sacred every moment is, and how I cherish every single day I spend free of the agonizing pain of my cancer.

Just like the other thrivers, my life seems more authentic now because it feels more comprehensible. It seems to have more meaning and feel more manageable, and perhaps the gift of the thrivers you have read about is their invitation to you to begin your healing now even before you feel sick.

12/7 and 9/11

I met two healers today. Just before I sat down to work on this chapter, I met two men at different points in their healing and thriving journeys. I had taken a break from writing this book to go Christmas shopping. Compared with my wife, I have very little shopper's stamina. I often tell her that her shopper's math of "spaving" or "spending to save" that provides much of the energy behind her shopping eludes me.

To regain my strength and patience, I sit down in the mall and people-watch. I am often joined by several other men seeking escape from shopping or sent to wait and package-hold by wives not wanting to be slowed down by their husbands' reluctant sulking pace. Like a group of children sent to the principal's office, we usually sit in a kind of embarrassed silence, but today was different. It was there that I met the two men who are models of healing, the third component of the thriving response.

On one side of me sat a veteran of the attack on Pearl Harbor on December 7, 1941. On my other side sat a young fireman who had survived the collapse of the World Trade Center towers caused by the terrorist attacks on September 11, 2001. The World War II veteran was in Honolulu for a memorial ceremony and had come to rest while his wife was "spaving" for souvenirs. One of the mall security guards was a Hawaiian man who recognized me. We exchanged greetings in Hawaiian, and when the guard left, the veteran said, "You are so lucky to live in Hawaii. It's so beautiful here, but it wasn't so beautiful when they bombed Pearl Harbor. I will never forget that day." When I learned who he was, I immediately began to ask him questions about his experience on December 7.

The man on my other side stuck out his hand for both of us to shake. "Excuse me," he said, "I'm a firefighter from New York. I survived the collapse of the towers on September 11. As a gift of *aloha*, the State of Hawaii gave a lot of us free trips to the islands." Looking at the veteran, he saluted him, and the veteran saluted back. The fireman said, "I guess you and I have a lot in common. We're both survivors of attacks on our country." The veteran answered, "I am very honored to meet you. I'll bet we could talk for hours about what we experienced." I got up to allow the two men to talk directly to one another, but the fireman said, "That's okay. Stay where you are. I read your book about miracles and your cancer. You will understand what we are talking about."

The three of us talked until the fireman's wife and children came to get him. The fireman spoke of having nightmares and flashbacks of his narrow escape. He said he was often awakened in the middle of the night by the sounds of tweeting, the noise made by the homing devices that are activated when a firefighter falls. He added, "All of us guys who went through that day are changed forever by it. You guys both know what I mean. Sooner or later, you get stronger and recover and go on."

The veteran answered with tears in his eyes, "I know I will never be back here for another ceremony at the *Arizona* Memorial. I think you are right about recovering, but that has not been enough for me. It took me all these years to do more than get over what happened. Something about the ceremony yesterday helped me finally get past it. I felt so much pride and love for the guys I saw and the guys we lost. I felt pride for my country and I felt good that I can go home now and finally feel more alive again. In all these years since that day, I think I have only been surviving, but the ceremony yesterday made it all finally fit together for me. It was very healing for all of us and I think it will help us enjoy the rest of our short lives."

The fireman seemed entranced by the veteran's words, and I was encouraged to hear this wise old man put into words precisely what I was trying to write about in my book about thriving. The fireman said, "So, it looks like I might be in for about 60 years or so of trying to really get-my life back in order?" We all laughed, but I thought about the wisdom of the fireman's statement. It had been more than a dozen years since my near-death from cancer. Like the veteran, I had survived and recovered, but I felt I was still in the process of trying to become more alive. The veteran said, "Whatever years the three of us have are more than those who lost their lives. It's up to us to do more than just survive. Healing takes a very long time and maybe forever. You have to get things together in your mind, and that takes a really long time."

The fireman introduced us to his wife and children, hugged us both, and left with his family for a day at the beach. As he walked away, he turned and gave us the thumbs-up sign. The veteran's wife arrived just after the fireman left. He introduced me to her, and she said, "I hope he didn't talk your ear off. He hasn't stopped talking since the ceremony at the *Arizona* yesterday. I don't think I've seen him smile as much as he has since then. He used to sit around and cry a lot, and I had to be the one to get him going. Now, the crazy old man even wants to try surfing. It's like he got new life from that ceremony."

As the couple walked away, I promised myself I would include in this chapter a description of our meeting in the mall. I thought it served as an example of going beyond survival and recovery to the more vital wholeness of the true healing I saw in so many thrivers. I thought the two men's experiences and healing processes revealed another important warning about thriving and healing, that it is possible to live long and never be healed. Healing is a choice to make the difficult journey to becoming whole again, not an automatic response that makes us feel good again.

Making Sense of It All

The three components of Antonovsky's sense of coherence concept are guides to developing the strong explanatory style characteristic of thrivers' ability to heal through the horrible times in their lives. Thrivers show his idea of comprehensibility by being able to make sense of whatever happens to them even amid the disordered chaotic nature of life. For example, Izzie described the passing of Mosha as "her great escape. She would have suffered in the most horrible ways had she lived, so God saw to it that she could get away." In a description of the healing process that fits the reports of the thrivers I interviewed, Antonovsky wrote, "Death, war, and failure can occur, but such a person [thriver] can make sense of them."[11] No matter what happens, thrivers remain mentally persistent. They keep seeking to put their lives not only back together again but back together in a stronger and more adaptive way.

The second component of mental coherence is manageability. This way of construing life events refers to the extent to which we can see that we have an available "match" between whatever events impact us and our way of thinking about and dealing with them. Antonovsky wrote, "To the extent that one has a high sense of manageability, one will not feel victimized by events or feel that life treats one unfairly. Untoward things do happen in life, but when they do occur, one will be able to cope and not grieve endlessly."[12]

To not grieve endlessly is a key to healing. It is a characteristic of those who have what Buddhist scholar Alan Watts called "forgettory."[13] Watts used the concept of "forgettory" to represent the counterpart of memory. He pointed out that there are times when we need to have a bad memory and totally forget things that happen to us. He suggests that we need both a good "forgettory" and memory to be able to feel that we can manage the challenges of our lives.

The emphasis on recalling everything accurately may not always be helpful for thriving. Sometimes we need our own mental "delete" key. When I was going through my bone marrow transplant and was destined to spend many more months in the hospital, I regularly hit my own mental "delete" button. I would block out the pain I had already suffered and try to forget the long struggle doctors told me was still ahead.

The third component of Antonovsky's sense of coherence is meaningfulness. He defined this way of construing life as "the extent to which one feels that life makes sense emotionally, that at least some of the problems and demands imposed by living are worthy of investing energy in, are worthy of commitment and engagement, and are challenges that are 'welcome' rather than burdens that one would much rather do without."[14] In other words, for those engaged in healing, life matters a great deal no matter what happens, and is always worth our full engagement.

While Izzie had every reason to give up and disengage from life while in the death camp, he remained a full-time participant in the process of doing all he could, mentally and emotionally, to shape his own destiny.[15] He had an excellent "forgettory" for the terrible tortures and horrors he witnessed and experienced, but he also had a very good memory for healing issues such as Mosha's invisible orchestra. Without these two crucial mental skills, Izzie's healing would have been much more difficult.

A Healing Mental Diet

You have read that thriving is not just taking things and events into our consciousness and reacting to them. It is a healing process through which we intentionally try to change the content of our consciousness and think in new ways to find more coherence in our lives. Jean Piaget was the renowned cognitive psychologist who first applied the metaphor of eating and digesting to mental processes.[16] I have used his work to help my patients understand Antonovsky's sense of coherence concept. In discussing this healing component of thriving, I put Piaget's general concepts in the framework of a "diet book for the mind," and I offer these principles to my patients as guides for developing a healing mind.

When we encounter a difficult idea or event, we sometimes say, "That's a lot to digest," or "I'll have to chew on that for a while." If the concept is particularly challenging to our current explanatory system or the way we construe the world, we may say, "That makes me sick to my stomach." You have learned that research in psychological immunity shows that how and what we think about what happens to us can make us sick. It is also possible to become well by "feeding ourselves" a healthier mental diet.

Piaget used the word "aliment" to refer to a new idea, concept, or event that we try to understand. Like food, an aliment is something that nurtures us and is necessary for our survival and ability to cope with life's stresses. The alimentary canal is our digestive system that processes the "aliments" we eat, and much the same process is involved when we encounter a mental aliment such as bad news or a stressful event. We have to take in what we encounter, try to digest it and absorb it, and make it part of us. This "mental diet" concept is not merely metaphorical. Our thoughts do literally "become" us. When we are told, "We are what we eat," that includes the mental diet we are feeding ourselves.

Piaget used the word "schema" to refer to the organization of our thoughts and experiences in our mind. In a way, our schema eats and digests the aliments of our living, those things our attention causes us to put on our minds. Unlike other animals, however, we do not have to be passive mental grazers. We can exert control over our mental diet because we can determine what goes into our consciousness. All day every day, we are constantly feeding ourselves, and by doing so, we are creating our own consciousness. When we say, "Food for thought," we might also say, "Thought is food."

When our schema assimilates aliments, it simply mentally "eats" whatever it is we perceive and passes it through our mental system into our consciousness without sufficient mental digestion or significant change in who we are, or how we are, or how we think. It is a process similar to gorging ourselves on junk food. We may become aware of something, but we fail to attend to it. Attention researchers Thomas H. Davenport and John Beck wrote, "Awareness becomes attention when information reaches a threshold of meaning in our brains and spurs the potential for action."[17] The word "assimilate" is defined as "to become of the same substance." When we mentally assimilate, our consciousness responds and becomes aware but it does not change. When we accommodate, not only what we choose to pay attention to and mentally take in significantly changes. Our consciousness and how it attends to the world are also altered.

In learning about thriving, my patients have found it helpful to pay more attention to what they were putting in their minds. They used the following "mental diet plan" I provided as a tongue-in-cheek (another part of the digestive system) way of learning about the healing aspect of thriving.

The Healing Mental Diet Plan
Breakfast
- The moment you wake up, don't get up. Lie there and take a mental dietary supplement. Think about why you are alive, your family, and the thrill of being able to live another day. Remember, the first mental food of your day will set your mental tone for the entire day.

- When you get up and get ready for your day, remember to eat a healthy mental breakfast. Feed yourself only happy, hardy, optimistic thoughts during breakfast. Don't read the newspaper. It usually contains mostly bad news. Talk with your family or just daydream about the good things in life.

Lunch
- Have a few mental snacks before lunch. Put some positive thoughts into your consciousness by remembering positive events and the people you love.

- Take a "consciousness break." Stop working and mentally reacting, and spend a few moments thinking about what you want to think about, not responding to and dealing with an endless stream of outside pressures.

- During lunch or any meal, use your "forgettory" to avoid chewing on stale mental food, old thoughts that upset your mental and emotional system. Focus on what you're tasting and the people with whom you are eating, not problems, hassles, and stressful events.

- Have a nutritious mental lunch by avoiding mental aliments such as work, war stories, or recollections of ongoing stressors.

- Avoid "overchewing" (ruminating) on negative thoughts.

Afternoon
- Avoid junk aliments. When you find yourself thinking hopelessly or angrily, have a mental nibble on thoughts that calm you down. Always have a few positive aliments with you to snack on when you need them. Think of some of the best things that ever happened to you or a person you love dearly. Whenever you find yourself eating nothing but junk aliments, take a bite of one of your healthier memories and chew on that for a while.

- If you're feeling sick, stay home and think about it. If you're really feeling blue about your present situation, think about some of the really bad things that happened to you in the past and compare them with your general life situation right now. Remember the positive psychology research finding that occasionally thinking about negative past events tends to lead to the most positive emotions. The times when you're sick are good times to engage in the luxury of some comparative thinking that might make your present situation seem a little brighter.

- Remember to stay on a strict "adrenalin diet." When you feel your psychological immune system alerting you and making you feel that you should fight or flee, sit down and shut up. That means stop and take time to block the thoughts that are upsetting your systems, and try to think of more calming images. Sometimes the most important aspect of attention is not taking information in but screening it out.

- Take a "mental afternoon nap." For just a few moments just sit back, put your feet up, and try to watch the thoughts going by in your brain. Watch them as if they are children playing and don't focus on them or try to "discipline" them. Just sit down, shut up, calm down, and wait a few moments before going back to your normal mental activities.

Dinner
- Have a balanced mental dinner. Mentally review the day from the perspective of what you learned that made your life better or made you think about life in a new, more creative, and positive way.

- Don't try to feed yourself mental aliments while watching television or multi-tasking. Good mental digestion requires your full attention, so if you're watching TV, pay attention to it no matter how simple and mundane it may be. Don't be psychologically absent by being mentally other places than where you are.

Bedtime
- Have a light and enjoyable mental snack before bed. Like warm milk before bed, thinking some wonderful calming thoughts before you fall asleep will help energize you for the next day.

- Don't worry if you mentally feed yourself some junk aliments once in a while. Your schema or consciousness digestive system is highly adaptive. It's okay to snack on the sad, angry, anxiety-inducing thoughts as long as your general mental diet is a calm, contented, and joyful one.

General Mental Healing Diet Tips

- Watch your mental diet when you're sick! Your psychological and physiological immune systems are strengthened by thoughts that help you accommodate what is happening to you, why you became sick, and what it takes to become stronger because you have been sick.

• It's okay to occasionally skip what others may describe as mentally healthy foods that are good for you. Mental dieting is informed selective mental eating, and research shows that denial can be as important to healing as "total self-honesty" and "facing the facts."[18]

• Keep a mental dietary "pick-me-up" handy. Carry a picture of someone you love or of a favorite place or event. Wear a piece of jewelry worn by someone close to you who is no longer with you. Whenever you feel that your mental digestive system is becoming upset, take a dose of that mental aliment to settle your system. Such thoughts can act as mental "antacids."

• Special Caution: It's not so much what you eat but what is eating you that upsets your system. Take charge of what you are feeding your consciousness.

While my patients and I had fun with the healing mental diet plan, and the patients themselves came up with many more mental diet recommendations of their own, they said the basic idea that the thoughts we feed ourselves directly impact our health and healing helped them pay more attention to how they were nurturing their minds.

One woman said, "I was laughing a lot about your stupid mental diet program until I realized that I was actually mentally poisoning myself with negative and angry thoughts about the past, present, and future. I was gorging myself on constant junk thoughts and sometimes didn't even know I was eating them. It was like automatically snacking on junk food and not paying attention to what and how much you are eating. I keep your idea about watching my mental diet on my mind a lot. It is really not that silly to know that the quality of my consciousness is a result of what I keep feeding it. That's a pretty heavy-duty thing to think about. I think it's something good for me to mentally digest."

Some Healing Thoughts

One of my patients engaged in learning the thriving response said, "My life is a vicious circle. I just got my life together after my divorce. My kids had a terrible time in school and I just got them settled with a good teacher and then she leaves. I worked out and lost weight, and now my doctor tells me I have lupus. The better things seem to get, the worse they get. It's just one big vicious circle."

Basing my answer on what I had learned about thriving and healing, I answered, "You might want to think of your life more like a spiral than a circle.

If you decide to see it as spiraling down, that's likely to be its direction for you. Your doctor didn't seem to help you much by presenting the challenge of your lupus without helping you comprehend its meaning for you and how you might decide to manage it. You can figure your way through this, but not if you think of yourself as going around in circles to keep hitting the same old problems and certainly not if you considered yourself cursed rather than challenged."

To help you work on your own sense of coherence, I've tried to state the following healing thoughts in mentally provocative and often paradoxical ways. Even if you disagree with these thoughts or find yourself arguing with them, you are still in the process of revamping your explanatory system and developing a sense of coherence essential for healing. It's your own sense of coherence, not mine or anyone else's, that is crucial for the healing component of thriving. If you will take some time to contemplate these ideas, they might even help boost your psychological immunity. At the very least, that could be used for some of your mental diet snacks.

Some Healing Thoughts from Thrivers

• *What we see is what we get.* If we define events as real, they become real in their consequences. How we construe what happens to us has profound consequences for what will and can actually happen to us in the long run.

• *Protect your own sense of coherence.* Don't frame your problems or allow others to frame them in ways that block your ability to comprehend what is happening to you from a meaningful and manageable perspective.

• *Where there's the breath of life, there's still time to find meaning in life.* So long as there is a breath of life left within us, we are in some measure healthy and still capable of healing.[19]

• *Don't let your life be dictated by death.* Life is a sexually transmissible condition with a 100 percent mortality rate. Fighting that fact is futile, but we can enjoy being alive if we put our minds to it and take charge of what our lives will mean to others and us.

• *Think "us," not "me."* When we get sick, we can choose to fight or take flight, or we can tend and befriend. It's the second choice that leads to healing and thriving.[20]

- *Take charge of your thoughts, not always the situation.* Sometimes the ultimate feeling of control comes when we know when and how to gracefully give up trying to control the events in our lives. Sometimes managing a problem is knowing when it is not manageable and when it's time to just go with the flow.

- *Make some sense of your sickness.* Look for life meanings that lead to a sense of control even when circumstances seem beyond your control. Studies in nursing homes showed that patients who were being moved involuntarily to a new home did better with the unavoidable stress when staff encouraged rather than helped them.[21]

- *Master the Art of Self-Disputation.* As if your own critical and hopeless thoughts were coming from an insensitive stranger unfamiliar with your true strengths, dispute your own negativity.

- *Be reason-able.* Of course things happen for a reason. The challenge is to find their purpose. Healing and thriving require remaining fully engaged with adversity on all levels long enough to find or at least make up a good reason for what happens to you that works for you in managing it.

- *Commend your body. It's doing the best it can.* The human body is neither naturally fragile nor robust. It is a bundle of compromises that has evolved over the years. For each strength and advantage it has, it has a built-in price. Sickness and its discomfort are the costs of our miraculous capacity to heal and be well.[22] Don't refer to "your bad back" or "bad heart." They're doing their best, so encourage them by thinking positively about them. Remember, your psychological immune system is listening.

- *Use your psychological immunity to help your physical immunity.* Autoimmune diseases such as rheumatoid arthritis and lupus are the healing price we pay for having such a strong immune system. Sometimes, the sicker we feel, the more powerful our physiological immune system is showing itself to be. What you think and feel about your illness may not save your life or cure you, but it can help boost your psychological immunity so you can have a happier and more meaningful life.

- *You don't "have" cancer, you're "cancering."* Cancer is the healing price we pay for having been given body tissue capable of growing and repairing itself. The same growth process that creates life can get out of control and crowd it out.

Cancer is not a "thing" we have, but it can "have us" if we allow it to determine the content of our consciousness and the course of life. As horrible as it is, cancer is the natural process of rapidly growing cells gone too far, so think of it as a process that changed once and can thus change again.

• *Don't rely on unnatural remedies for dealing with natural processes.* For example, contrary to the pathogenic view that menopause is a disease, it isn't. The emotional and physical discomforts of menopause are natural occurrences. It is the price the females of our species pay so we will give more attention to and invest our interest in the children we already have rather than being distracted by the drive to have more of them. Think first of natural ways to reduce symptoms of what pathogenisists are often too willing to call a "disease." Hormonal replacement therapies may not be therapeutic and may even be dangerous. Replacing painful knees may not help and might make matters worse. Before you ask yourself what you should do about your problem, ask yourself what it is for. What is it telling you about your life and your way of living, and what can you do and think to grow through and because of it?

• *Reach out and touch someone.* All healing is ultimately a form of reconnection. Feelings can follow behaviors, so you don't have to wait to feel connected before you show it. When you're hurting, don't wait to be touched, start holding on for dear life. From the youngest child to the oldest adult, the damage of physical and emotional stress can be reduced by the simple act of hugging, holding, and embracing. Research shows that doing nothing more than picking up a baby laboratory mouse and handling it for a few minutes each day strengthens that mouse's immune system.[23]

• *Be a healer, not a patient.* Nothing promotes healing more than being in the role of healer to others. In the pathogenic model, patients are "done to" and "treated." In the salutogenic model, maintaining a sense of challenge, commitment, and control even when we're very sick is crucial to the healing process. Don't wait for flowers to be sent to you. Send them. Don't wait to be comforted. Comfort.

• *Take "pain pauses."* Look for and celebrate even the briefest pain-free healthy moments. Accept and learn from the sick times, and embrace firmly the healthy times. There could be no health without its opposite, sickness.

- *Trust in the healing power of suffering.* Sickness means your life is getting better in often very paradoxical or mysterious ways. Pain is made worse by anger and despair over the inevitable and necessary suffering all of us experience at some time in our lives.

- *Remember stress hardiness.* If you've had a lot of sickness and suffering in your life and learned to thrive through these stressful times, you may be stronger than most people who haven't suffered as much. Even dogs can show immuno-toughness.[24] Dogs born and bred in a research laboratory are more likely to succumb to sickness than their life-toughened dog pound cousins. The street strays captured and sent to the laboratories seem to find at least a "dog-level" kind of meaning through their street suffering as strays, and this allows them to have more stamina. They seem to figure out that while the laboratory is a horrible place, they can rely on some of their prior stress experience to toughen them somewhat against it.

- *Use your "forgettory."* Don't try to control in the present what happened in the past. Don't blame yourself for not having the right attitude or thinking enough positive loving thoughts. We get sick and die not because we didn't have the right attitude but because we are mortal.

- Primum non nocere. *(First, do no harm.)* Don't hurt yourself by trying too hard to cure yourself. Before you act, think and reflect. Healing is not only a matter of comprehending and finding meaning in sickness. It's also a matter of managing our situation with the right strategy and force. The trick seems to be to meet "the problem of the match." The challenge is to make the right choice of fighting or giving in. After getting all the information we can, we have to know when to match our fighter's skills to our problem or to match our "enlightened quitter's" approach. We have to remember that strength is not always perseverance and that some problems are best dealt with by disengaging and moving on.

    Thrivers get good information about their condition and act assertively to remediate it when possible. But remember, sometimes there is power in just waiting and doing not much at all. In many instances, our sickness can get better on its own, so just reflectively waiting is sometimes a healing act. Neurophysiologist Robert M. Sapolsky quoted a phrase that summarizes this principle. "In the face of strong winds, let me be a blade of grass. In the face of a strong wall, let me be a gale of wind."[25]

• *Remember the power of positive psychology*. When things become unbearable, it's okay to mentally run away. Pathogenic psychology says that strategies such as intentionally deluding yourself, fantasizing, compartmentalizing, denial, and all sorts of self-deception techniques are "sick," but positive psychology says they can sometimes be helpful. Social worker Katherine Northcraft refers to "transcenders" [thrivers] as people who "in the worst of times, envision themselves as elsewhere, imagine that they can do great things despite their surroundings."[26] When I went through the pain of my bone marrow transplant, I told my wife, "I'll be leaving for Maui in my mind. I'll be back after this is over."

Another Get-Well Card from Patsy

The lessons of thriving's hardiness, happiness, and healing you have learned so far all relate to a fundamental concept regarding the nature of healing and thriving. To find the sense of coherence, thrivers seem to be able to be "palindromatic" thinkers. A palindrome is a word or phrase that reads the same way and means the same thing forward and backward (e.g., madam).

You have read that thrivers have the ability to "go with the flow." They seem to be able to swing back and forth with the stresses of life. They remain mentally creative by looking for the comedy in their tragedy and remaining aware of the tragic in the comic. While their general psychological trajectory is always upward, they can deal with sickness by thinking creatively in all directions.

My cancer unit neighbor Patsy gave me a get-well card. She had drawn a picture in crayon of a little girl on a swing. She had written underneath it, "Some days I feel up, other days I feel down." When I asked her to tell me about the card, she went into one of her wise teaching stories. " It's like I'm playing on our swing at home and going back and forth and way up and way down. I would get afraid sometimes when I was going way up high, but it was kind of exciting. Then, when I would go really down fast, I knew I would be going higher again. You get afraid but you have fun and get excited anyway. You can't swing good if you just go up a little bit up and a little bit down or when you just sit on the swing doing nothing. The fun is because you go up and down, up and down, up and down." Once again, the thriving little philosopher had shown us another secret of the healing aspect of thriving.

12 Hoping for All Times

"Every good thought you think is contributing its share to the ultimate result of your life."

—*Grenville Kleiser*

Learning to Be Optimistic

"Doctor, you have to help me," said the frustrated mother to the child psychiatrist. "I have two wonderful, identical, five-year-old twin boys. They differ in only one way. Steve is an eternal optimist and Stewart is an unrelenting pessimist. How do I balance them up and make Steve a little more pessimistic and Stewart more optimistic?" The doctor answered, "That's easy. On their birthday, fill Stewart's room with an amazing and overwhelming array of the best toys you can find. Fill Steve's room with a large pile of horse manure." The mother said she thought the suggestion a little odd but that she would try it.

A few weeks later the disappointed mother returned to the therapist's office. "Nothing changed at all," she reported. "When Stewart saw all the toys, he just whined and said, 'Look at all this junk. The other kids have newer and better versions of these toys. I'm so unlucky I never get anything good.' When Steve opened the door to his room to find his gift, he immediately began digging gleefully through the pile of horse manure. He screamed in delight, 'You can't fool me! Wherever there's horse manure there must be a pony!' I'm afraid they were just born they way they are and there isn't anything anyone can do about it."

Are we naturally born optimists or pessimists, or can we learn to be more generally positive in our outlook? According to Dr. Martin E. P. Seligman, who is one of the strongest advocates for the field of positive psychology, optimism can be learned. He wrote, "Pessimists can in fact learn to be optimists, and not through mindless devices like whistling a happy tune or mouthing platitudes, but by learning a new set of cognitive skills."[1] These skills constitute the fourth foundation of thriving, a resilient and creative consciousness characterized by a persistent hopefulness that helps us maintain an upward psychological trajectory.

A Joyful Heart

Dr. Seligman is a professor of psychology at the University of Pennsylvania. As former president of the American Psychological Association, he gave testimony at the congressional meeting on the issue of preventive medicine. He emphasized the need for a more optimistic and positive psychology and pointed out that there has been far too great a focus on what makes people sick and how to avoid these factors than on natural human strengths and competencies.[2] Like Kobasa's research on hardiness (stress resistance), Csikszentmihalyi's work on happiness (flow), and Antonovsky's studies on healing (a sense of coherence), Seligman's exploration of the nature of hopefulness (learned optimism) has helped advance the field of positive psychology and done much to clarify why so many of us manage to thrive through the trying times in our lives.

Seligman's primary research interest has been in the area of the cornerstone of thriving, our explanatory style. He defines it as the manner in which we habitually explain to ourselves why events happen. He wrote, "Your way of explaining to yourself determines how helpless you can become, or how energized, when you encounter the everyday setbacks as well as momentous defeats. I think of your explanatory style as reflecting 'the word in your heart.'"[3] He says that "word" is a "no" or a "yes," and for thrivers that word is almost always "yes." While a little rational pessimism is essential to prudent living, a hopeful heart is what gives our lives a joyful purpose and helps us thrive through the traumas of our lives.

The Thriver's Antidote

According to Greek mythology, Pandora was the first woman. She was created by Prometheus's brother, and the gods became jealous of her extraordinary beauty and presented her with the gift of a mysterious box with the instructions that she must never open it. As the gods suspected, Pandora was unable to resist the temptation and lifted the lid to peek inside. The result of her curiosity let loose misery upon the world. Before she could slam the lid back down, disease, madness, malaise, and other plagues had sprung forth from the box. At the last minute, one compassionate god took pity on Pandora and allowed her to close the lid with one thing left inside—the antidote that not only can render life's miseries bearable but can make it possible for us to thrive through its adversities: that magical antidote was hope.

Webster's dictionary defines hope as "cherishing a desire with expectation."[4] All of us have desires and expectations, but my interviews of thrivers indicate that much of the energy behind their upward emotional spiral is their "yes" heart and cherishing life no matter how many setbacks they are handed.

Because their goals are related to finding more meaning in life and not things, and their expectations are for a loving, joyful life and not a bigger pile of toys, they are able to make their way through the "manure" they encounter. By focusing their hope on the simple pleasures of life, they avoid setting themselves up for the disappointment that leads to pessimism. They go far beyond a wish list of things they want to the more deeply personal goal of celebrating life irrespective of its external circumstances. Because of this kind of hope, the world remains a pretty great place, no matter what has happened to them.

One of my patients who barely survived a heart attack illustrated the life-cherishing kind of optimism and enduring hope. He said, "Before my heart attack, I had a wish list a mile long and I could be a really cynical sourpuss when things didn't go my way. I hoped for this and I hoped for that. Now I have a focused hope, to love and cherish my life as long as I can."

The Best of All Possible Worlds

If we allow it to, the trauma in our lives can focus our attention on what we really need instead of on what we have spent a lifetime thinking we want. If we overextend and squander our "hope-capital," we end up squandering its immense power to help us thrive when we really need it. One of my fellow cancer patients said, "I was always hoping for this and hoping for that, but when I found out I had cancer, I learned to stop spreading my hope so thin and used it to help me enjoy what life I had."

The kind of hope that constitutes the fourth component of the thriving response is one based on a life explanatory system that construes the world we live in as the best of all possible worlds, even when things seem to go so terribly wrong. Patsy, the little philosopher you have been reading about, had a simple phrase that all of us on the cancer unit knew well. When things seemed at their worst for any of us, she would say, "Hey you guys, none of us gets our way. We get the way."

Despite the suffering she had experienced throughout her young life, Patsy persisted in explaining whatever happened to her from the perspective of "oh yes" rather than " oh no." Because of her explanatory style, neither she nor her parents ever lost hope. After Patsy died, her parents overheard a medical resident crying. They heard her say through her tears, "A lot of good their hope did them." They went to the young doctor to offer her their comfort. They put their arms around her as Patsy's mother said, "Hope did everything for us. It was the energy that kept us all going upward instead of feeling like we were always sliding backwards. Hope doesn't guarantee you won't die, only that you can enjoy living. Patsy loved to swing, and our hope kept swinging us up even after the many down times. Without it, we would have ruined our last days with her. Doctor, that's the good hope did us."

Leibniz's Lighthearted Logic

Henry David Thoreau said he intentionally used to stay in bed a few minutes every morning to take the time to remind himself of how good life was and that he was living in the best of all possible worlds. Philosopher Gottfried Wilhelm von Leibniz would have understood Thoreau's daily celebration of life. Although Leibniz was one of the world's greatest logicians, he could also be seen as one of the first cognitive psychologists. He discussed optimism as a way of thinking characterized by the reasoned judgment that good would predominate in some way and some form over evil, even if that goodness was associated with and developed through suffering. Although telling us that Leibniz had a brilliant mind, one of my philosophy professors said that Leibniz's ideas were often based on unrealistic, pie-in-the-sky, implausible, and often overly simplistic reasoning.

Valid logic or not, I found Leibniz's concept of optimism to be life-affirming, helpful in developing my own explanatory style during my cancer, and related to the current positive psychology research on optimism.

The life philosophy most often associated with Leibniz's thinking is Voltaire's parodistic phrase, "This is the best of all possible worlds."[5] In his novel *Candide* (1759), Voltaire was highly critical of what he considered the shallowness of an optimistic perspective. While the critical and ever rational Voltaire himself was far from being optimistic about the world, and thought that random chance determined the outcome of our lives, his satirical summary of Liebniz's thinking is more in line with how thrivers see the world.

Why does Leibniz's thinking matter to the modern world and positive psychology? It does because his definition of an optimistic person was someone who arrived at a reasoned conclusion that eventually something good will come from evil. He did not see optimism as a state accepted on blind faith, a state of naive happiness or feigned contentment or as freedom from setbacks and disappointments. Leibniz's concept of creative construing through adversity is the kind of optimism most related to the flourishing of thrivers through crisis, and the idea that all life events can be defined in terms of a constructive goal state.

Leibniz reasoned that if God is all-wise, then His wisdom allowed Him to know of all possible worlds. If God was all-powerful, then His power allowed Him to create whatever world He chose. If God was good, then His innate infinite goodness would have made it impossible for Him to create any world other than the best of all possible worlds. Thrivers seem to catch a glimpse of God's wonderful world because they experience it in all of its intensely complex, sometimes miserable, but always wonderful glory.

The optimism of thrivers does not mean that they are not also pessimistic. Even when they feel pessimistic and down in the dumps, they seem able to think optimistically about their situation. They develop an optimistic mental habit positive psychologists call explanatory style, a generally positive long-term view of the eventual outcome of even the most devastating circumstances. In terms of thriving, it doesn't matter if Leibniz or Voltaire was right. It's Leibniz's way of thinking and explanatory style that demonstrates the kind of creative construing that the thrivers I interviewed most often showed.

As a result of their hard-earned insight, the thriver's optimism, or hopeful thinking, as I detected it in their interviews, is not only about them or their specific situation but also for the whole world no matter what the world seems to have done to them. Whatever kind of hope thrivers had going into their traumas, and even if their logic didn't hold up to Voltaire's skeptical rationalism, they seemed to use their optimism to come out of their crisis with renewed trust in the ultimate mysteries of the world and a hope that is infinite, sacred, and unconquerable.

So What's So Wonderful?

Traditional pathologenically oriented psychology spends little time looking for what's right with us and the world. The skepticism regarding our potential to thinking "thrivingly" as expressed by writers such as Sophocles, Nietzsche, and Freud notwithstanding, the new positive psychology's research is showing that other writers such as Socrates, Condorcet, Maslow, and Rogers had it right. We are capable of remarkable acts of conscious creation and of not being just helpless victims doing our best to survive in a cruel world.

Those who have not yet learned to flourish in their lives tend to see thrivers as Pollyannas, but they are not. After one of my lectures on the hope component of thriving, one man said, "It all sounds too Pollyanna-ish to me. Life isn't as wonderful as you're making it sound. It all depends on your definition of wonderful." I answered, "That's exactly it. It all depends on how you construe your life and how you decide what will constitute a wonderful life for you. For most thrivers, it's wonderful just being alive to reflect on such issues."

Thrivers' optimism is born from their struggle to find meaning through their painful experience of the kind of random chance events that Voltaire proposed characterize life. They would have no quarrel with Voltaire because their hope extends far beyond being upbeat, strong-willed, having a positive attitude, or clinging to cheerful blind faith. They know well how tough life can be, but their creative consciousness helps them develop their own individual, unshakable, optimistic philosophy honed by their firsthand experience with the natural chaos of life.

Because of how thrivers come to construe their world, any degree of stress or suffering becomes further evidence of the intensity of being fully alive. They don't necessarily take bad news any differently or better than pessimists, but it's what they eventually do with that news that allows them to thrive. In the long run, they don't let it get them down, and they keep their psychological trajectory up. Seligman's research shows that they do this by the three Ps. They don't take negatives personally, see them as pervasive, or consider them permanent.

Whether or not all thrivers subscribed to Leibniz's faith or Voltaire's rationalism, my interviews indicated that they all seemed to eventually come to the point in their thriving that caused them to embrace this world as the best of all possible worlds and their lives as the best of all possible lives, even when their lives seemed so much worse than other lives and their world so much crueler. Their crises somehow had caused them to carry Pandora's last gift forever in their hearts and minds, allowing them to cherish their lives and world with great expectations.

Hoping for Life

When I was dying of cancer, I often wondered about and sometimes doubted and cursed a Supreme Power or universal force that would allow cancer and caused children like Patsy to suffer and die from it. I could feel my waning hope transforming to anger and even hate, but I had plenty of time to think and reflect about the nature of the universe, the meaning of life and death, and why the world seemed so innately terrible. Over time and after endless hours of working on my explanatory style and with the help of co-thrivers such as my wife, family, caring medical staff, and thriving role models like Patsy, I felt a new kind of "big league" hope coming over me. I began to take my misery much less personally, to see my bad luck much less pervasively, and to view my suffering as not being permanent.

Like the thrivers I interviewed, I learned that thriving is a lifelong process. I could see the suffering and agony all around me, but I finally came to think of both as evidence that the intensity of the energy associated with my pain might paradoxically be creating a deeper sense of being more alive. I knew that the one sure thing that would stop my pain would be my death, and as a result, I sometimes became worried when the pain would stop because I feared that it meant I was dying.

The looming presence of death seemed to make life all the more real for me and made me want to embrace life more fully and intensely than ever before. I began to sense that living in what seemed the worst of all possible worlds was allowing me the opportunity to sense the paradoxical and mysterious energy that was associated with a world with wonders that, without deep suffering or unless we learn to thrive before we suffer, may always be beyond our comprehension.

Olympic-Size Hope

I have a neighbor on the Big Island of Hawaii whom you may know of. His name is Matt Biondi, and he was a member of the 1988 U.S. Olympic swimming team. He was expected to follow in the footsteps—or should I say, the wake—of Olympian Mark Spitz, who had won seven gold medals in 1972. Unfortunately, adversity struck. Matt finished a disappointing third in his first event and missed the gold medal in his next event by milliseconds. A life of sacrifice and rigorous training had resulted in terrible disappointment. Everyone thought that Matt's devastating defeats would result in his recovering only in time to win a medal in one of his future events. But they had greatly underestimated the power of hope, optimism, and the thriving response.

Biondi not only survived and recovered from his defeats; he went on to win five gold medals in his next five events. In preparing to write this book, I asked Matt about his extraordinary achievement. He said, "I never lost hope. I was actually becoming more optimistic than ever because of those losses. They seemed to awaken a new resolve within me." Biondi's statement reflects the way thrivers manage to construe failures and setbacks in such a way that they become challenges more than problems and indicators of what needs to be done next more than what they failed to do.

Dr. Seligman would not have been surprised to hear of Matt Biondi's victorious comeback. Earlier in the year of the Olympics, Seligman had done an experiment that predicted Matt's thriveability.[6] As part of a study conducted at a swimming demonstration event designed to showcase Biondi's best time, his coach was asked to tell Matt that he had earned a time slower than he actually had achieved. Seligman's study was designed to assess the impact of "bad news" as related to optimism, and Biondi did what thrivers do.

When he received the surprising and disappointing slow time, he remained mentally engaged, construed his "failure" as a challenge rather than a problem, and tried again. This time his time—which was already actually very good—was even better. He did not just show resilience. He seemed to get stronger and thrive because of the negative feedback. When his other less optimistically thriving teammates received their false slow times, their second scores were lower than their first.

Leibniz's Hope or Murphy's Law?

Hope is the counter-emotion to despair. It is the emotional antibody our psychological immune system provides for us so we can avoid falling into the apathy and depression of adversity or the languishing of those who never learn to thrive. It helps alter our psychological trajectory back up to an upward direction after life events force it downward. Like hardiness, happiness, and healing, hope does not just happen to us. You may remember that Izzie said he was not "an optimist by nature" and had to "work at it." We can all choose to work at it by following the model of thrivers—by cherishing our opportunity to remain engaged in a full life, and constantly modifying our explanatory system to one that allows for expectations for better times coming from the bad. Even if we have to fool ourselves to do it, thinking hopefully is crucial to the ability to thrive.

Hope is a way of feeling about life, and optimism is the way of thinking that makes us feel that way. Because we determine the content of our own consciousness and are the ones who feed ourselves our own mental diet, we have the choice of using Murphy's Law or Liebniz's philosophy as our guide. We can worry as Murphy's Law warns that anything that can go wrong will, and think that we are like the tiny ball rolling around the roulette wheel and by chance dropping into winning or losing slots. If we elect to thrive, however, we can be guided by Leibniz's idea that even with its random harshness, the world is still as Voltaire satirized Liebniz's view and truly the best it could possibly be. Thrivers show the ultimate form of hope, the benefit-finding skill that allows them even at the worst of times in the world to feel gratitude for the time they have and will still have to live in it.

The word "optimism" derives from the Latin word *ops,* meaning "power," and also from *optimus,* meaning "the best." When we hope, we intentionally exert mental power over our consciousness to help us make the best of the way things turn out. Hoping is having an "apt attitude," the view that things are apt to change for the better or at least be the best they can be. This is the way of thinking that teaches our heart to say Seligman's "yes" word. It is feeling and thinking that we are apt or suitable for the challenge that faces us.

Having an Apt Attitude

There is a subtle difference between what has come to be called "the power of positive thinking" and the kind of hopeful optimism I detected in the thrivers. They did not engage in rote statements of positive affirmations and personal pep talks. Instead, they were busy working on developing an explanatory system that could accommodate the changes and stressors in their lives. Their feelings of hope seemed to stem from a consciousness of creativity committed to optimism no matter how many bad things happened to them.

In my interviews of thrivers, you will note an underlying hopeful theme that permeated every story they told themselves about their lives. They show a hopefulness based on acceptance of their limitations and those imposed upon them, tempered by a clear and creative assessment of the possibilities still open to them for growth through their challenges. As best they can, they not only return to normal after a major setback, but seem able to transcend what was usual for them to discover an even more authentic and meaningful life because of their suffering.

Thrivers do not bring their suffering upon themselves by an act of will. Their general mental momentum is away from the role of martyr and toward the expectation that how they think and imagine their world will be is how eventually it turns out. One thriver was a 97-year-old Taiwanese woman. She had endured serious illness most of her life, lived in abject poverty, and recently lost several members of her family in an earthquake. She told me, "If you think of your life as a garden constantly being destroyed by drought and wind, that is what your life becomes for you. If you think of it as a flourishing garden that keeps regrowing even more beautifully after each storm, that is how life will be for you."

Another example of the thriving style of hopefulness is that of the young mother of a five-year-old girl dragged from the safety of the porch of her home while playing a board game with one her friends. She was found days later at the side of the highway, raped and murdered. When the distraught mother granted an interview to the news media and a reporter asked how she was coping with her tragic loss and its horrible circumstances, she responded tearfully but with a thriver's hope. She said, "I have to make every cell in my body all over again just to get through the next day. I have to remake myself and my life, but I will do it because of what happened to my daughter. I will always be Samantha's mother, always. Nothing changes that. It's my love for her that will help me remake my life."

Despite this mother's grief and rage, and with stress hormones surging through her body, she remained hopeful about her life. She refused to allow her identity as a mother to be taken from her. Her hope was based on the creativity of her consciousness that allowed her to travel the path of reconciliation, even though the pattern of her life had been ravaged in one violent act.

The Advantage of Being Moody

Psychologist Lionel Tiger defines optimism as "a mood or attitude associated with an expectation about the social or material future—one which the evaluator views as socially desirable, to his or her advantage, or for his or her pleasure."[7] Popular psychology has tended to encourage putting up a good front, but often neglects the more difficult issue of how our consciousness works. Most self-help books say that we are supposed to think positively and try to at least show that we are in a good or upbeat mood. Even if we're feeling blue, our automatic answer to "How are you?" is supposed to be "Great!" We all know of course that we are not always feeling and doing great, because we are by our nature moody beings.

We are moody because our psychological immune system is always working, changing, and adapting. A "mood" is a reflection of what is on our mind, and an active mind has many and ever changing moods to match whatever challenges it perceives. Getting stuck in one mood is a reflection of a static consciousness and not a thriving mind.

Thriving requires paying attention to our moods, reading them, and asking ourselves what is going on in our mind that is leading to our mood of the moment. By trying to stay in or to broadcast a "good mood," we fail to listen to what our consciousness is trying to tell us about what we need to be working on to maintain a legitimately adaptive and upward psychological trajectory.

One of my patients was a physician who had come to my clinic because her son told her she was "excessively moody." Her son was a therapist who described himself as a "trainer in positive thinking." She said he was worried she "had too much negative energy" and was not "thinking positive thoughts." She said, "My son seems to think I need to work on my moodiness, but I don't really agree. When I'm in a good mood, I don't jump around smiling and announce it to the world. I don't make a big deal about it. When a bad mood comes over me, I like to think a little about what is on my mind that is causing my mood. I think Charlie is mistaking my pensiveness for not being positive enough. I don't really want to be a positive thinker. I just want to be a thinker. If I have to think about always being positive, I can't think about the real issues in my life."

This doctor's words express the importance of not trying to contrive or fake a positive mood and of learning from our moods rather than just trying to change them to fit the current psychological code of conduct.

What Good Is Hope?

Pathogenically oriented psychology often sees hope and its associated optimistic philosophy much as the playwright Sophocles and philosopher Nietzsche did, as ways of prolonging inevitable human suffering. The assumption seems to be that it is somehow more mature to just face the cold, hard facts of the cruel realities of life and dispense with the mental games of trying to think optimistically. The salutogenic orientation of positive psychology, however, sees hope and optimism as essential to surviving, recovering from, and eventually thriving because of adversity. In this view, there are no "cold, hard facts," only events that we mentally comprehend, assign our own meaning to, and learn to mentally manage because we exercise our choice of how we will construe our lives.

Our psychological immune system sees to it that no emotional state will last, so hope and optimism are built into us. If we open our minds and hearts, we can usually feel the subtle stirrings of hope within us even in the direst circumstances. It may be that evolution made us naturally hopeful beings. Any of our primitive ancestors who constantly sat pessimistically outside the cave, thinking that the tigers seemed to always chase only them and that they were doomed to this fate for life, probably became a meal for a more optimistic tiger hunting in hopes of just such a submissively passive game.

Our optimism provides our determination, and our hoping enables us to be open to discovering the pathways to thriving through crisis.[8] Hoping is the feeling that we can eventually come up with a plan to successfully reach our goal.

Optimistic thinking helps us reach that goal or find another one. These ways of thinking and feeling allow us to remain mentally engaged long enough at times of crisis to be able to come up with a different mental angle or different and more attainable goal.

Life in a Fuzzy World

Are being realistic and being optimistic two different orientations to life?[9] Optimism exists because, no matter how hard we try, we can never be all that realistic. There is too much uncertainty in the way the world works to assert that anything is unqualifiedly and permanently true. Optimism works for us because it allows us to live in a world in which nothing is certain.

Positive psychologist Sandra L. Schneider has written that optimism is a positive mental strategy because so much of the knowledge about our world is what she called "fuzzy." She pointed out that, despite our vast scientific achievements, our knowledge of our environment lacks the precision we seek. Particularly when it comes to the important issues such as the meaning of life, death, love, joy, and misery, we know very little about the whys and what fors of such things, and optimism is essential for dealing with just such issues.

Schneider wrote, "Fuzzy meaning provides leeway for each of us to extract personal meaning from our experiences."[10] "Fuzzy," as Schneider used the word, refers to the fact that we have just enough mental "wiggle room" to be able to enhance and focus on what we choose to see as the potential for favorable outcomes in our life experiences.

Seligman's Three Ps of Optimism

We all feel helpless and despairing when major crisis strikes. You have read that for at least a while, we all tend to make things worse by kindling or willfully suffering as victims. Those who turn the emotional corner and head their psychological trajectory upward toward thriving have one thing in common: they do not remain very long in their pessimistic way of framing their trauma. They seem to take a pessimistic peek into negative thinking just long enough to look into potential dangers and then search for a new range of mental options.

Seligman writes, "Pessimistic explanatory style . . . consists of certain kinds of explanations for bad events: personal ('It's all my fault'), permanent ('It's always going to be like this'), and pervasive ('It's going to undermine every aspect of my life')."[11] Thrivers tend to see the world in exactly the opposite way. They see all crises as temporary variations in a generally wonderful world and as challenges to their life point of view that are confined to this one time and instance. They know the difference between taking up the challenge and responsibility for dealing with adversity and seeing crises as their own fault and representative of failures in all areas of their lives and that will characterize their lives forever.

Thrivers have their bouts of pessimism, but they use them constructively. They use their negative thinking to take a few steps back and to think twice about their actions, how they are framing what has happened to them, and the ifs, ands, buts, and so whats of their situation. Their periods of pessimism protect them from making rash or foolhardy decisions about how to deal with adversity.

Dr. Seligman points out that hope depends primarily on not being stuck in the "personal, pervasive, and permanent" mode of thinking.[12] Thrivers figure out ways of thinking about their stressors that assign them to temporary and specific causes, not global life influences and not some "negativity magnet" implanted somewhere inside them. They already have an unalterable global view of the world as being a wonderful place, so individual crises are seen as painful but necessary variations on the wonderful world theme.

One of the thrivers I interviewed had experienced the theft of two of her new cars in the same month. This happened the same month she was told by her doctor that she was diabetic and would have to begin giving herself insulin injections. She came to my clinic to discuss her situation, but she was already clearly showing the nonpersonal, nonpervasive, nonpermanent kind of hopefulness of her thriving mode.

She said, "Can you believe the odds? Two cars, two thefts, and then this lousy news about the needles? What a fluke. My mother said I seem to have a dark cloud over my head, but I really don't see it that way. I think I'm generally a pretty lucky gal and most of my life is going just great, thank you. The economic problems in Detroit now are causing an increase in crime, but it always goes down eventually when things get better. I hate trying to give myself the injections, but I'm glad they found out about the diabetes before it had worse effects. I'm not in denial, am I?" I told her that she might be, but that it seemed to be an enlightened and mild form essential for growing through her problems.

Eternal Hope

One of the most significant and perhaps most adaptive and helpful aspects of thriving is a special kind of hope I call "eternal hope." This is hope not just for this time or the immediate future but for all time. It is a life beacon and perennial optimism that serves as a guiding life philosophy.

Thrivers, especially those like me who faced their own death, seem to think of two futures. One is just around the corner and one is the infinite and forever future. Eternal hope results in the long-range optimism characterized by a different mental and emotional take on Seligman's three Ps of pessimism.

• *Eternal hope is highly personal.* The hope of the forever future is faith in "something more" that is often difficult to describe to others. It may take the form of a formalized set of religious beliefs, but more often it is expressed as one thriver put it: "I'm not religious, but I have faith that there is more than just this world and this life and that my problems are nothing compared to the major scheme of things."

• *Eternal hope is pervasive.* It tends to extend into all phases of a thriver's life. One thriver who was a photographer said, "I think all the crap that happens in my life is an exception and not the rule. When I go on streaks of bad luck, I know I'm in for a winning streak eventually. If you think of your bad luck as snapshots in your life that will eventually fade away, you don't get stuck telling yourself you're a natural-born loser in every area of you life."

• *Eternal hope is permanent.* Many psychologists suggest that our most basic source of suffering is related in some way to our fear of the end of the self.[13] They suggest that all terror results ultimately from our awareness of our vulnerability and mortality. In the final analysis, we are all concerned with self-preservation, so contemplating the end of the self is not something in which most of us easily engage. However, thrivers seem to convert this nagging fear of death into being more profoundly aware of the importance of enjoying life now. Because thrivers "flow" by totally immersing themselves in life, they are comforted by the fact that the loss of a sense of self can be a source of joy.

Patsy, the thriving superstar, showed her eternal hope in her typical profound innocent wisdom. We all knew that she knew she was dying, but it seemed to make her all the more alive in the present. As weak as she was, she often seemed more full of life than the patients who were doing much better physically than she was. She never used the words "death" or "dying," but one day she told me, "You know, Dr. Pearsall, I really love to play and pretend. The doctor said I should calm down now because I'm too sick to play, but I feel safer when I'm acting silly. I feel stronger when I pretend I'm a fairy princess with magical powers to stop the burning in my body. I hope they play in Heaven."

A new doctor came to our cancer unit. Everyone said she was one of the most brilliant cancer researchers in the world, and she visited us during medical rounds every morning. I met her several years after my cancer was cured. I had just given a talk to a medical group about the "eternal kind of hope" related to the thriving response. She met with me for a few minutes after my talk and told me how happy she was that my treatment had been successful. I remembered that she seldom spoke about people or feelings, so referring to the success of something concrete like treatment seemed more comfortable for her. As we talked, she said she felt I had failed to point out in my lecture that the eternal kind of hope I was speaking of was more like a mental opiate and self-delusion we all use to prevent us from having to face the fact that life is essentially what she called "a brief biophysical event."

She went on to say, "The kind of eternal hope you just talked about sounds nice, but I think everyone knows down deep that it is just a pleasant human farce that helps us avoid seeing that we are really not much more than a bag of cells that live for a while and then die. If the kind of hope you described works for patients, that's fine, but I think as scientists we have to remember what is really going on."

As the doctor walked away I remembered why, at our private late-night patient meetings on the cancer unit, we had called this doctor the "iron maiden." She was held prisoner by the pessimism of her pathogenic point of view. The most we could hope for from her was a morning when she didn't point out how vulnerable we were and what might go wrong. She seemed blind to the essential nature of eternal hope—that it is not only possible but also essential for thriving.

Novelist Albert Camus suggested that we should recognize those times in our lives when the quality of life depends on our ability to make a 100 percent commitment to something about which we are only 51 percent sure.[14] This is the kind of commitment that is at the core of eternal hope.

Some Optimistic Principles

I end this chapter about the role of hope in thriving with some of the principles of optimism as revealed by research in positive psychology, my own experience with cancer, and my interviews of thrivers who mentally concocted a combination of mental hardiness, emotional happiness, meaningful healing, and enduring hoping. I hope you will reflect on them as a way to review some of the concepts of learned optimism that portray it as a vital energy behind the capacity to thrive through life's tragedies.

• *Hope itself is happiness.* Hopeful feelings elevate us. They result in feeling happier and hardier, and that in turns increases our chances for healing. Samuel Johnson wrote that "hope is itself a special kind of happiness, and, perhaps, the chief happiness which this world affords."[15] When a group of young Germans was asked what they considered to be the most beautiful word in human speech, "hope" topped the list over such emotional heavyweights as "joy," "love," and "happiness."[16]

• *Hoping is not just looking favorably to the future but also being forgiving in our evaluation of past events.* We become hopeless not only when we look to the future with anxiety but also when we look to the past with regrets and self-recrimination. Hope requires giving ourselves the benefit of the doubt and an emotional break. We seldom wake up in the morning deciding to intentionally mess things up for ourselves or others, so a little loving leniency and "forgettory" action regarding our own past mistakes helps us to not lose hope.

• *Hope requires accepting uncertainty as a challenge to find new meaning in our lives.* While the fact that life is so uncertain can be a cause of anxiety, those who learn to hope are able to thrive because they know that in the final analysis, there are very few facts of life. They are heartened by the "fact" that, in the absence of certainly, there is nothing wrong with hope.

• *Hoping is mental reframing.*[17] Thriving requires our most creative construing when we experience severe adversity. The hope component of thriving is not fabricating or faking a positive attitude. It is doing hard mental work to find meaning by creating a perspective that is truthful enough to assure but not mislead us, and positive enough to comfort us without setting us up for major disappointment.

• *Hoping is a willful lowering of expectations.* Positive psychologists call this aspect of hoping adopting a relatively moderate threshold of minimum acceptability. Sometimes it is better not only to hope for the best but also to lower our criterion for and the meaning of what constitutes "best" and "better." I remember complaining that it was raining on the day of one of our family picnics. My grandmother said, "Better a rainy family picnic than no family or no picnic. When it rains, you can see it as a drizzle or a downpour. It all depends on how much rain you decide it will take to ruin a picnic. It's all really up to you."

- *Hoping is "benefit finding" by discovering positive aspects even in the worst situations.* There was a terrible tornado in Michigan while I was in the cancer unit. The sky turned pitch black and the warning sirens wailed. Patsy came quickly, wheeling her chair into my room, and I assumed that she was frightened. Instead, she rolled to the window and said, "Isn't this cool? Let's look for the funnel clouds. We're all here safe and cozy with lots of doctors and security guards and people to take care of us. This is a good day to have cancer."

- *Hoping is collecting and making memories of the wonderful simple things in life.* Most of our lives are spent engaging in routine activities. We often do so mindlessly as if we were on mental autopilot.[18] To develop our hoping, we need to turn off that autopilot once in a while and pay more attention to our lives. We need to look back to the good memories and pay attention to the fact that right now in our lives we are making the memories that will enrich them. When I was first able to walk alone to the bathroom after leaving the intensive care unit, I remember how important and wonderful it seemed that I could turn on the faucet myself, feel the water go from cold to warm, brush my own teeth, and swish the water around in my mouth. I doubt that you are looking forward to brushing your teeth tomorrow morning as much as I do now, but I hope my example might draw your attention to what a simply wonderful event it can be to start your day thriving.

- *Hoping is getting unused to life.* You read earlier about the process of habituation, or getting used to what we are doing and experiencing. Positive psychologists define the process of intense appreciation as "dishabituation." Appreciation requires dealing with all of life's activities, even the most ordinary and simple ones, in a less habitual way. It is intentionally paying attention so that we and not our life circumstances will determine the content of our consciousness.

- *Hoping is beyond comparison.* As you learned in chapter 9, a comparative approach to life ultimately leads to unhappiness. Maintaining an optimistic outlook requires that we find positive anchors in our lives that are not based on a competitive view and that are referenced to our lives, not that of others.

- *Hoping is being aware of being.* Another finding about optimism from positive psychology shows that happiness comes not from what we have done or think we may be able to do. It comes from being fully absorbed in what and how we are doing in the present moment.[19]

• *Hoping is not wishful thinking.* There is a significant difference between the reflective reasoning of enlightened hoping and passive wishing. Enlightened optimism helps us think in more creative, open, and adaptive ways that help us focus our wishes so that they become conscious acts of creation.[20] As I pointed out in my book *Wishing Well: Making Your Every Wish Come True,* the power of a wish ultimately derives from the degree of reasoned hope and philosophical optimism with which we make it.

Toward a New Story

You have now learned about the four components of thriving. At the time of your next life challenge, it will be up to you to keep hoping, aspiring, and searching for new ways to grow through your crisis. It will be up to you to be willing to accept what you will never know or fully understand while maintaining the optimism and hope that you can always learn and understand more.

Positive psychologist Sandra L. Schneider's research supports the principles of hoping listed above. You have read that she emphasizes the point that reality is "fuzzy" because there is no one exact and perfect truth in the world. She points out that even if there were a remarkably constant truth that perfectly predicted future events, most of us are not in the mental, emotional, or spiritual position to be able to recognize it. The best we can do is to keep seeking our own best estimate of the truths that seem to apply to our own life.

If there is one truth, it might be that that life is an eternal challenging chaos in which we are active participants as well as causes. Like some clever and wise teacher, it seems that the universe enjoys provoking and aggravating us into learning more and more, even though we will never learn enough.

Philosopher and theologian Thomas Berry pointed out that what is needed in order to thrive is a better new story about our lives. Thrivers are masters at composing such stories. He wrote that we all need a basic story: "Our narrative of how things came to be, how they came to be as they are, and how the future can be given some satisfying direction. We need a story that will educate us, a story that will heal, guide, and discipline us."[21] While Berry was referring to a story like those provided by traditional religions, we also need to keep writing, editing, refining, and creating our individual life stories capable of accommodating life's tortures and horrors as well as its blessings. This is the challenge of an optimistic creative consciousness that allows us to thrive through stress.

Dr. Schneider wrote, "The illusion of the good life is likely to break down for those who lull themselves into complacency with self-deceptive beliefs, but the illusion is likely to become a reality for those who are optimistic within the fuzzy boundaries established by active engagement in life."[22] As you have read, it is just this kind of creative and eternally hopeful engagement that results in the ordinary magic of our capacity to thrive through the tragedies of this wonderful world.

Izzie always carried a yellowed and torn piece of paper in his wallet. He said it served as a reminder to never lose hope. The paper had a statement by the Persian poet Nizami, and it can serve as reminder to all of us about the importance of an optimistic explanatory style and the miracles wrought by a thriving mentality. It said, "In the hour of adversity be not without hope. For crystal rain falls from black clouds."

Epilogue:
Grandma's Recipe for Thriving

"Cry with me as I die, but not for me. I'm crying because I will miss the precious moments of my life. No matter what happens to you, always remember to make the ordinary things sacred. Focus more on who you are with than what you do. Then, grandson, you will cry as I am not because you are dying but because you have so fully lived."

—My Grandma Leita Schlieman

Grandma's Wisdom

My grandmother was a thriver. She had suffered through the poverty of the Great Depression and had to struggle every day to provide for the safety and welfare of my mother and her sister. She held several menial jobs and had to spend hours on streetcars and buses to get back and forth to work. Although her own health was always poor, she managed to care for my grandfather, who himself was in even poorer health. He had nearly died from bleeding ulcers and barely survived being crushed through a small wooden door by a garbage truck at the city yard where he worked. For the last years of his life, my grandfather had become senile, difficult to manage, and often abusive. He lost complete control of his bladder and bowels, yet even through her own failing health, my grandmother continued to care for him. Despite her stressful life, Grandma remained the strong center of our family.

Grandma's house is where we all went to celebrate and sometimes to grieve. She cooked the Thanksgiving and Christmas turkeys and the post-funeral meals. It was the supreme honor to be asked to spend the night at Grandma's house because you were sure you would hear remarkable stories. As I began my study of the thriving response, I recognized that I had spent my young years knowing and loving a woman who exemplified the thriving response I was trying to understand.

Like most of the thrivers you have read about in this book, Grandma was not always upbeat, optimistic, positive thinking, and confident. She was often despondent and cried openly, and it was her vulnerability as much as her strength that comforted and encouraged us. She would speak of her trials and tribulations, and would not be seen by today's popular psychology as a model of positive attitude and personal power, but she was nonetheless a model of the invincible spirit and capacity to thrive that has been the focus of this book.

What was special about Grandma was not that she was an extraordinary person but that she was so ordinary, vibrant, vulnerable, and strong all at the same time. Her hardiness in the face of her trials inspired us. Her ability to seem to flow with happiness through so many crises encouraged us. The way she found a sense of coherence in the chaos of her life instructed us. And perhaps most important, her eternal optimism comforted us and made us feel safe. We felt comfortable sharing our worst fears and problems with Grandma, not because she was an exceptional person but because she wasn't. She was an ordinary woman thriving through extraordinary times, and it was her way of viewing life that we all longed to emulate. She often said and made us feel that if Grandma could do it, so could we.

Grandma's Ingredients for Thriving

When my grandmother was dying, I visited her as often as I could. I had completed my Ph.D. in clinical and educational psychology and finished my internship so as to begin my work as a clinical neuropsychologist at Sinai Hospital of Detroit. My grandmother was extremely proud of me, and when I visited her at her deathbed, she began to talk to me not only as the grandson she had helped so many times before, but as someone who might be able to help her through her last days.

She was in terrible pain, facing amputation of an infected foot, and often cried and shared her fears. She said, "I know you're sad that you're losing me, but I'm sadder because I'm losing all of you. You each lose one but I lose everyone. You must help me deal with my loss and not be frightened by my tears. You must help me make sense of this." I didn't know then that I would feel exactly this way years later when I faced my own death from cancer.

At first I was uncomfortable with Grandma's sharing. I still felt like her little grandson, but I could sense that she needed to see me differently now, and for both of us, I needed to see her differently as well. Later, when I almost died from cancer, I would feel as Grandma must have. I had always been seen as the strong one in the family to whom everyone else turned for support and advice, but my cancer made me long to be helped and guided by others. I learned then the message you read earlier about hardiness, that it is a matter of much grace and grit. It is as much knowing when to give up control as it is trying to exercise it.

Grandma clearly needed me now to help her complete her life story. I listened for hours to what she had to say about her life as she faced her death, and I share her messages with you now as a way to help you integrate what you have read about the hardiness, happiness, healing, and hope that constitute your thriveability. I end this book with the gift Grandma gave me as she died. She had said these things to us many times before, whenever we brought her our problems, and along with the words quoted at the beginning of this chapter, she spoke about them again as she attempted to give meaning through her dying. I realize now that the list I have had for all these years is an expression of the nature of the thriving I have spent years trying to understand.

As a way of reviewing the points I have made about thriving, I hope you will take some time to reflect on each item from Grandma's list as a prescription for thriving. Her exact words are in italics, followed by my interpretations of them. I use the word "recipe" because Grandma was famous in our family for her cooking. I think you will find Grandma's recipe not too dissimilar from the one someone in your own family may have taught you as you grew up. In many of my interviews of thrivers, a grandmother or grandfather was very often their thriving role model, so perhaps you will find it helpful to look to your own ancestors for reminders as to how to enhance your natural thriving talent.

Grandma's Recipe for Thriving

• *Everything bad is a blessing in disguise.* If we remain engaged long enough with our adversities and try to construe them from an optimistic point of view, we can learn that our most difficult challenges can be our most life-affirming.

- *This too shall pass.* No emotional state lasts. Unless we choose to cling to an emotion, our feelings are in a constant state of flux. There is immense thriving power in having the persistent patience to "just wait and see how things work out."

- *Things always get worse before they get better.* When things seem to be falling apart, it is a sign they are coming together again in a new, different, and more challenging way. Despite popular psychology's emphasis on finding life balance, life is never in balance. By the time you have finished reading this sentence, your mind, thinking, spirit, and even the cells in your body are no longer what they were when you began reading. No matter how bad things are, sometime and some way, they will get better.

- *What is meant to be is meant to be.* There are reasons for everything, and thriving is continuing our search not only for those reasons but also for their underlying purpose no matter what adversity we face. We may never find "the reason," but because thriving is a lifelong process of weaving our life story, continuing to look for reasons can help us go beyond surviving and resilience to the experience of being a thriver.

- *Life is what you make it.* While we often can't do anything to alter the events in our lives, we can create our own consciousness and internal experience of them. The mental diet we feed our consciousness ultimately determines what we are and can become. Life is fuzzy, uncertain, and has few if any universal truths, so it is up to us to construe it in such a way that it has creative and adaptive meaning for us. Thriving is constantly editing, modifying, and strengthening our explanatory style.

- *Be careful what you wish for.* Wishing is an expression of our hopes, and hoping has immense power. Thrivers have eternal hope, so their wishes are made in the context of a lifelong philosophy and not immediate need.

- *Remember to make good memories.* Since we are constantly creating our own consciousness, we are forever in the process of re-creating ourselves. Who we are and the content of our minds is the compilation of the memories we choose to hold and retrieve and also of what we choose to intentionally relegate to our unremembered past. To be able to thrive, we need both a good memory and a good forgettory.

- *Things are never as bad as they seem.* Things could not only be worse, they could be much worse. What we see as adversity might be seen by someone else at a different place in his or her life as nowhere near as traumatic as we have construed it to be.

- *What goes around, comes around.* It not only seems that bad things happen to good people but that very good things happen to some very bad and undeserving people. In the long run, how we choose to see the world and how we behave in terms of our explanatory system will come back to us sometime in some way. Thrivers have the patience, broadness of thinking, and emotional will to wait for their suffering to pass, and their rewards, in whatever mysterious ways they might, to finally come.

- *When you're feeling sorry for yourself, start feeling sorry for someone else instead.* Thrivers tend to use their own suffering to spark within them thoughts of how they might be able to reduce the suffering of others. Grandma told me that I would know when I was doing the most important things in my life because doing such things always seems to cost the most in terms of personal pain, sacrifice, and selflessness. One of her favorite phrases was, "If you are feeling sorry for yourself, you're thinking far too much about yourself and not nearly enough about someone else."

- *Don't forget to say your prayers.* Research shows that praying lowers blood pressure and strengthens our physical immunity. When it's performed in a group, it also provides the benefits of social support. Praying usually involves a conversation with a Higher Power, so the relationship between the person praying and the One prayed to can reduce feelings of loneliness and isolation. Whatever your belief system, praying regularly seems to result in improved mental health and enhances our thriveability.[1] In her usual irascible and often irreverent way, Grandma said, "Listen and learn when you pray, don't just talk and ask. Even if you don't believe in God, you'd better be pretty damn sure something a hell of a lot wiser than you are believes in you."

- *I'll always be with you.* Grandma was right. She always said that, no matter what, she would always be with us. Thrivers seem to convey an eternal hope far beyond a good immediate future. They know that the meaning of their living and ultimately their dying is a matter of how they elect to find meaning while they are alive. Because thrivers so deeply and profoundly connect with life and with us, it seems that their energy stays with us. Perhaps, if we could listen like Beethoven did, we might even be able to hear the voices of thrivers who have passed.

Two Times to Thrive

I hope my Grandma's recipe for thriving will be as much help to you as it has been to me. I read her simple words almost every day at two special times. My first time for daily thriving is when I wake up in the morning. I try to do what Thoreau did, and resist the temptation to spring out of bed and get busy with my day. Instead, I spend just a few extra moments trying to truly and fully awaken to my life rather than just get up to try to lead it. Instead of trying to get up and get going, I try to wake up and start being. I lie in bed thinking about Grandma's words or reflect on how very lucky I am to be living for another day in the best of all possible worlds and how much I hope to learn about that world in the coming day.

My second time for daily thriving is when I go to bed at night. I try to remember to ask myself: What thoughts and feelings did I have today that I hope to remember for the rest of my life? Sometimes I write down my answer and read it again when I wake up the next morning.

I have found that practicing these two thriving rituals has helped me remain on the upward trajectory course I know allows me to keep learning how to thrive. I don't always remember to set aside these special times, and sometimes feel too busy, too tired, or too distracted to do so. When I feel rushed, upset, angry, impatient, or unfairly treated, I begin to feel that spending these two thriving times is silly and that Grandma's recipe is too unrealistic or overly simplistic. Fortunately, whenever I begin to feel this way, I seem to have a dream or see an image of Grandma that inspires me to start spending more time again in learning what it means to thrive.

Several times when I was dying, I saw images of Grandma. Perhaps it was an illusion, a delusion, a dream, a result of oxygen deprivation, or a medication side effect, but I am sure I saw and heard her. She was sitting in her wheelchair and holding up her hand. She kept saying softly, "Go back, you must tell them." She said, or perhaps with Beethoven's type of hearing I thought I heard her saying, those same words over and over again. Doctors told me I said these words out loud when I was coming out of anesthesia. Whatever was happening, I hope Grandma is proud that I have shared her recipe. I hope she's happy to know that because of her loving wisdom, she and I are both invincible.

Endnotes

Preface

1. C. L. M. Keyes. "Complete Mental Health: An Agenda for the 21st Century." In C. L. M. Keyes and J. Haidt (Editors). *Flourishing: Positive Psychology and the Life Well-Lived*. Washington, D.C.: American Psychological Association, 2002, p. 294.

2. E. S. Fisher and H. G. Welch. "Avoiding the Unintended Consequences of Growth in Medical Care: How Might More Be Worse?" *Journal of the American Medical Association*, 1999, Volume 282, Number 5, pp. 445–453.

3. C. K. Meador. "The Last Well Person." *New England Journal of Medicine,* Volume 330, Number 6, 1994, pp. 440–441.

4. C. R. Snyder and S. J. Lopez, *The Handbook of Positive Psychology*: Oxford: Oxford University Press, 2002.

5. W. James. *The Varieties of Religious Experience.* New York: New American Library, 1902/1958, p. 77.

6. Ibid., p. 86.

Introduction

1. This research is discussed in Andrew Sullivan's article "Lacking in Self-Esteem? Good for You!" *Time*, October 14, 2002, p. 102.

2. F. B. Bryant. "A Four-Factor Model of Perceived Control: Avoiding, Coping, Obtaining, and Savoring." *Journal of Personality*. Volume 57, 1989, pp. 773–797.

3. Positive psychologists Kennon M. Sheldon and Laura King offer this definition in the article "Why Positive Psychology Is Necessary." *American Psychologist,* May 2001, Volume 56, Number 3, pp. 216–217.

4. D. Meyers. "The Friends, Funds, and Faith of Happy People." *American Psychologist,* January 2000, Volume 55, pp. 56–57.

5. For a brilliantly thorough discussion of the concept of a fall from paradise and its influence on our psyche and spirit, see R. Heinberg. *Memories and Visions of Paradise.* Los Angeles: Jeremy P. Tarcher, 1989.

6. M. E. P. Seligman. *Authentic Happiness*. New York: Free Press, 2002, p. xii.

7. See D. K. Goodwin's history of the life of Franklin and Eleanor Roosevelt titled *No Ordinary Time*. As quoted in M. E. P. Seligman. *Authentic Happiness*. New York: Free Press, 2002, pp. xii–xiii.

8. E. S. Fisher and H. G. Welch. "Avoiding the Unintended Consequences of Growth in Medical Care: How Might More Be Worse?" *Journal of the American Medical Association*, 1999, Volume 281, pp. 445–453.

9. For a discussion of the research softening and balancing the absolute negativism of many health warnings and presenting a more positive outlook on the issue of "risk," see Robert Ornstein's and David Sobel's classic book *Healthy Pleasures*. Reading, MA: Addison-Wesley, 1989.

10. This example is used and developed in the insightful and carefully researched book by cardiologist Dean Ornish titled *Love and Survival: The Scientific Basis for the Healing Power of Intimacy*. New York: HarperCollins, 1997.

Chapter 1

1. H. Benson. *Your Maximum Mind.* New York: Random House, 1987.

2. C. S. Carver. "Resilience and Thriving: Issues, Models, and Linkages." *Journal of Social Issues,* Volume 54, Number 2, p. 251.

3. Variations of these reactions are outlined in V. E. O'Leary and J. R. Ickovics. "Resilience and Thriving in Response to Challenge: An Opportunity for a Paradigm Shift In Women's Health." *Women's Health: Research on Gender, Behavior and Policy,* Volume 1, 1995, pp. 121–142.

4. The kindling metaphor was first offered by social psychologist P. D. Kramer. *Listening to Prozac: A Psychiatrist Explores Antidepressant Drugs and the Remaking of the Self.* New York: Viking Penguin, 1993.

5. Author Daniel Goleman discusses what he calls the "ventilation fallacy" in his book titled *Emotional Intelligence.* New York: Bantam Books, 1995, pp. 64–65.

6. D. Tice. As reported in Ibid., p. 58.

7. As quoted in A. H. Berger. "Are You're a Chronic Worrier?" *Complete Woman*, October 1987, p. 58.

8. As quoted in B. Q. Hafen, et al. *Mind Body Health.* Boston: Allyn Bacon, 1996, p. 205.

9. As quoted in C. L. Wallis (Editor). *The Treasure Chest.* San Francisco: Harper and Row, 1965, p. 232.

10. Ibid., p. 226.

11. L. Roemer and T. Borkovec. "Unwanted Cognitive Activity That Controls Unwanted Somatic Experience." In D. Wegner and J. Pennebaker (Editors). *Handbook of Mental Control. Volume 5,* Englewood Cliffs, NJ: Prentice Hall, 1993.

12. In researching the issue of worrying, I came across a quote from an unnamed source that was also titled "Why Worry?" It was very similar to the old Hawaiian's words. A similar phrase is in L. Romer and T. Borkovec, Op. cit., p. 228.

13. J. Gottman. *What Predicts Divorce: The Relationship Between Marital Processes and Marital Outcomes.* Hillsdale, NJ: Lawrence Erlbaum Associates, 1994.

14. D. Goleman. Op. cit., pp. 13–14.

15. J. Haidt. "Elevation and the Positive Psychology of Morality." *Flourishing.* Washington, D. C.: American Psychological Association, 2002, pp. 275–289.

Chapter 2

1. *Webster's Third New International Dictionary.* Springfield, MA. Merriam-Webster, 1993, p. 2332.

2. Ibid., p. 1932.

3. C. S. Carver. "Resilience and Thriving: Issues, Models, and Linkages." *Journal of Social Issues*, Volume 54, 1998, pp. 245–267.

4. Ibid., p. 53.

5. R. S. Lazarus. "From Psychological Stress to the Emotions: A History of Changing Outlooks. *Annual Review of Psychology*, 1993, pp. 1–22.

6. As quoted in D. Shaw. *The Pleasure Police*. New York: Doubleday, 1996, p. 17.

7. As reported by Dr. Martin Seligman in his book about the new field of positive psychology titled *Authentic Happiness*. New York: Free Press, 2002, p. 6.

8. These findings are presented by S. E. Taylor and J. D. Brown. "Illusion and Well-Being: A Social Psychological Perspective on Mental Health." *Psychological Bulletin*, 1988, pp. 193–210.l

9. As quoted in C. Jabs. "New Reason to Be an Optimist." *Self*, September 1988, pp. 170–173.

10. W. L. Wilbanks. "The New Obscenity." *Reader's Digest*, December 1988, p. 23.

11. As quoted in B. Siegel. "Mind Over Cancer. An Exclusive Interview." *Prevention*, March 1998, pp. 59–64.

12. Study reported in M. E. P. Seligman. *Learned Optimism*. New York: Alfred A. Knopf, 1991.

13. Ibid., p. 178.

14. The term "pleasure police" was coined by author David Shaw. Op.cit., p. ix.

15. This percentage is a manufactured one. There are many good studies of the negative effects of eating too much meat, and there is no doubt that there are cardiovascular and other health risks associated with an unbalanced diet and too much animal protein. Nonetheless, most of us can think of relatives who were lifelong carnivores who to the best of our knowledge never developed heart disease. There are few headlines announcing, "A small percentage of people with lousy diets have no health problems at all!"

16. For a description of "passive volition" as described in psychological and parapsychological research, see my book about the power of wishing or intent. P. Pearsall. *Wishing Well: Making Your Every Wish Come True*. New York: Hyperion, 2000.

Chapter 3

1. E. Forbes. *Thayer's Life of Beethoven*. Princeton, NJ: Princeton University Press, 1969, p. 286.

2. As quoted at *Classical Music Pages Homepage*, created by Matt Boynick, February 1, 1996.

3. These and the other quotes from Beethoven's writings can be found in biographies such as the Forbes work listed above and many other books about the composer and his music. The website *Beethoven: The Immortal* is a particularly rich source of information on his life, work, suffering, and thriving. I also suggest a reading of Beethoven's "Heilgenstadt Testament," his powerfully insightful last will and testament that serves as a treatise on thriving.

4. As quoted at *Classical Music Pages Homepage*, created by Matt Boynick, February 1, 1996.

5. Charles C. Carver. "Resilience and Thriving: Issues, Models, and Linkages." *Journal of Social Issues*, Volume 54, Number 2, p. 248.

6. Ibid., p. 250.

7. J. Piaget. *The Child's Conception of the World*. Paterson, NJ: Littefield Adams, 1963.

8. C. McMillen, S. Zuravin, and G. Rideout. "Perceived Benefits from Child Sexual Abuse." *Journal of Consulting and Clinical Psychology*, Volume 63, 1985, pp. 1037–1043.

Chapter 4

1. M. Biondi. "The Illusion of Success." In P. Pearsall. *Toxic Success: How to Stop Striving and Start Thriving*. Makawau, HI: Inner Ocean Publishing, 2002.

2. M. Csikszentmihalyi. *Flow: The Psychology of Optimal Experience*. New York: HarperCollins, 1991, p. 20.

3. For an example of the process of "meaning reconstruction," see R. A. Neimeyer. *Meaning Reconstruction and the Experience of Loss*. Washington, D. C.: American Psychological Association, 2001.

4. This point is made by K. W. Saakvitne, H. Tennen, and G. Affleck in "Exploring Thriving in the Context of Trauma Theory: Constructivist Self Developmental Theory." *Journal of Social Issues*, Volume 54, Number 2, Summer 1998, pp. 279–299.

5. W. Kaminer. *I'm Dysfunctional, You're Dysfunctional*. New York: Addison-Wesley, 1992, p. 3.

6. Ibid., p. 281.

7. This danger is explained and discussed in an excellent book by William Ryan. *Blaming the Victim*. New York: Pantheon, 1971.

8. Ibid., p. 281.

9. Psychologist Charles C. Carver develops this point. "Resilience and Thriving: Issues, Models, and Linkages." *Journal of Social Issues*, Volume 54, Number 2, 1998, p. 262–263.

Chapter 5

1. For an excellent description of the important social and cultural role of shame, see J. B. Twitchell. *For Shame*. New York: St. Martin's Press, 1997.

2. W. R. Miller and J. C'deBaca. "Quantum Change: Toward a Psychology of Transformation" In T. F. Heatherton and J. L. Weinberger (Editors). *Can Personality Change?* Washington, D. C.: American Psychological Association, 1994, pp. 253–280.

3. For a discussion of these sudden personal reappraisals and transformations during trauma, see M. A. Greenbert. "Cognitive Processing of Traumas: The Role of Intrusive Thoughts and Reappraisals." *Journal of Applied Social Psychology*, Volume 25, 1995, pp. 1262–1296.

4. In his forward to E. E. Werner and R. S. Smith. *Vulnerable But Invincible: A Study of Resilient Children*. New York: McGraw Hill, 1982, p. xvi.

Chapter 6

1. W. A. Tiller, W. E. Dibble, and M. J. Kohane. *Conscious Acts of Creation: The Emergence of a New Physics*. Walnut Creek, CA: Pavior Publishing, 2001.

2. As defined in *Webster's New World Dictionary*. New York: Simon and Schuster, 1988, p. 710.

3. Ibid., p. 711.

4. J. R. Ickovics and C. L. Parks. "Paradigm Shift: Why a Focus on Health is Important." *Journal of Social Issues*, Volume 54, Number 2, 1998, p. 237. For an excellent presentation of the research related to this "value-added" orientation to thriving, see R. G. Tedechi, C. L. Park, and L. G. Calhoun (Editors). *Posttraumatic Growth: Positive Changes in The Aftermath of Crisis*. Mahwah, NJ: Lawrence Erlbaum Associates, 1998.

5. K. Bryant. "I Won't Take 'See You Later' For Granted." *Newsweek*, December 24, 2001, p. 9.

6. Ibid., p. 9.

7. M. E. P. Seligman and M. Csikszentmihalyi. "Positive Psychology: An Introduction." *American Psychologist*, January 2000, p. 7.

8. A. Antonovsky, *Health, Stress, and Coping: New Perspectives on Mental and Physical Well-Being*. San Francisco: Jossey-Bass, 1979.

9. Ibid., p. xii.

10. M. E. P. Seligman and M. Csikszentmihalyi. Op. cit., p. 7.

11. J. R. Ickovics and C. L. Park. "Paradigm Shift: Why a Focus on Health is Important." *Journal of Social Issues,* Volume 54, Number 2, 1998.

12. For a description of the process of enlightened denial, see D. Goleman. *Vital Lies, Simple Truths.* New York: Simon and Schuster, 1985.

13. L. L. Lanager. *Holocaust Testimonies: The Ruins of Memory.* New Haven, CT: Yale University Press, 1990.

14. Ibid., p. 59.

15. This systematic selective evaluation and the power of "positive illusion" are described in S. E. Taylor. *Positive Illusions: Creative Self-Deception and the Healthy Mind.* New York: Basic Books, 1989.

16. M. Rutter. "Psychosocial Resilience and Proactive Mechanisms." *American Journal of Orthopsychiatry,* Volume 57, 1987, pp. 316–331.

17. As described by another pioneer in resilience research psychiatrist George E. Valliant. "Adaptive Mental Mechanisms: Their Role in a Positive Psychology." *American Psychologist,* January 2000, pp. 89–98.

18. For a discussion of this research, see R. Ornstein and D. Sobel. *The Healing Brain.* New York: Simon and Schuster, 1987.

19. E. E. Werner and R. S. Smith. *Vulnerable but Invincible: A Study of Resilient Children.* New York: McGraw Hill, 1982. See also E. E. Werner and R. S. Smith. *Kauai's Children Come of Age.* Honolulu, HI: University of Hawaii Press, 1977.

20. E. E. Werner and R. S. Smith. *Vulnerable but Invincible: A Study of Resilient Children.* Op.cit., p. 3.

21. As quoted in W. E. Barton. *Abraham Lincoln and His Books: With Selections from the Writings of Lincoln and a Bibliography of Books in Print Relating to Abraham Lincoln.* Folcroft, PA: Folcroft Library Edition, 1976.

22. M. J. Lerner. "The Desire of Justice and Reactions to Victims." In J. Macaulay and L. Berkowitz (Editors). *Altruism and Helping Behavior.* New York: Academic Press, 1970, pp. 205–229.

23. For a current review of the data on the variance of what really seems to lead to a sense of well-being, see Diener, et al. "Subjective Well-Being: Three Decades of Progress. *Psychological Bulletin,* Volume 125, 1999, pp. 276–302.

24. For a discussion of how we "cognitively process" or "construe" everything that happens to us, see J. Bruner. *Actual Minds, Possible Worlds.* Cambridge, MA: Harvard University Press, 1986.

25. This process is described in S. Scarr. "How Genotypes and Environments Affect Coping: Development and Individual Differences." In N. Bogler, et al. (Editors). *Persons in Context: Developmental Process.* New York: Cambridge University Press, 1988, pp. 217–244.

26. I first heard the term "conscious acts of creation" used by my friend and esteemed physicist Dr. William Tiller. For a comprehensive presentation of the science of how our consciousness can literally impact and change external events, see his book *Conscious Acts of Creation: The Emergence of a New Physics.* Walnut Creek, CA: Pavior, 2001.

27. S. Lyubomirsky. "Why Are Some People Happier Than Others?" *American Psychologist,* March 2001, pp. 239–249.

28. Examples of some of the pioneering studies on resilience are: E. J. Anthony. "The Syndrome of the Psychologically Vulnerable Child." In E. J. Anthony and C. Koupernik (Editors). *The Child in His Family: Children at Psychiatric Risk.* New York: Wiley, 1974, pp. 529–545. See also N. Garmezy. "Stress Resistant Children: The Search for Protective Factors." In J. E. Stevenson (Editor). "Recent Research in Developmental Pathopathology."

Journal of Child Psychology and Psychiatry Book Supplement Number 4, Oxford, England: Pergamon Press, 1985, pp. 213–233. Also L. B. Murphy and A. E. Moriarity. *Vulnerability, Coping, and Growth: From Infancy to Adolescence.* New Haven, CT: Yale University Press, 1976.

29. E. Roskies, M., et. al. "Life Changes as Predictors of Illness in Immigrants." In C. D. Spielberger and I. G. Srason (Editors). *Stress and Anxiety.* Washington, D. C.: Hemisphere, 1977, pp. 3–21.

30. Research on Irish immigrants supports what this man said. See W. F. Adams. *Ireland and Irish Emigrations in the New World.* New Haven, CT: Yale University Press, 1932. See also G. J. Drolet. "Epidemiology of Tuberculosis." In B. Goldberg (Editor). *Clinical Tuberculosis.* Philadelphia: F. A. Davis, 1946.

31. S. E. Snodgrass. "A Personal Account." *Journal of Social Issues,* Volume 54, Number 2, 1998, pp. 373–380.

32. Ibid., pp. 378–379.

33. S. Massey, A. Cameron, S. O. Kobasa, and M. Fine. "Qualitative Approaches to the Study of Thriving: What Can Be Learned?" *Journal of Social Issues*, Volume 54, Number 2, 1998, pp. 340–341.

34. Ibid., p. 377.

35. E. E. Werner and R. S. Smith. *Overcoming the Odds: High Risk Children from Birth to Adulthood.* Ithaca, NY: Cornell University Press, 1992.

Chapter 7

1. As quoted in S. Carpenter. ""We Don't Know Our Own Strength." *Monitor on Psychology,* October 2001, p. 82.

2. P. McCarthy and J. A. Loren (Editors). *Breast Cancer? Let Me Check My Schedule!* Boulder, CO: Westview Press, 1997.

3. This research appeared in the July edition of *The Journal of Personality and Social Psychology.* Reporter Lee Brown in "Positive Outlook Extends Life Span" describes it. *Honolulu Star Bulletin,* July 29, 2002, pp. A1 and A10.

4. Ibid., p. A1.

5. I described the research on the power of intent to alter physical systems and life events in my book *Wishing Well: Making Your Every Wish Come True*: New York: Hyperion, 2000.

6. This issue is discussed in depth in E. S. Epel, B. S. McEwen, and J. R. Ickovics. "Embodying Psychological Thriving: Physical Thriving in Response to Stress." *Journal of Social Issues*, Volume 54, Number 2, 1998, pp. 301–322.

7. Ibid., p. 302.

8. B. McEwen. "Protective and Damaging Effects of Stress Mediators." *New England Journal of Medicine,* Volume 338, 1998, pp. 171–179.

9. This syndrome is described as it applies to elderly populations in R. Verdery. "Failure to Thrive in the Elderly." *Clinics in Geriatric Medicine,* Volume 1, 1995, pp. 653–659.

10. I described this phenomenon in my book *The Heart's Code.* New York: Broadway Books, 1999.

11. D. Goleman. *Emotional Intelligence.* New York: Bantam Books, 1995, p. 75.

12. Ibid., p. 75.

13. This study is reported in Ibid., p. 208. It was a study described by neurochemist Rachel Yehuda, who is director of the Traumatic Stress Studies Program at the Mount Sinai School of Medicine in New York. See also D. Goleman. *The New York Times,* October 6, 1992.

Chapter 8

1. D. M. Lang. Armenia: *The Cradle of Civilization*. London: G. Allen and Unwin. 1970.

2. For an insightful perspective on the combination of the mobilization of social and individual resources in response to risk and threat that can lead to both personal and social growth, see M. Karakashian. "Armenia: A Country's History of Challenges." *Journal of Social Issues,* Volume 54, Number 2, 1998, p. 390.

3. For a clear and fascinating discussion of nationalistic thriving, see A. Bakalian. *Armenian-Americans: From Being to Feeling Armenian*. New Brunswick, NJ: Transaction Publishers, 1993.

Chapter 9

1. As quoted in J. Fishman. "Getting Tough." *Psychology Today,* December 1987, pp. 26–28.

2. R. J. Wheeler and M. A. Frank. "Identification of Stress Buffers." *Behavioral Medicine,* Summer 1988, pp. 78–79. See also B. Justice. *Who Gets Sick: Thinking and Health*. Houston, TX: Peak Press, 1987.

3. These studies are reported by Blare Justice in "Those Who Stay Healthy." *New Realities*, July/August 1988.

4. S. Cholar. "The Miracle of Resilience." *American Health*, 1994, p. 74.

5. H. S. Friedman, et al. "Psychosocial and Behavioral Predictors of Longevity." *American Psychology*, February 1995, pp. 69–78.

6. C. S. Carver and M. F. Scheier. "Three Human Strengths." In L. G. Aspinwall and U. M. Staudinger, (Editors). *A Psychology of Human Strengths: Fundamental Questions and Future Directions for a Positive Psychology*. Washington, D.C.: American Psychological Association, 2003.

7. E. E. Werner and R. S. Smith. *"Overcoming the Odds. High Risk Children from Birth to Adulthood."* Ithaca, NY: Cornell University Press, 1992.

8. As quoted in S. Cholar. "The Miracle of Resilience.*"American Health*, April 1994, p. 74.

9. Werner and Smith. Op. cit., p. 228.

Chapter 10

1. Cited in J. Freedman. *Happy People: What Happiness Is, Who Has It, and Why*. New York: Harcourt Brace Jovanovich, 1978.

2. C. S. Wallis (Editor). *The Treasure Chest*. San Francisco: Harper and Row, 1965, p. 63.

3. B. L. Frendrikson. "The Role of Positive Emotions in Positive Psychology: The Broaden-and-Build Theory of Positive Emotions." *American Psychologist*, March 2001, pp. 218–226.

4. Ibid., p. 218.

5. As reported in R. Ornstein and D. Sobel. *Healthy Pleasures*. Reading, MA: Addison-Wesley, 1989, p. 217.

6. See P. Long. "Laugh and Be Well?" *Psychology Today*, October 1987, pp. 28–29.

7. K. M. Dillon, B. Minchoff, and K. H. Baker. "Positive Emotional States and Enhancement of the Immune System." *International Journal of Psychiatry in Medicine*. 1985–1986, Volume 15, pp. 13–17.

8. As quoted in Ibid., p. 18.

9. Dr. Meeker calls himself a "human ecologist," but his work contributes to the field of positive psychology. J. W. Meeker. *The Comedy of Survival*. Tucson, AZ: The University of Arizona Press, 1997, p. 10.

10. Ibid., p. 15.

11. Ibid., p. 14.

12. Ibid., p. 15.

13. As defined in *Webster's Third New International Dictionary*. Springfield, MA: Merriam-Webster, 1993, p. 2118.

14. I discuss the salutary effect of laughing and happiness in my book *Super Joy: Learning to Celebrate Everyday Life*. New York: Doubleday, 1988.

15. For a description of research related to this emotion, see B. L. Fredrickson. "What Good Are Positive Emotions?" *Review of General Psychology*, Volume 2, 1998, pp. 300–319.

16. B. T. Yanowski. *The Bad Stuff Is the Good Stuff*. St. Pete Beach, FL: Hari, Inc., 2001, p. 182.

17. For a summary of the research related to this emotion, see C. E. Izard. *Human Emotions*. New York: Plenum, 1977.

18. S. Lyubomirsky. "Why Are Some People Happier Than Others?" *American Psychologist,* March 2001, pp. 239–249.

19. Ibid., p. 241.

20. S. Freud. *A General Introduction to Psychoanalysis*. New York: Washington Square Press, 1952, p. 365 (original work published in 1920).

21. Ibid., p. 365. See also Freud. *Beyond the Pleasure Principle*. New York: Liveright, 1950 (original work published in 1920).

22. H. M. Lefcourt. "Humor." In C. R. Snyder and S. J. Lopez. *Handbook of Positive Psychology*. New York: Oxford University Press, 2002, pp. 619–631.

23. E. T. Higgins. "Beyond Pleasure and Pain." *American Psychologist*, December 1997, pp. 1280–1300.

24. P. Brickman and D. T. Campbell. *Reports of Happiness*. Chicago: Aldine, 1965.

25. Ibid., p. 821.

26. S. Lindner. *The Harried Leisure Class*. New York: Columbia University Press, 1970.

27. P. Pearsall. *Toxic Success: How to Stop Striving and Start Thriving*. Makawau, HI: Inner Ocean Publishing, 2002.

28. M. Csikszentmihalyi. "If We Are So Rich, Why Aren't We Happy?" *American Psychologist*, October 1999, p. 824.

29. J. Martin. "Relative Deprivation: A Theory of Distributive Injustice for an Era of Shrinking Resources." *Research in Organizational Behavior,* Volume 3, 1981, pp. 53–107.

30. P. Shaver and J. Freedman. "Your Pursuit of Happiness." *Psychology Today,* August 26, 1976, p. 29.

31. S. Pinker. *How the Mind Works*. New York: Norton, 1997.

32. As quoted in Ibid., p. 390.

33. M. Csikszentmihalyi. Op.cit., pp. 821–827.

34. This description of feeling "too busy to be concerned with being happy" and an afterglow that occurs after flowing is described in W. Adlai-Gail. *Exploring the Autotelic Personality*. Unpublished Doctoral Dissertation, University of Chicago, 1994.

35. As reported in R. A. Clay. "Researchers Harness the Power of Humor." *American Psychological Association Monitor*, September 1997, pp. 15 and 18.

36. As quoted in R. A. Clay. "Laughter May Be No Laughing Matter." *American Psychological Association Monitor,* September 1997, p. 16.

37. As quoted in Ibid., p. 10.

Chapter 11

1. L. Dossey. "In Praise of Unhappiness." *Alternative Therapies,* January 1996, Volume 2, Number 1, p. 10.

2. See his groundbreaking book about the difference between a pathogenic and saluto-genic orientation to health and healing. *Unraveling the Mystery of Health*. San Francisco: Jossey-Bass, 1987.

3. B. Azar. "A New Take On Psychoneuroimmunology." *Monitor on Psychology,* December 2001, pp. 34–36.

4. Ibid., p. 34.

5. Ibid., p. 35.

6. D. P. McAdams. *The Stories We Live By: Personal Myths and the Make of the Self.* New York: Morrow, 1993.

7. E. S. Epel, B. S. McEwen, and J. R. Ickovics. "Embodying Psychological Thriving: Physical Thriving in Response to Stress." *Journal of Social Issues,* Volume 54, 1995, pp. 301–322. See also, R. G. Tedeschi, C. L. Park, and L. G. Calhoun (Editors). *Posttraumatic Growth: Positive Changes in the Aftermath of Crisis.* Mahwah, NJ: Lawrence Erlbaum Associates, 1997.

8. C. L. Park. "Assessment and Prediction of Stress-Related Growth." *Journal of Personality,* Volume 64, 1996, pp. 71–105.

9. For a description of this new field that studies the salutary effects of illness from the evolutionary perspective, see R. M. Nesse and G. C. Williams. *Why We Get Sick: The New Field of Darwinian Medicine.* New York: Times Books, 1994.

10. Ibid., p. 35.

11. A. Antonovsky. *Unraveling the Mystery of Health: How People Manage Stress and Stay Well.* San Francisco: Jossey-Bass, 1987, p. 17.

12. Ibid., p. 18.

13. As quoted in L. Dossey. "Forgetting." *Alternative Therapies,* Volume 8, 2002, p. 13.

14. A. Antonovsky. Op. cit., p. 18.

15. This point is made by Aaron Antonovsky in his book *Health, Stress, and Coping: New Perspectives on Mental and Physical Well-Being.* San Francisco: Jossey-Bass, 1979, p. 128.

16. J. Piaget. *Biology and Knowledge.* Chicago: University of Chicago Press, 1971.

17. T. H. Davenport and J. C. Beck. *The Attention Economy.* Boston, MA: Harvard Business School Press, 2001, p. 22.

18. Research on women who underwent mastectomy showed that those who employed denial did better and lived longer than the patients who stoically faced their problem. K. W. Pettingale, et al. "The Biological Correlates of Psychological Responses to Cancer." *Journal of Psychosomatic Research,* Volume 25, 1981, pp. 453–458.

19. Ibid., p. 3.

20. B. Adjar. "A New Stress Paradigm for Women." *Monitor on Psychology,* July/August 2000, p. 42.

21. The literature on nursing homes is reviewed in J. Rodin. "Aging and Health: Effects of the Sense of Control." *Science,* Volume 233, 1986, p. 1271.

22. Ibid., p. 236.

23. M. Meaney, et al. "Effect of Neonatal Handling on Age-Related Impairments Associated with the Hippocampus." *Science,* Volume 239, 766.

24. M. E. P. Seligman. *Helplessness.* New York: W. H. Freeman. 1992.

25. As quoted in R. S. Sapolsky. *Why Zebras Don't Get Ulcers: A Guide to Stress, Stress-Related Disease, and Coping.* New York: W. H. Freeman, 1994, p. 280.

26. As quoted in K. Pelletier. *Sound Mind, Sound Body: A New Model of Lifelong Health.* New York: Simon and Schuster, 1994, p. 57.

Chapter 12

1. M. E. P. Seligman. *Learned Optimism.* New York: Alfred A. Knopf, 1991. p. 5.

2. M. Seligman. Opening Remarks: (Testimony) *Congressional Briefing on Prevention.* Washington, D. C.: U. S. Congress, 1998.

3. M. E. P. Seligman. *Learned Optimism.* New York: Alfred A. Knopf, 1991, p. 15.

4. *Webster's Third New International Dictionary.* Springfield, MA: Merriam-Webster, 1993, p. 1089.

5. As quoted in J. Jones and W. Wilson. *An Incomplete Education.* New York: Ballantine Books, p. 313.

6. This study is reported in M. E. P. Seligman. *Learned Optimism.* New York: Knopf, 1991.

7. L. Tiger. *Optimism: The Biology of Hope.* New York: Simon and Schuster, 1979, p. 18.

8. This model was developed by psychologist C. R. Snyder, et al. "Development and Validation of the State Hope Scale." *Journal of Personality and Social Psychology.* Volume 70, 1996, pp. 321–335.

9. S. L. Schneider. "In Search of Realistic Optimism." *American Psychologist,* March 2001, pp. 250–263.

10. Ibid., p. 252.

11. M. E. P. Seligman. Op. cit., p. 76.

12. Ibid., pp. 48–49.

13. This point is made by S. Solomon, J. Greenbert, and T. Pyszezynksi. "A Terror Management Theory of Social Behavior: The Psychological Functions of Self-Esteem and Cultural World Views." *Advances in Experimental Social Psychology,* Volume 24, 1991, pp. 93–159.

14. As quoted in D. G. Myers. *The Pursuit of Happiness.* New York: William Morrow and Company, 1992, p. 204.

15. As quoted in Ibid., p. 201.

16. W. Tatarkiewica. *Analysis of Happiness.* The Hague: Martinus Nijhoff, 1976, p. 1.

17. B. E. Ashford and G. E. Kreiner. "How Can You Do It? Dirty Work and the Challenge of Constructing a Positive Identity." *Academy of Management Review,* 1999, pp. 413–434.

18. E. Langer. *The Power of Mindful Learning.* Reading, MA: Addison-Wesley, 1997.

19. M. E. P. Seligman. Op. cit., p. 826.

20. G. Oettinger. "Positive Fantasy and Motivation." In P. M. Golwitzer and J. A. Bargh (Editors). *The Psychology of Action: Linking Cognition and Motivation to Behavior.* New York: Guildford, 1996, pp. 236–259.

21. T. Berry. *The Dream of the Earth.* San Francisco: Sierra Club Books, 1988, p. 124.

22. S. L. Schneider. Op. cit., p. 261.

Epilogue

1. There are several studies of the salutary effects of prayer. For an interesting recent report on the power of prayer to influence mental health and how we construe events in our lives, see J. B. Meisenhelder and E. Chandler. "Prayer and Health Outcomes in Church Members." *Alternative Therapies,* Volume 6, Number 4, July 2000, pp. 56–60.

A Glossary of Terms from the Field of Positive Psychology

Accommodating A term used by psychologist Jean Piaget to describe making significant changes in thinking and how we think when encountering a new idea, concept, or event in our lives. Contrast with *assimilation*.

Aliment A term used by psychologist Jean Piaget to describe an event, thought, or emotion that is either accommodated or assimilated into our way of thinking.

Allostasis The process of the body adapting to stress. Allostasis tends to increase over time as we encounter and thrive through stress.

Anabolic This involves conserving the body's energy, as when we are relaxed, calm, contented, and feeling connected. It is essential for counterbalancing catabolic, or energy-burning, processes.

'A'ole pilikia A Hawaiian phrase meaning "no problem" and reflecting the highly adaptive and accommodating oceanic way of thinking.

Assimilation A term used by psychologist Jean Piaget to describe dealing with new ideas or life events without making a significant change in our thinking or how we think. Contrast with *accommodating*.

Beethoven Factor Based on the great composer's thriving through his hearing loss to create the "Ode to Joy" symphony and other great works, it refers to the capacity to thrive through adversity and rise to new levels of creativity and growth.

Benefit-finding A characteristic of thriving involving mentally seeking and finding gains, personal growth, and/or enhanced interpersonal relationships from even the worst life crises.

Catabolic This term refers to the burning of the body's energy, as when we are anxious, agitated, angry, and competitive. It is a metabolic process primarily designed for survival but eventually destructive when prolonged without relief.

Catecholamines These are stress hormones (adrenalin and norepinephrine) that cause the heart to race, blood vessels to constrict, and muscles to tense— "the fight response." They are catabolic, or energy-burning, neurohormones.

Catharsis This term refers to expressing one's deepest feelings to vent or achieve purgation. It is wrongly assumed to be a way to dispel angry feelings.

Cold Reactor This is a general temperament of low sensitivity, underreaction, and tendency toward slower and less intense reactivity to life events.

Construing A word meaning to discover and apply meaning to the events in our lives. Thrivers are highly adaptive "creative contruers."

Corticosteroids These are stress hormones, including cortisone and cortisol— catabolic, or energy-burning, hormones that over time weaken the body's defenses.

Darwinian Medicine Also referred to as evolutionary medicine, this is the field of study that applies the principles of evolutionary biology to the problems of medicine. It seeks to understand why sickness has not become extinct and what evolutionary advantages are associated with suffering and the symptoms of illness.

Elevating This term refers to feelings of increased energy, optimism, altruism, and warmth in the chest and heart area resulting from dilation of the blood vessels caused by highly positive emotions and their accompanying hormones.

Entropy This is a term from Newtonian physics referring to the idea that everything is slowly but surely disorganizing and falling apart. It refers to the general tendency of the universe toward death and disorder.

Explanatory Style A concept from the field of cognitive psychology, this refers to our individually unique way of assigning meaning to the events in our lives. A highly dynamic explanatory style promotes thriving.

Flourishing This is feeling intensely and authentically alive, physically well, filled with emotional vitality, intensely and lovingly connected with others, and having optimistic thoughts and hopeful feelings about work, life, play, and interpersonal relationships.

Flow This concept, developed by psychologist Mihaly Csikszentmihalyi, refers to a state of mental focus so complete that it results in a loss of sense of time, place, and self. Problems seem to disappear and we feel we are totally in tune and lost in what we are experiencing.

Gelontology The study of laughter.

Hardiness A concept developed by psychologist Suzanne Ouelette Kobasa, it is thinking of the events in our lives from the perspective of challenge, commitment, and control.

Hot Reactor This is a general temperament of high reactivity, sensitivity, and proneness to quick and intense reaction.

Invincible This term refers to our natural capacity to grow in some way through any life crisis, including the process of dying.

Kindling This is an overreaction to trauma, managing to worsen the situation.

Languishing A term meaning not mentally ill but lacking mental health. It is a silent but debilitating epidemic in the Western world, characterized by being devoid of positive emotions toward life, living in quiet despair, "going through the motions without high emotion," being weary, distracted, too busy to love and too tired to care. It is estimated that more than 75 percent of Americans suffer from this "life delight deficiency."

Learned Optimism This concept offered by psychologist Martin E. P. Seligman describes our ability to learn a less personal, pervasive, and permanent orientation to life's problems; in other words, a more optimistic explanatory style.

Neoteny This is a concept offered by anthropologist Ashley Montagu to describe a state of retaining a childish, playful, trusting orientation to life.

Nonlocality This is a quantum physics concept that describes how events can happen free of time and space limitations.

Pathogenic A word referring to a negative, pessimistic orientation that looks primarily for the causes of illness and emotional distress and the human vulnerabilities. (Contrast with *salutogenic.*) It asks, "Who gets sick and why?"

PIDS This is the abbreviation for "psychological immunity deficiency syndrome," which results from unawareness of or failure to think in terms of the principles of our natural emotional capacity to thrive through adversity.

Positive Psychology This refers to the scientific study of our natural human strengths and virtues, our "thriveability." It is sometimes called "optimum" psychology. It deals with the thriving skills of finding well-being, contentment, and satisfaction with our past, flow, happiness, and connection in our present life, and hope and optimism for our future. It asks, "Why do we stay well?" instead of, "Why do we get sick?" The first issue of the professional journal *American Psychologist* to deal directly and exclusively with this new field was published in January 2000.

Post-Traumatic Stress Disorder (PTSD) An emotional, mental, physical, and spiritual reaction to severe stress that occurs for prolonged periods of time after the trauma.

Post-Traumatic Thriving Response (PTTR) This refers to emotional, mental, physical, and spiritual strengthening, or "steeling," because of severe stress or adversity that continues throughout life.

Psychological Immune System This refers to our mental and emotional "defense system" that helps us construe ourselves out of, past, and beyond the adversities and stressors of our lives.

Psychoneuroimmunology This is the study of how the mind interacts with the immune system.

Resilience This refers to recovering to preadversity level, managing to recover.

Salutogenic This means a positive, optimistic orientation that looks primarily for human physical, spiritual, mental, and emotional resources. (Contrast with *pathogenic*.) It asks, "Who stays healthy, and why?"

Schema This is a term used by psychologist Jean Piaget to describe our way of thinking and current mental "set" or way of construing events in our lives.

Sense of Coherence This concept, developed by psychologist Aaron Antonovsky, is the sense that life is comprehensible and meaningful. A strong and adaptive explanatory style is related to a strong sense of coherence.

Shadenfreude This is a German word describing gaining pleasure from others' pain. It refers to a comparative orientation in one's joy requiring that we feel someone else is suffering more than we are.

Sickness Response The essential human reaction to stress, characterized by fatigue, withdrawal from sex and eating, and general malaise. It provides for necessary rest and reflection that can lead to thriving.

SIG (Stress Induced Growth) Rising above the level of functioning that existed prior to a life trauma.

Surviving This is about regaining most, but not all, of our original way of thinking and feeling in the aftermath of adversity; managing to exist.

Temperament This is a moderately stable emotional, mental, and behavioral way of reacting to the world present at a birth.

Thanatophobia This is the fear of death, and a primary, often unconscious, source of the anxiety that blocks the thriving response.

Thriving This means growing physically, mentally, emotionally, and spiritually because of trauma or adversity; managing to become.

Uncertainty Principle Proposed by 1932 Nobel prize–winning physicist Werner Heisenberg, this principle states that the act of observing either the acceleration or location of electrons "influenced" the state of the electrons. This principle has metaphorical relevance to thriving because it suggests that how we view the world may actually in some small way influence our world.

Zeitgeber This is a German word describing the "grabbing," or domination, of emotional time by those who are the most emotionally assertive and expressive.

Bibliography of Positive Psychology References

Adams, W. F. *Ireland and Irish Emigrations in the New World*. New Haven, CT: Yale University Press, 1932.

Adlai-Gail, W. "Exploring the Autotelic Personality." Unpublished Doctoral Dissertation, University of Chicago, 1994.

Anthony, E. J. "The Syndrome of the Psychologically Vulnerable Child." In E. J. Anthony and C. Koupernik (Editors). *The Child in His Family: Children at Psychiatric Risk*. New York: Wiley, 1974, pp. 529–545.

Antonovsky, A. *Health, Stress, and Coping: New Perspectives on Mental and Physical Well-Being*. San Francisco: Jossey-Bass Publishers, 1979.

———. "The Sense of Coherence as a Determinant of Health." In Matarazzo, J. D. et al. (Editors). *Behavioral Health: A Handbook of Health Enhancement and Disease Prevention*. New York: Wiley, 1984.

———. *Unraveling the Mystery of Health: How People Manage Stress and Stay Well*. San Francisco: Jossey-Bass Publishers, 1987.

Arcus, D. "Vulnerability and Eye Color in Disney Cartoon Characters." In J. S. Reznik (Editor). *Perspective on Behavioral Inhibition*. Chicago: University of Chicago Press, 1989, pp. 291–297.

Argyle, M. *The Psychology of Happiness*. London: Methune, 1987.

Ashford, B. E. and Kreiner, G. E. "How Can You Do It? Dirty Work and the Challenge of Constructing a Positive Identity." *Academy of Management Review*, 1999, pp. 413–434.

Aspinwall, L. G. and Staudinger, U. M. (Editors). *A Psychology of Human Strengths:*

Fundamental Questions and Future Directions for a Positive Psychology. Washington, D.C.: American Psychological Association, 2002.

Azar, B. "A New Stress Paradigm for Women." *Monitor on Psychology,* July/August 2000, pp. 42–43.

———. "A New Take on Psychoneuroimmunology." *Monitor on Psychology,* December 2001, pp. 34–36.

Bakalian, A. *Armenian-Americans: From Being to Feeling Armenian.* New Brunswick, NJ: Transaction Publishers, 1993.

Barton, W. E. *Abraham Lincoln and His Books: With Quotations from the Writings of Lincoln and a Bibliography of Books in Print Relating to Abraham Lincoln.* Folcroft, PA: Folcroft Library Edition, 1976.

Benson, H. *Your Maximum Mind.* New York: Random House, 1987.

Berger, A. H. "Are You a Chronic Worrier?" *Complete Woman,* October 1987, p. 58.

Berger, P. and Luckman, T. *The Social Consequence of Reality: A Treatise on the Sociobiology of Knowledge.* New York: Anchor Books, 1996.

Bernardo, R. "Love, Faith Cure Family's Ailments.'" *Honolulu Star Bulletin,* December 9, 2001, pp. 1 and 7.

Bloom, H. *The Lucifer Principle.* New York: Atlantic Monthly Press, 1995.

Brikman, P. and Campbell, D. T. *Reports of Happiness.* Chicago: Aldine, 1965.

Brikman, P., Coates, D., and Janoff-Bulman, R. "Lottery Winners and Accident Victims: Is Happiness Relative?" *Journal of Personal and Social Psychology,* Volume 36, 1978, pp. 917–927.

Bruner, J. *Actual Minds, Possible Worlds.* Cambridge, MA: Harvard University Press, 1986.

Byant, K. "I Won't Take 'See You Later' For Granted." *Newsweek,* December 24, 2001, p. 9.

Caroline, N. L. and Schwartz, H. "Chicken Soup Rebound and the Relapse of Pneumonia." *Chest,* Volume 67, 1975, pp. 215–216.

Carpenter, S. "We Don't Know Our Own Strength." *Monitor on Psychology,* October, 2001, p. 82.

Carver, C. S. "Resilience and Thriving: Issue, Models, and Linkages." *Journal of Social Issues,* Volume 54, Number 2, pp. 245–266.

Carver, C. S. and Scheier, M. F. "Three Human Strengths." In *A Psychology of Human Strengths: Fundamental Questions and Future Directions for a Positive Psychology.* Aspinwall, L. G. and Staudinger, U. M. (Editors). Washington, D.C.: American Psychological Association, 2003.

Cholar, S. "The Miracle of Resilience." *American Health*, 1994, p. 74.

Classical Music Pages Homepage, created by Matt Boynick, February 1, 1996.

Clay, R. A. "Laughter May Be No Laughing Matter.*" American Psychological Association Monitor*, September 1997, p. 16.

————. "Researchers Harness the Power of Humor." *American Psychological Association Monitor*, September 1997, pp. 15–18.

Csikszentmihalyi, M. *The Evolving Self*. New York: HarperCollins, 1993.

————. *Flow: The Psychology of Optimal Experience*. New York: Harper and Row, 1990.

————. "If We Are So Rich, Why Aren't We Happy?" *American Psychologist*, October, 1999, pp. 821–827.

DeAngelis, T. "Surviving a Patient's Suicide." *Monitor on Psychology*, November 2001, pp. 70–73.

DeSalvo, L. *Virginia Wolf: The Impact of Childhood Sexual Abuse on Her Life and Work*. New York: Ballantine Books, 1989.

Diener, E., et al. "Subjective Well-Being: Three Decades of Progress." *Psychological Bulletin*, Volume 125, 1999, pp. 276–302.

Dillon, K. M., Minchoff, B., and Baker, K. H. "Positive Emotional States and Enhancement of the Immune System." *International Journal of Psychiatry in Medicine*, 1985–1986. Volume 15, pp. 13–17.

Dossey, L. "In Praise of Unhappiness." *Alternative Therapies*, January 1996, Volume 2, pp. 7–10.

————. "The Great Wait: In Praise of Doing Nothing." *Alternative Therapies*, November 1996, pp. 8–13.

————. "Now You Are Fit to Live: Humor and Health." *Alternative Therapies*, Volume 2, 1996, pp. 8–13, and 98–100.

————. "Who Gets Sick and Who Gets Well." *Alternative Therapies*. September 1995, pp. 2–8.

Drolet, G. J. "Epidemiology of Tuberculosis." In B. Goldberg (Editor). *Clinical Tuberculosis*. Philadelphia: F. A. Davis, 1946.

Eliot, R. S. *Is It Worth Dying For?* New York: Bantam Books, 1984.

Engel, G. L. "Sudden and Rapid Death During Psychological Stress: Folk Lore or Folk Wisdom." *American Internal Medicine*, Volume 74, 1971, pp. 771–782.

Epel, E. S., McEwen, B. S., and Ickovics, J. R. "Embodying Psychological Thriving:

Physical Thriving in Response to Stress." *Journal of Social Issues,* Volume 54, Number 2, 1998, pp. 301–322.

Fishman, J. "Getting Tough." *Psychology Today,* December 1987, pp. 26–28.

Forbes, E. *Thayer's Life of Beethoven.* Princeton, NJ: Princeton University Press, 1969.

Frankl, V. *Man's Search for Meaning.* New York: Washington Square Press, 1963.

Fredrickson, B. L. "The Role of Positive Emotions in Positive Psychology: The Broaden-and-Build Theory of Positive Emotions." *American Psychologist,* March 2001, pp. 218–226.

———. "What Good Are Positive Emotions? *Review of General Psychology,* Volume 2, 1998, pp. 300–319.

Freedman, J. *Happy People: What Happiness Is, Who Has It, and Why.* New York: Harcourt Brace Jovanovich, 1978.

Freud, S. *A General Introduction to Psychoanalysis.* New York: Washington Square Press, 1952. (Original work published in 1920.)

———. *Beyond the Pleasure Principle.* New York: Liverright, 1950. (Original work published in 1920.)

Friedman, H. S., et al. "Psychosocial and Behavioral Predictors of Longevity." *American Psychologist,* February 1995, pp. 69–78.

Garmezy, N. "Stress Resistant Children: The Search for Protective Factors." In J. E. Stevenson (Editor). "Recent Research in Developmental Pathopathology." *Journal of Child Psychology and Psychiatry Book.* Supplement Number 4. Oxford, England: Pergamon Press, 1985, pp. 213–233.

Goleman, D. *Emotional Intelligence.* New York: Bantam Books, 1995.

———. *The New York Times.* October 6, 1992.

———. *Vital Lies, Simple Truths.* New York: Simon and Schuster, 1985.

Greenbert, M. A. "Cognitive Processing of Traumas: The Role of Intrusive Thoughts and Reappraisals." *Journal of Applied Social Psychology,* Volume 25, 1995, pp. 1262–1296.

Hafen, B. Q., et al. *Mind Body Health.* Boston: Allyn Bacon, 1996.

Higgins, E. T. "Beyond Pleasure and Pain." *American Psychologist,* December 1977, pp. 1280–1300.

Hoffman, E. *The Right to Be Human: A Biography of Abraham Maslow.* Los Angeles: Jeremy Tarcher, 1988.

Ickovics, J. R. and Park, C. L. "Paradigm Shift: Why a Focus on Health Is Important." *Journal of Social Issues,* Volume 54, Number 2, 1998, pp. 237–244.

Isen, A. M. "The Influence of Positive and Negative Affect on Cognitive Organization: Some Implications for Development." In N. Stein, et al. (Editors). *Psychological and Biological Approaches to Emotions.* Hillsdale, NJ: Lawrence Erlbaum Associates, 1990, pp. 75–94.

Izard, C. E. *Human Emotions.* New York: Plenum, 1977.

Jabs, C. "New Reason to Be an Optimist." *Self,* September 1988, pp. 170–173.

James, W. *The Varieties of Religious Experience.* New York: New American Library, 1902/1958, p. 77.

Jones, J. and Wilson, W. *An Incomplete Education.* New York: Ballantine Books, 1987.

Justice, B. "Those Who Stay Healthy." *New Realities,* July/August 1988.

Kagan, J. *Galen's Prophecy: Temperament in Human Nature.* New York: Basic Books, 1994.

Karakashian, M. "Armenia: A County's History of Challenges." *Journal of Social Issues,* Volume 54, Number 2, 1998, pp. 381–392.

Kelley, G. A. *The Psychology of Personal Constructs.* New York: W. W. Norton, 1955.

Keltner, D. and Harker, L. "Expressions of Positive Emotion in Women's College Yearbook Pictures and Their Relationship to Personality and Life Outcomes Across Adulthood." *Journal of Personality and Social Psychology,* Volume 80, 2001, pp. 112–124.

Keyes, C. M. and Haidt, J. *Flourishing: Positive Psychology and the Life Well Lived.* Washington, D. C.: American Psychological Association, 2002.

Kobasa, S. O. "How Much Stress Can You Survive?" *American Health,* September 1984, pp. 56–68.

Kramer, P. D. *Listening to Prozac: A Psychiatrist Explores Antidepressant Drugs and the Remaking of the Self.* New York: Viking Penguin, 1993.

Lanager, L. L. *Holocaust Testimonies: The Ruins of Memory.* New Haven, CT: Yale University Press, 1990.

Lang, D. M. *Armenia: The Cradle of Civilization.* London: G. Allen and Unwin, 1970.

Langer, E. *The Power of Mindful Learning.* Reading, MA: Addison-Wesley, 1997.

Lazarus, R. S. "From Psychological Stress to the Emotions: A History of Changing Outlooks." *Annual Review of Psychology,* 1993.

Lefcourt, H. M. "Humor." In C. R. Snyder and S. J. Lopez. *Handbook of Positive Psychology.* New York: Oxford University Press, 2002.

Lerner, M. J. "The Desire of Justice and Reactions to Victims." In J. Macaulay and L. Berkowitz (Editors). *Altruism and Helping Behavior*. New York: Academic Press, 1970, pp. 205–229.

LeShan, L. *The Dilemma of Psychology*. New York: Dutton, 1990.

Linder, S. *The Harried Leisure Class*. New York: Columbia University Press, 1970.

Long, P. "Laugh and Be Well." *Psychology Today*, October 1987, pp. 28–29.

Lyubomirsky, W. "Why Are Some People Happier Than Others?" *American Psychologist*, March 2001, pp. 239–249.

Martin, J. "Relative Deprivation: A Theory of Distributive Injustice for an Era of Shrinking Resources." *Research in Organizational Behavior,* Volume 3, 1981, pp. 53–107.

Massey, S., Cameron, A., Oulellette, S., and Fine, M. "Qualitative Approaches to the Study of Thriving: What Can Be Learned." *Journal of Social Issues,* Volume 54, Number 2, 1998, pp. 337–355.

Masten, A. S. "Ordinary Magic: Resilience Processes in Development." *American Psychologist*, March 2001, pp. 227–238.

Matilin, M. and Stang, D. *The Pollyanna Principle*. Cambridge, MA: Schenkman, 1978.

McAdams, D. P. *The Stories We Live By: Personal Myths and the Make of the Self.* New York: Morrow, 1993.

McCarthy, P. and Loren, J. A. (Editors). *Breast Cancer? Let Me Check My Schedule!* Boulder, CO: Westview Press, 1997.

McEwen, B. "Protective and Damaging Effects of Stress Mediators." *New England Journal of Medicine,* Volume 338, 1998, pp. 171–179.

McMillen, C., Zuravin, S., and Rideout, G. "Perceived Benefits from Child Sexual Abuse." *Journal of Consulting and Clinical Psychology*, Volume 63, 1985, pp. 1037–1043.

Meaney, et al. "Effect of Neonatal Handling on Age-Related Impairments Associated with the Hippocampus." *Science,* Volume 239, 1992, pp. 775–777.

Meisenhelder, J. B. and Chandler, E. "Prayer and Health Outcomes in Church Members." *Alternative Therapies,* July 2000, Volume 6, Number 4, pp. 56–60.

Meyer, D. *The Positive Thinkers: Popular Religious Psychology from Mary Baker Eddy to Norman Vincent Peale and Ronald Reagan*. Middletown, CT: Wesleyan University Press, 1988.

Miller, W. R. and C'deBaca, J. "Quantum Change: Toward a Psychology of Transformation." In T. F. Heatherton and J. L. Weinberger (Editors). *Can Personality Change?"* Washington, D. C.: American Psychological Association, 1994, pp. 253–280.

Murphy, L. B. and Moriarity, A. E. *Vulnerability, Coping, and Growth: From Infancy to Adolescence.* New Haven, CT: Yale University Press, 1976.

Myers, D. *The Pursuit of Happiness.* New York: William Morrow and Company, Inc., 1992.

Neimeyer, R. A. *Meaning Reconstruction and the Experience of Loss.* Washington, D. C.: American Psychological Association, 2001.

Nesse, R. M. and Williams, G. C. *Why We Get Sick: The New Field of Darwinian Medicine.* New York: Times Books, 1994.

Oettinger, G. "Positive Fantasy and Motivation." In P. M. Golwitzer and J. A. Bargh (Editors). *The Psychology of Action: Linking Cognition and Motivation to Behavior.* New York: Guildford, 1996, pp. 236–259.

O'Leary, V.E. and Ickovics, J. R. "Resilience and Thriving in Response to Challenge. An Opportunity for a Paradigm Shift in Women's Health." *Women's Health: Research on Gender, Behavior, and Policy,* Volume 1, 1995, pp. 121–142.

Ornstein, R. and Sobel, D. *The Healing Brain.* New York: Simon and Schuster, 1987.

———. *Healthy Pleasures.* Reading, MA: Addison-Wesley, 1989.

Pearsall, P. *Superimmunity: Master Your Emotions and Improve Your Health.* New York: McGraw Hill, 1987.

———. *The Heart's Code.* New York: Broadway Books, 1999.

———. *Super Joy: Learning to Celebrate Everyday Life.* New York: Doubleday, 1988.

———. *Toxic Success: How to Stop Striving and Start Thriving.* Makawau, HI: Inner Ocean Publishing, 2002.

———. *Wishing Well: Making Your Every Wish Come True.* New York: Hyperion, 2000.

Peck, S. *The Road Less Traveled.* New York: Simon and Schuster, 1978.

Pelletier, K. *Sound Mind, Sound Body: A New Model of Lifelong Health.* New York: Simon and Schuster, 1994.

Peterson, C. "The Future of Optimism." *American Psychologist,* January 2000, pp. 44–55.

Piaget, J. *Biology and Knowledge.* Chicago: University of Chicago Press, 1971.

———. *The Child's Conception of the World.* Patterson, NJ: Littlefield Adams, 1963.

———. *Psychology and Epistemology: Towards a Theory of Knowledge.* New York: Viking Press, 1971.

Pettingale, K. W., et al. "The Biological Correlates of Psychological Responses to Cancer." *Journal of Psychosomatic Research,* Volume 25, 1981, pp. 453–458.

Pinker, S. *How the Mind Works*. New York: Norton, 1997.

Rodin, J. "Aging and Health: Effects of the Sense of Control." *Science,* Volume 233, 1986, pp. 1269–1272.

Roemer, L. and Borkovec, T. "Unwanted Cognitive Activity That Controls Unwanted Somatic Experience." In D. Wegner and J. Pennebaker (Editors). *Handbook of Mental Control*. Volume 5. Englewood Cliffs, NJ: Prentice Hall, 1993.

Roskies, E., et al. "Life Changes as Predictors of Illness in Immigrants." In C. D. Spielberger and I. G. Sarason (Editors). *Stress and Anxiety*. Washington, D. C.: Hemisphere. 1977, pp. 3–21.

Royce, J. "Psychology Is Multi-: Methodological, Variant, Epistemic, World View, System, Paradigmatic, Theoretic, and Disciplinary." In *Nebraska Symposium on Motivation, 1975. Conceptual Foundations of Psychology*. Lincoln, NE: University of Nebraska Press, 1976.

Rutter, M. "Psychological Resilience and Proactive Mechanisms." *American Journal of Orthopsychiatry,* Volume 57, 1987, pp. 31–33.

Ryan, W. *Blaming the Victim*. New York: Pantheon, 1971.

Saakvitne, K. W., Tennen, H., and Affleck, G. "Exploring Thriving in the Context of Trauma Theory: Constructive Self Development Theory." *Journal of Social Issues*, Volume 54, Number 2, 1998, pp. 279–299.

Sapolsky, R. S. *Why Zebras Don't Get Ulcers: A Guide to Stress, Stress-Related Disease, and Coping*. New York: W. H. Freeman, 1994.

Scar, S. "How Genotypes and Environments Affect Coping: Developmental and Individual Differences." In N. Bogler, et al. (Editors). *Persons in Context: Developmental Process*. New York: Cambridge University Press, 1988, pp. 217–244.

Scheier, M. F. and Carver, C. S. "Dispositional Pessimism and Physical Well-Being: The Influence of Generalized Outcome Expectations on Health." *Journal of Personality*, Volume 55, 1987, pp. 169–210.

Schneider, S. L. "In Search of Realistic Optimism." *American Psychologist,* March 2001, pp. 250–263.

Seligman, M. E. P. *Authentic Happiness*. New York: Free Press, 2002.

Seligman, M. E. P. *Helplessness*. New York: W. H. Freeman, 1994.

———. *Learned Optimism*. New York: Knopf, 1991.

———. "Opening Remarks: (Testimony)." *Congressional Briefing on Prevention*. Washington, D.C.: U.S. Congress, 1998.

———. "Response from Martin E. Seligman." *Monitor on Psychology,* November 2001, p. 10.

Seligman, M. E. P. and Csikszentmihalyi, M. "Positive Psychology: An Introduction." *American Psychologist,* January 2000, pp. 5–14.

Shaver, P. and Freedman, J. "Your Pursuit of Happiness." *Psychology Today,* August 26, 1976, p. 29.

Shaw, D. *The Pleasure Police.* New York: Doubleday, 1996.

Shay, J. *Achilles in Vietnam: Combat Trauma and the Undoing of Character.* New York: Atheneum, 1994.

Sheldon, K. M. and King, L. "Why Positive Psychology Is Necessary." *American Psychologist*, March 2001, pp. 216–217.

Siebert, A. *The Survivor Personality*. New York: Berkley Publishing, 1996.

Siegel, B. "Mind Over Cancer: An Exclusive Interview." *Prevention,* March 1998, pp. 59–64.

Snodgrass, S. E. "A Personal Account." *Journal of Social Issues,* Volume 54, Number 2, 1998, pp. 373–380.

Solomon, S., Greenbert, J., and Pyszezynski, T. "A Terror Management Theory of Social Behavior: The Psychological Functions of Self-Esteem and Cultural World Views." *Advances in Experimental Social Psychology,* Volume 24, 1991, pp. 93–159.

Snyder, C. R., et al. "Development and Validation of the State of Hope Scale." *Journal of Personality and Social Psychology,* Volume 70, 1996, pp. 321–335.

Snyder, C. R. and Lopez, S. J. *The Handbook of Positive Psychology.* Oxford: Oxford University Press, 2002.

Starker, S. *Oracle in the Supermarket: The American Preoccupation with Self-Help Books.* New Brunswick, NJ: Transactions, 1989.

Tatarkiewica, W. *Analysis of Happiness.* The Hague: Martinus Nijhoff, 1976.

Taylor, S. E. *Positive Illusions: Creative Self-Deception and the Healthy Mind.* New York: Basic Books, 1989.

Taylor, S. E. and Brown, J. D. "Illusion and Well-Being. A Social Psychological Perspective on Mental Health." *Psychological Bulletin*, 1988, pp. 193–210.

Tedeschi, R. G. and Calhoun, L. G. *Trauma and Transformation.* Thousand Oaks, CA: Sage, 1995.

Tedeschi, R. G., Park, C. L, and Calhoun, L. G. (Editors). *Posttraumatic Growth: Positive Changes in the Aftermath of Crisis.* Mahwah, NJ: Lawrence Erlbaum Associates, 1998.

Thomas, A. and Chess, S. *Temperament and Development.* New York: Brunner Mazel, 1977.

Tiger, L. *Optimism: The Biology of Hope*. New York: Simon and Schuster, 1979.

Tugade, M. and Fredrickson, B. L. "Resilient Individuals Use Positive Emotions to Bound Back from Negative Emotional Arousal." Manuscript in preparation.

Valliant, G. E. "Adaptive Mental Mechanisms: Their Role in a Positive Psychology." *American Psychologist*, January 2000, pp. 89–98.

Verdery, R. "Failure to Thrive in the Elderly." *Clinics in Geriatric Medicine*, Volume 1, 1995, pp. 653–659.

Wallis, C. S. (Editor). *The Treasure Chest*. San Francisco: Harper and Row, 1965.

Walsh, R. and Shapiro, D. H. "In Search of a Healthy Person." In Walsh, R. and Shapiro, D. H. (Editors). *Beyond Health and Normality*. New York: Van Nostrand Reinhold Company, 1983.

Webster's Third New International Dictionary. Springfield, MA: Merriam-Webster, 1993.

Werner, E. E. and Smith, R. S. *Vulnerable But Invincible: A Study of Resilient Children*. New York: McGraw Hill, 1982.

————. *Overcoming the Odds. High Risk Children from Birth to Adulthood*. Ithaca, NY: Cornell University Press, 1992.

Wheeler, R. J. and Frank, M. A. "Identification of Stress Buffers." *Behavioral Medicine*, Summer 1988, pp. 78–79.

Wilbanks, W. L. "The New Obscenity." *Reader's Digest*, December 1988, p. 23.

Wilbur, K. *The Spectrum of Consciousness*. Wheaton, IL: Quest, 1977.

Yannowski, B. T. *The Bad Stuff Is the Good Stuff*. St. Pete Beach, FL: Hari, Inc., 2001.

Index

Hampton Roads Publishing Company

. . . for the evolving human spirit

Hampton Roads Publishing Company
publishes books on a variety of subjects,
including metaphysics, health,
visionary fiction, and other related topics.

For a copy of our latest catalog, call toll-free
800-766-8009, or send your name and address to:

Hampton Roads Publishing Company, Inc.
1125 Stoney Ridge Road
Charlottesville, VA 22902

e-mail: hrpc@hrpub.com
www.hrpub.com